WILLIAMS-SONOMA

# Italian Favorites

The Best of Williams-Sonoma Kitchen Library

# Italian Favorites

GENERAL EDITOR
CHUCK WILLIAMS

RECIPE PHOTOGRAPHY
ALLAN ROSENBERG

# Contents

# Introduction

Europe's first true cuisine was born on the Italian peninsula. Cooks in ancient Rome, using not only their native ingredients but also the culinary know-how and pantries of their Greek and Anatolian counterparts, developed a sophisticated cookery and an appreciation of good eating. But with the collapse of the Roman Empire into a many independent states, culinary unity was lost forever; today, the cooking of Italy is the cooking of its regions.

Fish soup, a standard Italian menu item due to the long coastline and ancient seafaring tradition, is a good example of this resolute regionalism. Simply put, "Italian fish soup" does not exist. Instead, there are scores of provincial fish soups, from the famed mixed-fish *cacciucco* of Livorno to the mussel, squid, and prawn chowder of Capri, to the oyster-rich soup of Taranto, to the octopus-laden version of Elba.

Innovation and restraint also typify the Italian table. Throughout history, Italian cuisine has been enriched by a steady stream of foreign influences through trade, wars, invasions, and shifting borders. From early on, Italian cooks have learned to adapt what was new and make it their own. At the same time, a remarkably

large variety of raw ingredients—vegetables, fruits, herbs, seafood, poultry, meat—of the highest caliber and in great abundance has long encouraged Italian cooks to rely on the plain harmonies of natural flavors.

In other words, the best Italian cooking, whether a steaming plate of pasta, a tomato-strewn pizza, a perfectly cooked veal piccata, or a square of tiramisù, shows a healthy respect both for superb ingredients and utter simplicity.

## THE ITALIAN TABLE

Italy shuts down in the middle of the day—shops are shuttered, banks and post offices are locked tight, classrooms empty out—and many Italians, some of them with a break from work as long as three hours, head home for il pranzo (lunch), just as their parents and grandparents did before them. Unlike the quickly downed sandwich lunch of San Francisco or London, the Italian midday meal—and its evening counterpart—is still a leisurely affair where good food and spirited conversation are shared.

An Italian meal is often four or five modestly sized courses, each selected with the others in mind and all of them offering both regional tastes and seasonal ingredients. It usually begins with the *antipasto* (appetizer), which can be as spare as a few slices of prosciutto or as fancy as *vitello tonnato* (cold veal with a tuna mayonnaise). For a simpler meal, the cook will dispense with the antipasto and begin with the *primo*, or first course, which may be pasta, in a broth or tossed with a sauce; a risotto; or a soup, such as a light Tuscan *stracciatella* (egg drop soup), or the heartier *pappa al pomodoro* (bread and tomato soup) of the same region. The *secondo*, or second course, is commonly meat, poultry, or fish—perhaps grilled lamb chops in Umbria, a roast chicken with sage in Emilia-Romagna, braised tuna with capers in Sicily. The *contorno*, vegetable course, is served alongside the *secondo*; it must complement not only its table partner but everything that has gone before it as well. For example, if the *primo* were a bean and pasta soup, the *contorno* would never be *fagioli all'uccelletto* (white beans "in the style of little birds").

Sometimes a salad—usually greens, lightly dressed, and nothing more—follows the *secondo*. It helps to cleanse the palate, readying it for dessert, the final course. Nearly every lunch and dinner ends with fresh fruit. More elaborate desserts, such as fresh fruit *crostate* (tarts), cream-filled pastries, and buttery cakes, are reserved for Sunday lunch or special occasions.

## SALUTE!

The grapevine grows nearly everywhere in Italy, from the alpine north all the way to the rocky volcanic south, a profusion that has made wine the everyday beverage of the Italian table. Today, as in the past, Italians typically drink the much celebrated wines native to their region—wines that they believe best complement their own provincial dishes—with the Piedmontese favoring their Barolos, the Tuscans their Chiantis, the Romans their young, fresh Frascatis. While no firm rules apply when choosing which local wine to serve, however, lighter white or rose wines are usually preferred in the hot summer months and with simple foods, while their sturdier kin are reserved for cooler weather and rich, highly seasoned dishes.

Any meal is always a celebratory occasion and Italians often prepare themselves by preceding it with an *apertivo*, a usually low-in-alcohol beverage—Campari and soda, Punt e Mes, a sparkling wine—designed to stimulate as well as awaken the appetite. When the meal is done, a *digestivo*, such as Fernet Branca or Averna—bitter, but delicious, blends of alcohol and herbs—or grappa, a drink made from the grape residue left over from making wine, drunk both to promote and smooth the digestion.

## ONE COUNTRY, MANY CUISINES

For centuries, the Italian peninsula and its islands were a mosaic of warring city-states, duchies, and colonies, each with its own government, language, and culture, a separation that extended to the dinner table. The Apennine Mountains, which snake their way down the length of the boot, helped these political divisions and a warren of other isolated pockets to keep their identities, in the kitchen and elsewhere. Then, in 1861, the establishment of the Republic of Italy brought about a slow evolution of similar eating habits—a widely recognized Italian cuisine—throughout the country's twenty regions. But a longstanding tradition of individuality, fueled by geography, climate, economics, and culinary stubbornness, has kept Italian regional cooking alive.

Pasta is a good example of this regional loyalty. It is eaten throughout Italy, but its basic character shifts radically as its moves from south to north. From Sicily to the Abruzzo, it is usually factory made, tubular, egg free, and sold dried, such as spaghetti and penne. From the Piedmont and Lombardy to Rome, it is often home-made, flat ribbons, rich with eggs and used fresh, such as fettuccine and tagliatelle. Numerous exceptions exist on both sides of this pasta demarcation line, of

course, plus scores of regional specialties—the trenette (narrow, thin ribbons) of Liguria, the orecchiette (ear-shaped pasta) of Apulia, the tortellini of Emilia Romagna—flourish, further contributing to Italy's vast pasta world.

Cooking fats are geographically defined as well. A shortage of good pastures in the south limits livestock to goats, sheep, and pigs, and local cooks traditionally use olive oil—olive trees thrive in the mild, arid landscape—and lard. The far north, where grazing land and thus cattle are more abundant, is butter country. This same difference puts sheep's milk cheeses on southern tables and cow's milk cheeses on northern tables.

Some Italian specialties cannot be contained, however. Pizza was born in Naples, but pizza makers are now busy in every corner of Italy and around the world. Machine-made macaroni is Neapolitan as well, but it too has traveled widely. Still, many Italian specialties are seldom found on dinner tables outside their region, such as the *cima alla genovese* (stuffed veal breast) of Liguria, the *fonduta* (fondue) of the Piedmont, the *busecca* (tripe with onions) of Lombardy, and the *sarde in saor* (sardines in vinegar) of the Veneto—each dish is further evidence of the Italian commitment to regional kitchens and ingredients.

## A GLOBAL FEAST

The Italian table grew out of politics and geography. In the ninth century, the Arabs invaded southern Europe, remaining in sunny Sicily for some three hundred years. They brought with them not only the art of making ice cream and of constructing desserts of honey, almond paste, and candied fruits, but also sophisticated irrigation methods that transformed much of the parched landscape into a sea of citrus orchards, sugarcane fields, and vegetable gardens. Their culinary footprint is still seen today in such island specialties as *pasta con le sarde*, with sardines, currants, and pine nuts, and the marzipan-rich *cassata alla siciliana*.

At the opposite end of the country lies the Alto Adige, a rugged stretch of alpine terrain that was part of the Austrian Empire until World War I. Not surprisingly, much of the contemporary menu echoes the region's political past, with sauerkraut and goulash, dumplings and strudel common offerings. Even the vineyards, planted with Riesling, Gewürztraminer, and other German grape varieties, reflect a past that owes more to central Europe than to the Mediterranean.

# Starters, Soups & Salads

# Bruschetta

You can vary this *antipasto* with many other possible additions: small leaves of arugula (rocket) or watercress, shavings of Parmesan, drops of balsamic vinegar, or anchovy fillets. Or place a spoonful of mayonnaise (page 323) on top of the tomatoes and omit the oil.

Toast the bread slices in a toaster until the outsides are slightly crunchy but the insides are still soft.

Cut the garlic cloves in half lengthwise. Using a half clove for each bread slice, evenly and thoroughly rub one side of the toast with the cut side of the garlic. Cut each tomato into 6–8 wedges and divide the wedges evenly among the bread slices, arranging them on the garlic-rubbed sides. Sprinkle each toast with salt and pepper to taste and then drizzle with 1 tablespoon of the olive oil. Finally, garnish each toast with a basil leaf and serve.

*Serves 4*

4 thick slices coarse country bread

2 cloves garlic

2 tomatoes

Salt and freshly ground pepper

4 tablespoons (2 fl oz/60 ml) extra-virgin olive oil

4 fresh basil leaves

# Vegetables with Olive Oil Dip

This dish, called *pinzimonio* in Italian, is a way to enjoy seasonal vegetables. The extra-virgin olive oil must be one of exceptional flavor; if you like, add some minced garlic or fresh herbs to the oil.

2 heads Belgian endive
(chicory/witloof)

2 green (spring) onions

2 carrots, peeled

4 small celery stalks

1 yellow bell pepper
(capsicum), seeded, deribbed,
and cut into long, thin strips

4 radishes

1¼ cups (10 fl oz/310 ml)
extra-virgin olive oil

Salt and freshly ground pepper

Cut the endives, green onions, carrots, and celery stalks in half lengthwise.

Arrange all the vegetables on a large serving dish, leaving a space at the center for the bowl of dressing.

In a small bowl, stir together the oil and salt and pepper to taste. Place the bowl in the center of the dish and serve.

*Serves 4*

# Roasted Pepper Frittata

This frittata, or Italian-style flat omelet, is offered as a colorful and satisfying main dish. Garnish it with bell pepper (capsicum) slices and flat-leaf (Italian) parsley sprigs, if you wish.

Preheat the broiler (grill).

Cut the bell peppers in half lengthwise and remove the stems, seeds, and ribs. Arrange cut sides down on a baking sheet. Broil (grill) until the skins blacken and blister (see page 328). Transfer to a paper or plastic bag and let stand until the peppers cool and the skins loosen, about 10 minutes. Using your fingers or a small knife, peel off the pepper skins. Cut the peppers lengthwise into strips 1/4 inch (6 mm) wide. In a bowl, combine them with the garlic, vinegar, oregano, and salt and pepper to taste. Let marinate for 30 minutes.

In another bowl, whisk together the eggs, milk, and Parmesan until frothy. Add the bell pepper mixture and mix well. Season to taste with salt and pepper.

Preheat the oven to 400°F (200°C). In a 10-inch (25-cm) nonstick ovenproof frying pan over medium-high heat, warm the olive oil. When the oil is hot, add the egg mixture. When it starts to set, lift the edges of the frittata with a spatula so that some of the egg mixture runs underneath. Reduce the heat to medium and cook until the bottom is set but the top is still runny, 8–10 minutes. Transfer the pan to the oven and cook until the eggs are set on top and golden brown on the bottom, about 6–7 minutes.

Remove the frittata from the oven and loosen with a spatula. Invert the frittata onto a serving plate. Cut into wedges and serve hot or at room temperature.

*Serves 6*

1 red bell pepper (capsicum)

1 yellow bell pepper (capsicum)

1 green bell pepper (capsicum)

2 cloves garlic, minced

2 teaspoons balsamic vinegar

1/4 teaspoon dried oregano

Salt and freshly ground pepper

8 eggs

3 tablespoons milk

1/2 cup (2 oz/60 g) grated Parmesan cheese

1 1/2 tablespoons olive oil

# Rice Croquettes
# with Smoked Ham and Mozzarella

These croquettes — sometimes called by their Italian name *crocchete* — should have a crisp surface and soft interior. To make a simple meal, serve the croquettes with warm tomato sauce (page 323) and garnish with fresh basil.

4 cups (32 fl oz/1 l) Beef, Chicken, or Vegetable Stock (pages 320–321)

2 tablespoons unsalted butter

1½ cups (10½ oz/330 g) Arborio rice

½ cup (4 fl oz/125 ml) Simple Tomato Sauce (page 323)

½ cup (2 oz/60 g) grated Parmesan cheese

Salt and freshly ground pepper

1 egg yolk, beaten

1 slice smoked ham, 3 oz (90 g), cut into ¼-inch (6-mm) dice

½ cup (2½ oz/75 g) fresh peas or frozen peas, thawed, boiled for 1 minute and drained

3 oz (90 g) fresh or smoked mozzarella, cut into ¼-inch (6-mm) dice

2–3 cups (8–12 oz/250–375 g) dried bread crumbs (page 324)

Peanut oil for deep-frying

Pour the stock into a saucepan and bring to a boil. Reduce the heat to achieve a gentle simmer and maintain over low heat.

Meanwhile, in a large, heavy saucepan over medium heat, melt the butter. Add the rice and stir for 2 minutes to coat. Add a ladleful of the simmering stock and stir constantly. When the liquid is almost absorbed, add another ladleful. Stir constantly and add more stock, a ladleful at a time, when the previous ladleful is almost absorbed. The rice is done when it is firm but tender and the center of each grain is no longer chalky, 20–25 minutes.

Remove from the heat and stir in the tomato sauce, Parmesan, and salt and pepper to taste. Let cool completely, then stir in the egg yolk, mixing well. In a small bowl, toss together the ham, peas, and mozzarella.

Scoop up 2 tablespoons of the rice mixture. Using two fingers, make a cavity in the center. Fill it with a little of the ham mixture. Finish shaping the rice by hand to make a croquette the size of a large chicken egg. Roll in bread crumbs to coat completely. Repeat with the remaining rice and filling.

In a saucepan, pour in oil to a depth of 3 inches (7.5 cm) and heat to 350°F (180°C) on a deep-frying thermometer, or until a bit of bread turns golden within moments of being dropped into the oil. Add the croquettes, a few at a time, and fry, turning them to cook evenly, until deeply golden, 3–5 minutes. Using a slotted spoon, transfer to paper towels to drain. Serve immediately.

*Makes 24 croquettes; serves 6*

# Carpaccio

Prime beef is sliced to near-translucent thinness in this recipe, which originated at the famed Harry's Bar in Venice, Italy. If you like, add a little anchovy paste to the sauce.

1¼ lb (625 g) beef fillet, sirloin, or round, about 2½ inches (6 cm) thick, trimmed of all fat, rolled, and tied

FOR THE SAUCE:

1 egg yolk

2 teaspoons Dijon mustard

Pinch of salt

¾ cup (6 fl oz/180 ml) peanut oil or vegetable oil

2 tablespoons heavy (double) cream

1 tablespoon Worcestershire sauce

1 teaspoon Cognac or other brandy

Place the meat in a plastic freezer bag and place the bag in the freezer for 1 hour. This will make the meat very firm and easy to cut into thin slices.

Meanwhile, make the sauce: Combine the egg yolk and mustard in a blender or food processor. Process briefly to blend. Add the salt and let stand for 1 minute. With the motor running, slowly pour the oil into the yolk mixture in a thin, steady stream. The mixture will be quite thick. Add the cream, Worcestershire sauce, and brandy and process briefly to blend. Cover and refrigerate.

When the meat is chilled, remove it from the bag and place it on a cutting board. Cut the bag open along one side and the closed end so that you have one large plastic sheet. Spread the sheet over your work surface. Snip off the string and slice the meat ⅛ inch (3 mm) thick. Place the slices in pairs, side by side, on half of the plastic sheet. Fold the uncovered portion of the sheet over the meat and, using a rolling pin, gently roll over the meat to flatten the slices. They will quickly become translucent.

Cover a platter with the meat slices. With a spoon, drizzle the sauce over the meat in a zigzag pattern.

*Serves 6*

# Cold Veal with Tuna Mayonnaise

This classic Italian dish — *vitello tonnato* — pairs cold poached veal with a smooth mayonnaise-based sauce flavored with tuna and anchovies. Serve as part of a buffet lunch or dinner.

Combine the carrots, celery, clove-studded onion, parsley, bay leaf, coarse salt, peppercorns and 8 cups (64 fl oz/2 l) water in a Dutch oven or other heavy pot. Bring to a boil. Add the veal, reduce the heat to medium, cover with a tight-fitting lid, and simmer for 1 1/2 hours.

Remove the pot from the heat and let the veal cool in the cooking liquid. When it is cool, remove it from the liquid and wrap it tightly in plastic wrap. Refrigerate for at least 8 hours.

To make the sauce, combine the egg yolk and mustard in a blender. Process briefly to blend. Add the salt and let stand for 1 minute. With the motor running, slowly pour the oil into the yolk mixture in a thin, steady stream. The mixture will be quite thick. Add the lemon juice and process briefly to blend. Transfer to a bowl and set aside.

Drain the tuna. Place the tuna, anchovy paste, nutmeg, and ground black pepper to taste in the blender and process to a smooth purée. Add the mustard mixture and blend just until combined. Add the cream and blend for 10 seconds longer. Transfer to a bowl, cover, and refrigerate for up to 6 hours.

To serve, cut the veal against the grain into slices 1/8 inch (3 mm) thick. Arrange on a serving platter. Spoon the sauce over the top and garnish with the capers.

*Serves 6–8*

2 small carrots, peeled

2 celery stalks with leaves

1 yellow onion studded with 2 whole cloves

2 flat-leaf (Italian) parsley sprigs

1 bay leaf

2 teaspoons coarse sea salt

1/2 teaspoon *each* whole black and white peppercorns

3 lb (1.5 kg) boned rolled veal

1 egg yolk

1 teaspoon Dijon mustard

Pinch of salt

1/2 cup (4 fl oz/125 ml) peanut oil or vegetable oil

1 tablespoon fresh lemon juice

4 oz (125 g) canned tuna packed in olive oil

2 teaspoons anchovy paste

2 pinches ground nutmeg

Freshly ground black pepper

1 tablespoon heavy (double) cream

1 tablespoon capers, rinsed and well drained

# White Bean Soup with Rosemary and Parmesan

This sturdy soup is a meal in itself. It is popular in northern Italy, especially Tuscany, where the locals are nicknamed *mangiafagioli,* or "bean eaters." Feel free to substitute other dried beans such as chickpeas (garbanzo beans), white kidney beans, or cannellini beans.

1½ cups (10½ oz/330 g) dried small white (navy) beans

3 tablespoons olive oil

1 yellow onion, finely chopped

1 carrot, peeled and finely chopped

1 stalk celery, finely chopped

2 cloves garlic, minced

1 teaspoon minced fresh rosemary

7 cups (56 fl oz/1.75 l) Chicken Stock (page 320) or Vegetable Stock (page 321) or water

Salt and freshly ground pepper

½ cup (2 oz/60 g) grated Parmesan cheese

1 tablespoon chopped fresh flat-leaf (Italian) parsley

Pick over the beans, discarding any stones or misshapen beans. Rinse the beans. Place in a bowl, add cold water to cover, and soak for about 3 hours. Drain the beans and set aside.

In a soup pot over medium heat, warm the olive oil. Add the onion, carrot, and celery and sauté, stirring occasionally until the vegetables are soft, about 10 minutes. Add the garlic and rosemary and continue to sauté for 3 minutes. Add the drained beans and the stock. Bring to a boil, reduce the heat to low, and simmer gently, uncovered, until the beans are tender, 1–1½ hours. Remove from the heat and let cool slightly.

Place one-third of the bean mixture in a blender or food processor. Process to a smooth puree. Return the purée to the soup and reheat gently. Season to taste with salt and pepper.

Ladle the soup into warmed individual bowls. Garnish with the Parmesan and parsley and serve immediately.

*Serves 6*

# Cappelletti in Broth

Cappelletti is a pasta that is very similar to ravioli and is usually stuffed with meat or cheese. The name literally means "little hats" in Italian. If dried porcini mushrooms are unavailable, substitute white button mushrooms.

⅓ oz (10 g) dried porcini mushrooms or 6 oz (185 g) fresh white button mushrooms, stems removed, caps brushed clean and cut into slices 1/16 inch (2 mm) thick

1 tablespoon unsalted butter

2 chicken livers

2 bay leaves

¼ cup (2 fl oz/60 ml) dry Marsala wine

Salt and freshly ground pepper

6 oz (185 g) ham

2 egg yolks, lightly beaten

¼ cup (1 oz/30 g) grated Parmesan cheese

6 oz (185 g) Fresh Egg Pasta dough (page 322)

8 cups (64 fl oz/2 l) Chicken Stock (page 320)

If using porcini, place in a bowl with lukewarm water to cover and soak until softened, about 30 minutes. Drain, squeeze out excess water, chop finely, and set aside.

In a large frying pan over medium heat, melt the butter. Add the chicken livers and bay leaves. Sauté, stirring occasionally, until browned, about 5 minutes. Add the porcini and Marsala, stir well, and cook over low heat until the wine evaporates. (If using fresh mushrooms, sauté them with the chicken livers, then add the wine.) Season to taste with salt and pepper. Remove the pan from the heat and discard the bay leaves. Turn out the contents of the pan onto a cutting board and let cool. Add the ham and finely chop the mixture together. Place in a bowl, add the egg yolks and Parmesan, and mix well. Set aside.

Prepare the pasta dough according to the directions for Fresh Egg Pasta (page 322). Roll out the dough into a very thin sheet and, using a pastry cutter, cut it into 2-inch (5-cm) rounds. On the center of each round, place a small mound of filling. Moisten the edges with cold water and fold in half. Pinch to seal.

Working with one dumpling at a time, fold the sealed edge up to form a cuff. Holding the straight edge of the half circle against the tip of your index finger, wrap the pasta around your finger. Bring the 2 points together to seal. Set aside on a lightly floured work surface. Repeat to form the remaining cappelletti.

In a large pot, bring the stock to a boil. Add the cappelletti and cook until they rise to the surface, about 2 minutes. Ladle the pasta and broth into warmed individual bowls and serve at once.

*Serves 6*

# Minestrone with White Beans and Pasta

Brimming with vegetables, pasta, and beans, minestrone is Italy's best-known soup. Diced potato can replace the pasta and coarsely chopped broccoli or cauliflower can stand in for the cabbage.

½ cup (3½ oz/105 g) dried cannellini beans

2 tablespoons olive oil

1 yellow onion, finely chopped

1 clove garlic, finely chopped

5 cups (40 fl oz/1.25 l) Chicken Stock (page 320) or Vegetable Stock (page 321)

1 lb (500 g) canned plum (Roma) tomatoes with juice

1 large carrot

1 zucchini (courgette), chopped

4 savoy cabbages, thinly sliced with outer leaves removed

1½ teaspoons *each* dried basil and dried oregano

1½ teaspoons sugar

1 bay leaf

⅓ cup (2 oz/60 g) dried small pasta such as elbow macaroni

2 tablespoons balsamic vinegar

Salt and freshly ground pepper

2 tablespoons coarsely chopped fresh flat-leaf (Italian) parsley

⅔ cup (3 oz/90 g) grated Parmesan cheese

Pick over the beans, discarding any stones or misshapen beans. Rinse the beans. Place in a bowl, add cold water to cover, and soak for about 4 hours.

Drain the beans and place in a saucepan with water to cover by about 1 inch (2.5 cm). Bring to a boil, reduce the heat to low, cover partially, and simmer gently until the beans are tender and most of the liquid is absorbed, 1–1 ½ hours.

When the beans have been cooking for about 1 hour, warm the olive oil in a soup pot over medium heat. Add the onion and garlic and sauté until translucent, 2–3 minutes. Add the stock and the tomatoes, coarsely breaking up the tomatoes with a wooden spoon. Peel and chop the carrot. Then, add the carrot, zucchini, cabbages, basil, oregano, sugar, and bay leaf. Cover partially and simmer until the vegetables are tender-crisp, about 20 minutes. Add the pasta and simmer, uncovered, until the pasta is al dente, 8–10 minutes; the timing will depend on the type of pasta.

Drain the beans and add to the pot along with the balsamic vinegar. Season to taste with salt and pepper. Ladle the soup into warmed individual bowls. Garnish with the parsley and Parmesan and serve immediately.

*Serves 6–8*

# Stracciatella alla Fiorentina

*Stracciatella* means "little rag" in Italian, a fanciful description of the shreds that form when egg and Parmesan cheese are stirred into simmering stock to make this favorite soup.

In a large saucepan, bring the stock to a boil and reduce to a brisk simmer.

Meanwhile, in a bowl, lightly beat the eggs and then stir in the Parmesan. While stirring the stock constantly, drizzle in the egg mixture and then add the spinach. Simmer 2–3 minutes longer and serve immediately.

*Serves 4–6*

6 cups (48 fl oz/1.5 l)
Chicken Stock (page 320)

4 eggs

¼ cup (1 oz/30 g) grated
Parmesan cheese

1 cup (2 oz/60 g) firmly packed
thinly shredded spinach leaves

# Pasta and Kidney Bean Soup

Known as *pasta e fagioli* in Tuscany, this hearty first-course soup is also robust enough to be served as a main course, accompanied by crusty bread and a green salad. Substitute red kidney, pinto, or cranberry (borlotti) beans, if you like.

Pick over the beans, discarding any stones or misshapen beans. Rinse the beans. Place in a bowl, add cold water to cover, and soak for about 4 hours.

Drain the beans and place in a saucepan with water to cover by 2 inches (5 cm). Bring to a boil, reduce the heat to low, and simmer gently, uncovered, until the beans are tender, 45–60 minutes. Drain and set aside.

In a soup pot over medium-low heat, warm the olive oil. Add the pancetta, if using, onion, and garlic and sauté slowly, stirring until the onion is soft, about 12 minutes. Add the tomatoes, sage, red pepper flakes, and salt and black pepper to taste. Simmer for 20 minutes. Add the beans and stock and simmer for 30 minutes longer to blend the flavors. The beans will be very tender and the soup will become stewlike.

Add the pasta to the soup and simmer, uncovered, until the pasta is al dente, 12–15 minutes; the timing will depend on the type of pasta.

Ladle the soup into warmed bowls. Garnish with the cheese and serve immediately.

*Serves 6*

1 cup (7 oz/220 g) dried white kidney beans or cannellini beans

2 tablespoons extra-virgin olive oil

2 oz (60 g) pancetta or bacon, finely chopped (optional)

1 yellow onion, finely chopped

2 cloves garlic, minced

3 tomatoes, peeled, seeded, and chopped (fresh or canned)

1 tablespoon chopped fresh sage

Pinch of red pepper flakes

Salt and freshly ground black pepper

4 cups (32 fl oz/1 l) Chicken Stock (page 320) or Vegetable Stock (page 321) or water

3/4 cup (3 oz/90 g) dried small pasta such as elbow macaroni or tiny shells

6 tablespoons grated pecorino romano or Parmesan cheese

# Tomatoes and Mozzarella

A classic combination of Neapolitan cuisine, this salad is quick to prepare and extremely delicious, but only if you choose top-quality ingredients: vine-ripened tomatoes and the freshest mozzarella. If you like, use fresh oregano or thyme in place of the basil.

1 bunch fresh basil, stemmed

4 tomatoes, thinly sliced

3/4 lb (375 g) fresh mozzarella cheese, thinly sliced

1 tablespoon capers, rinsed and well drained

8 black olives

4 anchovy fillets, chopped

Salt

1/4 cup (2 fl oz/60 ml) extra-virgin olive oil

Set aside the best basil leaves for garnish.

Arrange the tomato and mozzarella slices and the remaining basil leaves on a serving dish, alternating the slices and the leaves. If you have any leftover tomato slices, arrange them in an attractive pattern in the center of the dish.

Decorate the plate with the capers, olives, and anchovies. Scatter the reserved basil leaves on top, tearing any large leaves. Sprinkle to taste with salt, drizzle the olive oil in a thin stream over the top, and serve.

*Serves 4*

# Orange and Onion Salad

Here is a popular Sicilian salad that makes an excellent appetizer or a side dish with chicken, duck, turkey, or any wild fowl. If you want to give the raw onion a milder taste, soak it in cold water to cover for 30 minutes, then drain and dry before combining it with the oranges.

Peel the oranges, carefully removing all the white membrane. Cut crosswise into thin slices and remove any seeds.

Arrange the slices on a large serving platter. Place the onion slices on top. Scatter the oregano over the onion. Sprinkle with salt and pepper to taste and then drizzle with the olive oil. Garnish with black olives. Refrigerate until ready to serve.

*Serves 4*

4 oranges

1 red onion, cut into paper-thin slices

1 teaspoon fresh oregano leaves

Salt and freshly ground pepper

1/4 cup (2 fl oz/60 ml) extra-virgin olive oil

Black olives for garnish

# Beef Fillet and Parmesan Salad

Here is a popular Italian raw beef salad that is both light and flavorful. Watercress, arugula (rocket), or any other peppery salad green can be used in place of the radicchio.

3/4 lb (375 g) beef fillet

1/4 cup (2 fl oz/60 ml) balsamic vinegar

Salt

6 tablespoons (3 fl oz/90 ml) extra-virgin olive oil

1 head radicchio, leaves torn into bite-sized pieces

2 oz (60 g) Parmesan cheese

Place the beef fillet in a plastic freezer bag and place the bag in the freezer for about 20 minutes. This will make the meat slightly firm and easier to slice.

Meanwhile, in a shallow bowl, stir together the vinegar and salt to taste until well mixed. Add the olive oil and stir vigorously until blended.

Make a bed of the radicchio on a large serving platter. Slice the beef fillet on the diagonal into slices so thin as to be almost transparent. Dip each slice into the oil mixture and then lay the slices on the radicchio.

Using a sharp knife or a vegetable peeler, cut the Parmesan into paper-thin shavings. Scatter them evenly over the meat and serve.

*Serves 4*

# Arugula and Fig Salad

Use red-colored figs, which are plump and have a thin skin. Wrapping the figs in a kitchen towel and refrigerating them for a couple of hours makes them easier to cut.

Wrap the figs in a kitchen towel and refrigerate for 2 hours.

Arrange the arugula on a serving platter. In a small bowl, stir together the olive oil and salt and cayenne pepper to taste until well mixed. Cut the unpeeled figs crosswise into thin slices and arrange atop the arugula. Scatter the cheese over the figs. Stir the dressing again, pour it over the salad, and serve.

*Serves 4*

8 red figs

4 oz (125 g) arugula (rocket), tough stems removed

5 tablespoons (3 fl oz/80 ml) extra-virgin olive oil

Salt

Cayenne pepper

6 oz (185 g) fresh goat cheese, crumbled

# Roasted Pepper Salad with Garlic Bread

Caper berries are larger than regular capers — about the size of an olive or a small cherry — and have long stems. Look for them in Italian delicatessens and specialty food stores. If unavailable, substitute ¼ cup (2 oz/60 g) regular capers, rinsed and well drained.

Preheat the broiler (grill). Cut the bell peppers in half lengthwise and remove the stems, seeds, and ribs. Arrange cut sides down on a baking sheet. Broil (grill) until the skins blacken and blister, about 10 minutes, Transfer to a paper or plastic bag and let stand until the peppers cool and the skins loosen, about 10 minutes. Using your fingers or a small knife, peel off the skins. Cut the peppers lengthwise into strips 1 inch (2.5 cm) wide.

To make the dressing, in a small bowl, whisk together the olive oil, red wine vinegar, and balsamic vinegar. Season to taste with salt and pepper. Set aside.

In a bowl, combine the bell pepper strips, ¼ cup (2 fl oz/60 ml) of the dressing (or as needed), and salt and pepper to taste and toss well. Arrange the bell pepper strips on a serving platter or individual plates and scatter the caper berries, olives, and basil over the top.

Toast the bread until lightly golden on both sides. Lightly rub the garlic halves over one side of each bread slice.

Tuck the garlic bread slices alongside the salad and serve.

*Serves 6*

4 large red bell peppers (capsicums), roasted and cut into strips 1 inch (2.5 cm) wide

4 large yellow bell peppers (capsicums)

Salt and freshly ground pepper

½ cup (3 oz/90 g) caper berries (see note)

⅓ cup (2 oz/60 g) well-drained Kalamata or Niçoise olives

½ cup (½ oz/15 g) loosely packed fresh basil leaves

5 tablespoons (3 fl oz/80 ml) extra-virgin olive oil

1 tablespoon red wine vinegar

1 tablespoon balsamic vinegar

Salt and freshly ground pepper

6 slices coarse country bread

2 cloves garlic, halved

# Spaghetti Salad with Tomatoes and Arugula

The puréed sauce for this salad resembles pesto, but the sweet, peppery flavor is quite different. The finished dish may be refrigerated for up to 6 hours, although it should be brought to room temperature before serving.

4 plum (Roma) tomatoes, peeled, halved, and seeded (page 329)

1¼ lb (625 g) dried spaghetti

2 oz (60 g) arugula (rocket), tough stems removed

Salt and freshly ground pepper

½ cup (4 fl oz/125 ml) extra-virgin olive oil

Bring a large pot three-fourths full of salted water to a boil. Add the spaghetti and cook until al dente, about 8 minutes.

Meanwhile, in a blender or food processor, combine the arugula and tomatoes. Season with salt and pepper to taste. With the motor running, add the olive oil in a slow, thin, steady stream. The mixture should be smooth and creamy.

Drain the pasta and transfer to a serving bowl. Pour half of the tomato sauce over the top and toss well. Spoon the remaining sauce over the top and let cool to room temperature before serving.

*Serves 6*

# Potato Salad with Tuna Dressing

A creamy tuna dressing accents chunks of red potato and crisp green beans. This is a substantial potato salad that can be served on a summer buffet with cold poached salmon and a cherry tomato salad.

Bring a large pot three-fourths full of water to a boil. Add salt to taste and the potatoes and cook until tender but slightly resistant when pierced with a fork, 25–30 minutes. Drain well and let cool, then cut into 1½-inch (4-cm) cubes and place in a bowl.

Meanwhile, bring a saucepan three-fourths full of water to a boil. Have a large bowl of ice water ready. Add the green beans to the boiling water and boil until tender-crisp, 5–7 minutes. Drain, immediately immerse in the ice water, and drain again. Add to the bowl with the potatoes.

To make the dressing, drain the tuna. In a blender or food processor, combine the mayonnaise, sour cream, drained tuna, lemon juice, anchovy paste, and ¼ teaspoon white pepper. Process until creamy.

Pour the dressing over the potatoes and green beans and mix gently until evenly coated. Taste and adjust the seasoning. Transfer to a serving bowl and garnish with the capers, tomato halves, and olives. Refrigerate for 1–2 hours before serving to chill and to allow the flavors to blend.

*Serves 6–8*

Salt

3 lb (1.5 kg) red potatoes, unpeeled and well scrubbed

1 lb (500 g) green beans, trimmed and cut on the diagonal into 1-inch (2.5-cm) pieces

FOR THE DRESSING:

6½ oz (200 g) canned white-meat tuna packed in water

1 cup (8 fl oz/250 ml) mayonnaise

¼ cup (2 oz/60 g) sour cream

3 tablespoons fresh lemon juice

2 teaspoons anchovy paste

Freshly ground white pepper

FOR GARNISH:

2 tablespoons capers, rinsed and well drained

Yellow pear or red cherry tomato halves

Niçoise olives

# Fusilli Salad
# with Bell Peppers and Mozzarella

The array of bell peppers (capsicums) now available to cooks gives this southern Italian pasta salad an especially colorful palette. The ingredients, except for the basil, can be assembled in advance and refrigerated. Creamy fontina may be substituted for the mozzarella.

3 red or yellow bell peppers (capsicums), or a mixture

1 clove garlic

2 anchovy fillets, drained

1 lb (500 g) dried fusilli

6 tablespoons (3 fl oz/90 ml) extra-virgin olive oil

2 tablespoons capers, rinsed and well drained

10 oz (315 g) mozzarella cheese, diced

12 fresh basil leaves, torn into small pieces

Salt and freshly ground pepper

Preheat the oven to 350°F (180°C).

Preheat the broiler (grill). Cut the bell peppers in half lengthwise and remove the stems, seeds, and ribs. Arrange cut sides down on a baking sheet. Broil (grill) until the skins blacken and blister, about 10 minutes. Transfer to a paper or plastic bag and let stand until the peppers cool and the skins loosen, about 10 minutes. Using your fingers or a small knife, peel off the skins. Cut lengthwise into strips about 3/8 inch (1 cm) wide. Set aside.

Place the garlic and anchovies in a small bowl. With a fork, mash them together to form a smooth paste. Set aside.

Bring a large pot three-fourths full of salted water to a boil. Add the fusilli and cook until al dente, 8–10 minutes.

Drain the pasta and transfer to a large, shallow serving bowl. Pour the olive oil over the pasta, add the anchovy-garlic paste and capers, and toss well. Let cool to room temperature.

Add the bell pepper strips, mozzarella, and basil. Season to taste with salt and pepper and toss well. Serve at room temperature.

*Serves 6*

# Italian Bread Salad with Tomatoes and Basil

In Italy, yesterday's stale bread can be made into today's fresh and flavorful *panzanella* salad. Use good-quality coarse country bread. Loaves made with unbleached flour are ideal, although those that include whole-wheat (wholemeal) or rye flour may also be used.

Cut the bread crosswise into slices 1 inch (2.5 cm) thick. Place in a large shallow container and pour 1 cup (8 fl oz/250 ml) water evenly over the slices. Let stand for 1 minute. Carefully squeeze the bread between your hands until dry. Tear the bread into rough 1-inch (2.5-cm) pieces and spread out on paper towels for 10 minutes to absorb any excess moisture .

In a bowl, combine the tomatoes, onion, cucumber, garlic, capers, basil, and bread. Toss together to mix well.

To make the dressing, in a small bowl, whisk together the olive oil, red wine vinegar and balsamic vinegar. Season to taste with salt and pepper. Add the dressing to the bread mixture and toss until evenly distributed. Cover and refrigerate for 1 hour.

Season to taste with salt and pepper and toss again. Transfer to a platter or individual plates and serve.

*Serves 6*

1 small loaf stale coarse country bread, about 1/2 lb (250 g)

6 tomatoes, seeded (page 329) and cut into 1/2-inch (12-mm) dice

1 small red onion, thinly sliced

1 cucumber, peeled, halved lengthwise, seeded, and cut into 1/2-inch (12-mm) dice

2 cloves garlic, minced

3 tablespoons capers, rinsed and well drained

1/2 cup (1/2 oz/15 g) loosely packed fresh basil leaves, torn into small pieces

1/2 cup (4 fl oz/125 ml) plus 2 tablespoons extra-virgin olive oil

2 tablespoons red wine vinegar

2 tablespoons balsamic vinegar

Salt and freshly ground pepper

# Blacksmith Salad

This oddly named salad was created in Modena, the ancient Italian city that gave the world balsamic vinegar. It is traditionally topped with Parmesan, although any type of hard or semihard cheese can be used.

3 small heads butter (Boston) lettuce, separated into leaves

2 tablespoons balsamic vinegar

Pinch of salt

3 tablespoons extra-virgin olive oil

1¹/₂ cups (3 oz/90 g) home-made croutons

3 oz (90 g) hard or semihard cheese such as Parmesan, Asiago, or Gruyère

Tear the large lettuce leaves in half and place all the lettuce in a salad bowl.

Sprinkle the vinegar and salt over the lettuce and toss well to mix. Drizzle with the olive oil, scatter the croutons over the top, and toss again.

Grate, shred, or shave the cheese and scatter it over the salad. Serve immediately.

*Serves 6*

# Lemon and Fennel Salad

Serve this refreshing salad alongside baked or grilled fish. The cumin seeds may be replaced with fresh dill, poppy seeds, or, for a slightly spicier flavor, mustard seeds.

Peel the lemon, carefully removing all the white membrane. Cut crosswise into very thin slices and remove any seeds.

Combine the fennel and lemon slices in a salad bowl. Add the cumin seeds and salt and green pepper to taste. Mix well. Drizzle with the olive oil and toss again. Let stand for 10 minutes to allow the flavors to blend, then serve.

*Serves 4*

1 lemon

3 fennel bulbs, trimmed and thinly sliced crosswise

2 tablespoons cumin seeds

Salt and freshly ground pepper

1/4 cup (2 fl oz/60 ml) extra-virgin olive oil

# Pizza & Calzones

# Pizza Margherita

A well-loved and widely traveled variety of pizza, this combination was the inspiration of nineteenth-century Neapolitan pizza maker Raffaele Esposito, who created it to honor Queen Margherita, wife of Italy's King Umberto I, on a royal visit to Naples in 1889.

Make the pizza dough. Preheat the oven to 450°F (230°C). If using a baking stone or tiles, place in the oven now.

Shape the pizza dough into one large pizza or 4 individual pizzas. Cover with the mozzarella and then the tomatoes. Scatter the basil over the top. Season to taste with salt and pepper and drizzle 3 tablespoons of the olive oil over the top. Transfer to the oven and bake for 10 minutes. Reduce the oven temperature to 400°F (200°C) and bake until the crust is golden, about 10 minutes longer. Drizzle the remaining 1 tablespoon olive oil over the top and serve immediately.

*Serves 4*

Basic Pizza Dough (page 318)

7 oz (220 g) mozzarella cheese, thinly sliced

8 fresh plum (Roma) tomatoes, peeled (page 329) and chopped, or canned plum tomatoes, drained and chopped

1/4 cup fresh basil leaves, torn into small pieces

Salt and freshly ground pepper

4 tablespoons (2 fl oz/60 ml) extra-virgin olive oil

# Fontina Cheese Pizza

The topping—a rich and creamy blend of fontina, Parmesan, and egg yolks—is especially good on miniature rounds of pizza dough. You can also scatter some crumbled, crisp bacon or cooked sausage over the pizza dough before adding the cheese.

Cornmeal Pizza Dough
(page 318)

10 oz (315 g) fontina cheese,
thinly sliced

3/4 cup (6 fl oz/180 ml) dry
white wine

1/2 cup (2 oz/60 g) grated
Parmesan cheese

3 egg yolks, lightly beaten

Salt and freshly ground pepper

Make the pizza dough. Preheat the oven to 450°F (230°C). If using a baking stone or tiles, place in the oven now.

Combine the fontina and wine in a heatproof bowl and place in a saucepan filled halfway with almost boiling water over medium-high heat, to create a bain-marie. When the fontina has melted, add the Parmesan and egg yolks and stir until the mixture is creamy and thickens, about 5 minutes. Do not let the mixture boil. Remove from the heat and season to taste with salt and pepper.

Shape the pizza dough into one large pizza or small hors d'oeuvre–sized rounds. Spoon the cheese mixture evenly over the top. Transfer to the oven and bake for 10 minutes. Reduce the oven temperature to 400°F (200°C) and bake until the crust is golden, about 10 minutes longer. Serve immediately.

*Serves 4, or more as hors d'oeuvres*

# Onion and Goat Cheese Pizza

The onions are cooked with sugar and vinegar until they are almost caramelized, resulting in a sweet-tart flavor perfectly suited to the fresh, creamy goat cheese that covers the dough. Shape four individual pizzas and serve them as a main course for a light lunch.

Potato Pizza Dough (page 319)

4 large yellow onions, thinly sliced

1 tablespoon unsalted butter

3 tablespoons extra-virgin olive oil

1 tablespoon sugar

3 tablespoons red wine vinegar

Salt

6 oz (185 g) fresh goat cheese, crumbled

1/2 cup (2 oz/60 g) chopped walnuts

Make the pizza dough. Preheat the oven to 450°F (230°C). If using a baking stone or tiles, place in the oven now.

In a frying pan over low heat, combine the onions, butter, and 2 tablespoons of the olive oil. Cover and cook, stirring often, until the onions are very soft, about 30 minutes, adding a little water occasionally if needed to prevent sticking. Add the sugar and vinegar and continue to cook until the vinegar evaporates, about 3 minutes. Add salt to taste.

Shape the pizza dough into one large pizza or 4 individual pizzas. Cover with the cheese. Scatter the walnuts over the top and then the onions. Transfer to the oven and bake for 10 minutes. Reduce the oven temperature to 400°F (200°C) and bake until the crust is golden, about 10 minutes longer. Drizzle the remaining 1 tablespoon olive oil over the top and serve immediately.

*Serves 4*

# Gorgonzola and Walnut Pizza

Although the pizza itself is contemporary, the pairing of blue-veined cheese with walnuts is a time-honored classic. Offer it after dinner, with a glass of Vin Santo or Port.

10 oz (315 g) Gorgonzola cheese

Whole-Wheat Pizza Dough (page 319)

4 tablespoons (2 fl oz/60 ml) extra-virgin olive oil

2/3 cup (2 oz/60 g) walnut halves

1 tablespoon lemon zest

Freshly ground pepper

Place the Gorgonzola in the freezer for 30 minutes, to make it easier to slice.

Make the pizza dough. Preheat the oven to 450°F (230°C). If using a baking stone or tiles, place in the oven now.

Thinly slice the gorgonzola. Shape the pizza dough and drizzle 2 tablespoons of the olive oil over the top. Cover with the Gorgonzola slices and then with the walnuts. Sprinkle evenly with the lemon zest and drizzle 1 tablespoon of the olive oil over the top. Season to taste with pepper. Transfer to the oven and bake for 10 minutes. Reduce the oven temperature to 400°F (200°C) and bake until the crust is golden, about 10 minutes longer. Drizzle the remaining 1 tablespoon olive oil over the top and serve immediately.

*Serves 4*

# Four-Cheese Pizza

Like four different pizzas in one, this recipe presents a quartet of distinctive toppings. Feel free to substitute whatever cheeses are available and appealing to you.

Place the Gorgonzola and goat cheese in the freezer for 30 minutes, to make them easier to slice.

Make the pizza dough. Preheat the oven to 450°F (230°C). If using a baking stone or tiles, place in the oven now.

Thinly slice the Gorgonzola, goat cheese, fontina, and mozzarella. Shape the pizza dough and top with the cheeses. Transfer to the oven and bake for 10 minutes. Reduce the oven temperature to 400°F (200°C) and bake until the crust is golden, about 10 minutes longer. Drizzle the olive oil over the top and serve immediately.

*Serves 4*

2 oz (60 g) Gorgonzola cheese

2 oz (60 g) fresh goat cheese

Potato Pizza Dough (page 319)

2 oz (60 g) fontina cheese

2 oz (60 g) mozzarella cheese

1 tablespoon extra-virgin olive oil

# Black Olive Pizza

An herb-flavored pizza dough distinguishes this modern-day version of a Roman classic, which conceals its cheese beneath the tomato sauce. For a more authentic pie, use Basic Pizza Dough (page 318). Shape the dough into four individual squares, if you like, for a rustic look.

Make the pizza dough. Preheat the oven to 450°F (230°C). If using a baking stone or tiles, place in the oven now.

In a frying pan over low heat, warm 3 tablespoons of the olive oil. Add the garlic and sauté, stirring occasionally, until translucent, about 2 minutes. Add the tomatoes, cover partially, and cook, stirring occasionally, until the liquid evaporates, about 40 minutes. Add the thyme and season to taste with salt and pepper.

Shape the pizza dough into one large pizza or 4 individual pizzas. Cover with the mozzarella. Cover with the tomato mixture and scatter the olives on top. Transfer to the oven and bake for 10 minutes. Reduce the oven temperature to 400°F (200°C) and bake until the crust is golden, about 10 minutes longer. Drizzle the remaining 1 tablespoon olive oil over the top and serve immediately.

*Serves 4*

Herb Pizza Dough (page 319)

4 tablespoons (2 fl oz/60 ml) extra-virgin olive oil

4 cloves garlic, chopped

1 1/4 lb (625 g) fresh plum (Roma) tomatoes, peeled (page 329) and chopped, or canned plum tomatoes with their liquid, chopped

2 tablespoons fresh thyme leaves

Salt and freshly ground pepper

7 oz (220 g) mozzarella cheese, thinly sliced

20 Gaeta or Greek black olives, pitted

# Potato, Onion, and Rosemary Pizza

This dish is a robust specialty of the pizzeria La Baia in Milan. If you wish, make this recipe with Basic Pizza Dough (page 318). Crumbled crisp bacon or pancetta scattered over the onions would be a delicious addition.

Whole-Wheat Pizza Dough (page 319)

2 boiling potatoes

1 yellow onion, sliced paper-thin

2 tablespoons fresh rosemary leaves, chopped if desired

4 tablespoons (2 fl oz/60 ml) extra-virgin olive oil

Salt and freshly ground pepper

Make the pizza dough. Preheat the oven to 450°F (230°C). If using a baking stone or tiles, place in the oven now.

Bring a saucepan three-fourths full of salted water to a boil. Add the potatoes and cook until tender, about 30 minutes. Drain, peel, and let cool, then slice thinly.

Shape the pizza dough and cover with the potatoes. Arrange the onion slices on top and sprinkle with the rosemary. Drizzle 3 tablespoons of the olive oil over the top. Season to taste with salt and pepper. Transfer to the oven and bake for 10 minutes. Reduce the oven temperature to 400°F (200°C) and bake until the crust is golden, about 10 minutes longer. Drizzle the remaining 1 tablespoon olive oil over the top and serve immediately.

*Serves 4*

# Roasted Bell Pepper Pizza

This preparation also works well with eggplant (aubergine), punctured in several places with a fork and roasted until soft, following the same instructions given below for peppers. For variety, shape the pizza into an oval, if you like.

Herb Pizza Dough (page 319)

3 red or yellow bell peppers (capsicums) or a mixture

4 tablespoons (2 fl oz/60 ml) extra-virgin olive oil

1/2 cup (2 oz/60 g) fine dried bread crumbs

3 cloves garlic, minced

3 large tomatoes, peeled (page 329) and thinly sliced

2 tablespoons capers, rinsed and well drained

Salt and freshly ground pepper

Preheat the broiler (grill). Cut the bell peppers in half lengthwise and remove the stems, seeds, and ribs. Arrange cut sides down on a baking sheet. Broil (grill) until the skins blacken and blister, about 10 minutes. Transfer to a paper or plastic bag and let stand until the peppers cool and the skins loosen, about 10 minutes. Using your fingers or a small knife, peel off the skins. Cut lengthwise into strips about 3/8 inch (1 cm) wide. Set aside.

Make the pizza dough. Preheat the oven to 450°F (230°C). If using a baking stone or tiles, place in the oven now.

In a frying pan over medium heat, warm 3 tablespoons of the olive oil. Add the bread crumbs and garlic and sauté, stirring until golden, about 3 minutes. Set aside.

Shape the pizza dough and cover with the bell pepper strips. Arrange the tomato slices on top and sprinkle with the capers. Season to taste with salt and pepper. Transfer to the oven and bake for 10 minutes. Reduce the oven temperature to 400°F (200°C) and bake until the crust is golden, about 10 minutes longer. Drizzle the remaining 1 tablespoon olive oil over the top and sprinkle with the fried bread crumbs. Serve immediately.

*Serves 4*

# Fresh Herb Pizza

Serve this pizza as an appetizer or on its own as a simple main course. Feel free to use your own favorite fresh herbs, or substitute dried herbs, halving the quantities. You can also use mixed dried spice seeds such as fennel or coriander, using 1 tablespoon seeds in all.

Make the pizza dough. Preheat the oven to 450°F (230°C). If using a baking stone or tiles, place in the oven now.

On a lightly floured work surface, knead 2 tablespoons of the olive oil and the rosemary into the pizza dough for 1–2 minutes.

Shape the pizza dough and sprinkle evenly with all the remaining herbs and the onion and garlic. Drizzle the remaining 2 tablespoons olive oil over the top. Season to taste with salt and pepper. Transfer to the oven and bake for 10 minutes. Reduce the oven temperature to 400°F (200°C) and bake until the crust is golden, about 10 minutes longer. Serve immediately.

*Serves 4*

Potato Pizza Dough (page 319)

4 tablespoons (2 fl oz/60 ml) extra-virgin olive oil

1 tablespoon minced fresh rosemary

1 tablespoon minced fresh marjoram

1 tablespoon minced fresh chives

1 tablespoon minced fresh basil

1 tablespoon chopped onion

1 clove garlic, minced

Salt and freshly ground pepper

# Onion Ring Pizza
# with Golden Potatoes

The earthy flavor of potato pizza dough is accented with crispy potatoes and onions in this hearty pizza. Serve as an autumn lunch or dinner. Save some sage leaves to use as garnish, if you like.

Potato Pizza Dough (page 319)

2 tablespoons all-purpose (plain) flour

1 yellow onion, sliced and separated into rings

5 cups (40 fl oz/1.25 l) olive oil or vegetable oil for deep-frying

1/2 cup (4 fl oz/125 ml) extra-virgin olive oil

4 boiling potatoes, peeled and cut into 3/4-inch (2-cm) dice

3 cloves garlic

Handful of fresh sage leaves

Salt and freshly ground pepper

1 tablespoon sesame seeds

Make the pizza dough. Preheat the oven to 450°F (230°C). If using a baking stone or tiles, place in the oven now.

Place the flour in a paper bag and add the onion rings. Shake the bag well to coat the onion rings fully, then take them out one by one, shaking off any excess flour.

Pour the 5 cups oil into a deep frying pan and heat to about 350°F (180°C) on a deep-frying thermometer. Slip the onion rings into the hot oil, a few at a time, and fry until they turn a deep gold, about 5 minutes. Transfer with a slotted spoon to paper towels to drain.

In a large frying pan over medium heat, warm the 1/2 cup (4 fl oz/125 ml) extra-virgin olive oil. Add the potatoes, garlic, and sage and cook, stirring occasionally, until the potatoes are a deep golden color, about 20 minutes. Transfer to paper towels to drain. Discard the garlic and sage. Season the potatoes with salt and pepper.

Shape the pizza dough and cover evenly with the potatoes, onion rings, and sesame seeds. Carefully transfer to the oven and bake for 10 minutes. Reduce the oven temperature to 400°F (200°C) and bake until the crust is golden, about 10 minutes longer. Serve immediately.

*Serves 4*

# Spinach and Goat Cheese Pizza

The cheese is blended with the vegetables and eggs in this pizza, creating an almost soufflélike topping. Swiss chard leaves, without the ribs, can be used in place of the spinach, if you wish.

Make the pizza dough. Preheat the oven to 450°F (230°C). If using a baking stone or tiles, place in the oven now.

Have a large bowl of ice water ready. Bring a saucepan three-fourths full of water to a boil. Add the spinach and cook for 2 minutes. Drain well, immediately immerse in the ice water, and drain well again. Squeeze the spinach dry.

In a frying pan over medium heat, warm 2 tablespoons of the oil. Add the spinach and sauté, stirring often, for about 3 minutes. Season to taste with salt and pepper. Remove from the heat and cool slightly, then stir in the eggs, nutmeg, and cheese.

Shape the pizza dough and drizzle with 1 tablespoon of the olive oil. Cover with the spinach mixture. Transfer to the oven and bake for 10 minutes. Reduce the oven temperature to 400°F (200°C) and bake until the crust is golden, about 10 minutes longer. Drizzle the remaining 1 tablespoon olive oil over the top and serve immediately.

*Serves 4*

Cornmeal Pizza Dough
(page 318)

1¼ lb (625 g) spinach, tough stems removed

4 tablespoons (2 fl oz/60 ml) extra-virgin olive oil

Salt and freshly ground pepper

2 eggs, lightly beaten

½ teaspoon ground nutmeg

6 oz (185 g) fresh goat cheese

# Marinated Zucchini Pizza

This marinating technique also works well with eggplants (aubergines). Covering the pizza with half green zucchini (courgette) and half yellow zucchini, alternating the slices, makes a tantalizing presentation.

Herb Pizza Dough (page 319)

5 cups (40 fl oz/1.25 l) olive oil or vegetable oil for deep-frying

4 zucchini (courgettes), about 13 oz (410 g) total weight, cut into slices 1/8 inch (3 mm) thick

1/4 cup (2 fl oz/60 ml) red wine vinegar

3 cloves garlic, chopped

Salt and freshly ground pepper

1 handful of fresh basil leaves, torn into small pieces

Make the pizza dough. Preheat the oven to 450°F (230°C). If using a baking stone or tiles, place in the oven now.

Pour the oil into a deep frying pan and heat until the temperature reaches 350°F (180°C) on a deep-frying thermometer. Slip the zucchini slices into the hot oil, a few at a time, and fry until they are barely golden, about 2 minutes. Transfer with a slotted spoon to paper towels to drain. When all of the slices have been fried, pour off all but about 1 tablespoon of the oil. Return the fried zucchini to the pan and pour in the vinegar. Place over medium heat, add the garlic, and cook until the vinegar evaporates and the zucchini begins to darken, about 5 minutes. Season to taste with salt and pepper.

Shape the pizza dough and evenly distribute the zucchini over top. Transfer to the oven and bake for 10 minutes. Reduce the oven temperature to 400°F (200°C) and bake until the crust is golden, about 10 minutes longer. Scatter the basil over the top and serve immediately.

*Serves 4*

# Smoked Salmon and Fennel Pizza

Smoked salmon has become a fashionable topping thanks to the new American approach to pizza. The mild, sweet anise flavor of fresh fennel goes nicely with the salmon, as does thinly sliced onion.

Make the pizza dough. Preheat the oven to 450°F (230°C). If using a baking stone or tiles, place in the oven now.

Shape the pizza dough. Transfer to the oven and bake for 10 minutes. Remove from the oven. Cover with the smoked salmon slices. Top with the fennel slices. Drizzle 3 tablespoons of the olive oil over the top and sprinkle with salt to taste. Quickly return the pizza to the oven, reduce the oven temperature to 400°F (200°C), and bake until the crust is golden, about 10 minutes longer. Drizzle the remaining 1 tablespoon olive oil over the top and serve immediately.

*Serves 4*

Basic Pizza Dough (page 318)

10 oz (315 g) smoked salmon, cut into thin strips

1 fennel bulb, trimmed and sliced paper-thin

4 tablespoons (2 fl oz/60 ml) extra-virgin olive oil

Salt

# Eggplant and Smoked Trout Pizza

In this up-to-date recipe, the gentle, smoky taste of the trout complements the eggplant's (aubergine's) earthy flavor, and both are highlighted by a hint of hot-sweet grated horseradish.

Herb Pizza Dough (page 319)

1 yellow bell pepper (capsicum), seeded, deribbed, and cut into long strips about 1/2 inch (12 mm) wide

2 eggplants (aubergines), about 10 oz (315 g) total weight, thinly sliced lengthwise

4 tablespoons (2 fl oz/60 ml) extra-virgin olive oil

Smoked trout fillet, skinned

1 teaspoon freshly grated horseradish

Salt

Make the pizza dough. Preheat a broiler (grill).

Brush the pepper strips and eggplant slices on both sides with 2 tablespoons of the olive oil and arrange them on a baking sheet. Broil (grill), turning once, until tender when pierced, about 2 minutes per side. Remove from the broiler and set aside.

Place the trout in a bowl and mash with a fork. Stir in the remaining 2 tablespoons olive oil and the horseradish.

Preheat the oven to 450°F (230°C). If using a baking stone, place in the oven now.

Shape the pizza dough and cover with the mashed trout mixture, eggplant, and bell pepper strips. Sprinkle with salt to taste. Transfer to the oven and bake for 10 minutes. Reduce the oven temperature to 400°F (200°C) and bake until the crust is golden, about 10 minutes longer. Serve immediately.

*Serves 4*

# Prosciutto and Egg Pizza

The flavors in this pizza make it an excellent dish to prepare for a special breakfast or brunch, although in Italy it would just as likely be served as a casual one-course dinner.

Make the pizza dough. Preheat the oven to 450°F (230°C). If using a baking stone or tiles, place in the oven now.

Shape the pizza dough and cover with the prosciutto and then the Fontina slices. Transfer to the oven and bake for 10 minutes.

Remove the pizza from the oven and break the eggs over it, positioning each egg so that it rests in the center of a quarter wedge of the pizza. Cover with the tomatoes and season to taste with salt and pepper. Drizzle 3 tablespoons of the olive oil over the top. Quickly return the pizza to the oven, reduce the oven temperature to 400°F (200°C), and bake until golden, about 10 minutes longer. Drizzle the remaining 1 tablespoon olive oil over the top and serve immediately.

*Serves 4*

Cornmeal Pizza Dough
(page 318)

¼ lb (125 g) prosciutto,
thinly sliced

¼ lb (125 g) fontina cheese,
thinly sliced

4 eggs

4 large fresh plum (Roma)
tomatoes, peeled (page 329)
and chopped, or canned plum
tomatoes, drained and
chopped

Salt and freshly ground pepper

4 tablespoons (2 fl oz/60 ml)
extra-virgin olive oil

# Sausage and Apple Pizza

This pizza is from the Alto Adige region of Italy, but its savory-sweet toppings point northward toward Austria. Use any high-quality, coarse-grain mustard, such as *moutarde de Meaux*.

Whole-Wheat Pizza Dough
(page 319)

2 tablespoons extra-virgin
olive oil

10 oz (315 g) sweet Italian
sausage, cut into slices
3/8 inch (1 cm) thick

2 tablespoons unsalted butter

4 Golden Delicious apples,
peeled, cored, and cut into
1-inch (2.5-cm) pieces

2 tablespoons coarse-grain
French mustard

Make the pizza dough. Preheat the oven to 450°F (230°C). If using a baking stone or tiles, place in the oven now.

In a frying pan over medium heat, warm 1 tablespoon of the olive oil. Add the sausage and cook, stirring occasionally, until it begins to turn golden, about 3 minutes. Set aside.

In another frying pan, melt the butter over medium heat. Add the apples and cook, stirring constantly, until translucent, about 10 minutes. Set aside.

Shape the pizza dough and brush with the mustard. Cover with the apples and sausage. Transfer to the oven and bake for 10 minutes. Reduce the oven temperature to 400°F (200°C) and bake until the crust is golden, about 10 minutes longer. Drizzle the remaining 1 tablespoon olive oil over the top and serve immediately.

*Serves 4*

# Goat Cheese, Olive, and Pesto Pizza

This topping is inspired by the Ligurian cuisine of northwestern Italy. If you like, add a garlic clove when puréeing the basil mixture. For a milder sauce, use Swiss cheese instead of the Parmesan and Romano.

Place the goat cheese in the freezer for 30 minutes, to make it easier to slice.

Make the pizza dough. Preheat the oven to 450°F (230°C). If using a baking stone or tiles, place in the oven now.

To make the pesto, in a blender or food processor, combine the basil leaves and a little salt. (The salt keeps the basil from darkening.) Process until finely chopped. With the motor running, slowly add 6 tablespoons (3 fl oz/90 ml) of the olive oil, the Parmesan, Romano, and pine nuts, and continue to process until a smooth, creamy mixture forms.

Slice the goat cheese. Shape the pizza dough and cover with the goat cheese slices. Drizzle the remaining 2 tablespoons olive oil over the goat cheese and then pour half of the basil mixture evenly onto the pizza. Scatter the olives over the top and season to taste with pepper. Transfer to the oven and bake for 10 minutes. Reduce the oven temperature to 400°F (200°C) and bake until the crust is golden, about 10 minutes longer. Pour the remaining basil mixture over the top and serve.

*Serves 4*

6 oz (185 g) fresh goat cheese

Basic Pizza Dough (page 318)

FOR THE PESTO:

3/4 cup (1 oz/30 g) firmly packed fresh basil leaves

Salt

8 tablespoons (4 fl oz/125 ml) extra-virgin olive oil

1/2 cup (2 oz/60 g) grated Parmesan cheese

1/4 cup (1 oz/30 g) grated Romano cheese

3 tablespoons (1 oz/30 g) pine nuts

1/3 cup (2 oz/60 g) Gaeta or Greek black olives, pitted and sliced

Freshly ground pepper

# Fried Pizzas with Prosciutto

Small, deep-fried pizzas are a favorite snack in the Emilia-Romagna region of Italy.
If you prefer to bake the disks: Preheat the oven to 450°F (230°C) and bake for 10 minutes,
then reduce the heat to 400°F (200°C) and bake until golden, about 10 minutes longer.

Basic Pizza Dough (page 318)

5 cups (40 fl oz/1.25 l) olive oil
or vegetable oil for deep-frying

7 oz (220 g) prosciutto,
thinly sliced

Make the pizza dough and divide it into 8 equal pieces.

Preheat the oven to 250°F (120°C). On a lightly floured work surface, use the palms of your hands to shape each piece of dough into a log about 1 inch (2.5 cm) thick. Cut each log crosswise into $1^{1}/_{2}$-inch (4-cm) pieces. On the floured surface roll out each piece of dough into a disk that is about $^{1}/8$ inch (3 mm) thick and 4 inches (10 cm) in diameter.

Pour the oil into a deep frying pan and heat to 350°F (180°C) on a deep-frying thermometer. Slip the disks into the hot oil, a few at a time, and fry until they puff and turn lightly golden, about 3 minutes. Transfer with a slotted spoon to paper towels to drain, then place in the oven with the door slightly ajar to keep warm until serving. Repeat with the remaining disks. Top each pizza with a slice of prosciutto and serve immediately.

*Makes about 30 pizzas; serves 4, or more as hors d'oeuvres*

# Neapolitan Pizza

Along with Pizza Margherita (page 49), this specialty of Naples is one of the most popular in Italy. It's a robust-tasting yet well-balanced combination of pizza dough, fresh tomatoes, and anchovies. For a twist on the classic, bake miniature pizzas and serve them as an hors d'oeuvre.

Basic Pizza Dough (page 318)

7 oz (220 g) mozzarella cheese, thinly sliced

4 anchovy fillets, cut in half lengthwise

¼ lb (125 g) fresh plum (Roma) tomatoes, peeled (page 329) and chopped, or canned plum tomatoes, drained and chopped

1 tablespoon dried oregano

Salt and freshly ground pepper

4 tablespoons (2 fl oz/60 ml) extra-virgin olive oil

Make the pizza dough. Preheat the oven to 450°F (230°C). If using a baking stone or tiles, place in the oven now.

Shape the pizza dough into one large pizza or small hors d'oeuvre–sized rounds. Cover with the mozzarella. Arrange the anchovies on top and then cover with the tomatoes. Sprinkle the oregano and salt and pepper to taste over the top. Drizzle 3 tablespoons of the olive oil over the top. Transfer to the oven and bake for 10 minutes. Reduce the oven temperature to 400°F (200°C) and bake until the crust is golden, about 10 minutes longer. Drizzle the remaining 1 tablespoon olive oil over the top and serve immediately.

*Serves 4, or more as hors d'oeuvres*

# Tuna and Egg Pizza

A favorite Roman recipe, this pizza nonetheless recalls the classic combination of ingredients found in a French Niçoise salad, particularly when made with a potato pizza dough. Canned salmon makes an excellent substitute for the tuna.

Make the pizza dough. Preheat the oven to 450°F (230°C). If using a baking stone or tiles, place in the oven now.

Shape the pizza dough and cover with the tomatoes. Evenly distribute the tuna and capers over the tomatoes. Drizzle 3 tablespoons of the olive oil over the top. Transfer to the oven and bake for 10 minutes. Remove from the oven. Season to taste with salt and pepper, arrange the egg slices on top, and sprinkle with the parsley. Quickly return to the oven, reduce the oven temperature to 400°F (200°C), and bake until the crust is golden, about 10 minutes longer. Drizzle the remaining 1 tablespoon olive oil over the top and serve immediately.

*Serves 4*

Potato Pizza Dough (page 319)

2 large tomatoes, peeled (page 329) and chopped

10 oz (315 g) canned tuna packed in olive oil, drained and flaked

2 tablespoons capers, rinsed and well drained

4 tablespoons (2 fl oz/60 ml) extra-virgin olive oil

Salt and freshly ground pepper

2 peeled hard-boiled eggs, sliced

1 tablespoon minced fresh flat-leaf (Italian) parsley

# Asparagus and Ham Pizza

You can, if you wish, use Gruyère or Emmentaler cheese in place of the mozzarella, and prosciutto for the ham. Swiss chard and spinach are other good vegetable choices.

Whole-Wheat Pizza Dough (page 319)

3/4 lb (375 g) asparagus

6 oz (185 g) cooked ham, thinly sliced

6 oz (185 g) mozzarella cheese, thinly sliced

4 tablespoons (2 fl oz/60 ml) extra-virgin olive oil

Freshly ground pepper

6 tablespoons (1 1/2 oz/45 g) grated Parmesan cheese

Make the pizza dough. Preheat the oven to 450°F (230°C). If using a baking stone or tiles, place in the oven now.

Have a large bowl of ice water ready. Bring a saucepan three-fourths full of salted water to a boil. Break off the tough end of each asparagus spear by bending it gently until it snaps. Discard the bottoms or reserve for another use. Add the asparagus tips to the pan and boil for 3 minutes. Drain, immediately immerse in the ice water, and drain again.

Shape the pizza dough. Arrange the asparagus, ham, and mozzarella on top. Drizzle 3 tablespoons of the olive oil over the top and season to taste with pepper. Transfer to the oven and bake for 10 minutes. Remove from the oven and sprinkle with the Parmesan. Quickly return the pizza to the oven, reduce the oven temperature to 400°F (200°C), and bake until the crust is golden, about 10 minutes longer. Drizzle the remaining 1 tablespoon oil over the top and serve immediately.

*Serves 4*

# Radicchio, Bacon, and Onion Pizza

This pizza can be made as one large pizza or 4 individual pizzas, if you like. You can replace the radicchio with Belgian endive (chicory/witloof), which can be broiled in the same way.

Make the pizza dough. Preheat the broiler (grill).

Brush the radicchio halves on both sides with 1 1/2 tablespoons of the olive oil and arrange them on a baking sheet. Broil (grill) for 2 minutes. Turn and broil the second side for 2 minutes. Remove and discard the charred outer leaves, as they are bitter. Set the radicchio aside. Brush the onion slices on both sides with the remaining 1 1/2 tablespoons olive oil, arrange in the same pan, and broil for 1 minute on each side, turning once. Remove and set aside. Then arrange the bacon slices in the pan and broil until lightly golden and crisp, about 2 minutes per side.

Preheat the oven to 450°F (230°C). If using a baking stone, place in the oven now.

Core the radicchio and separate the leaves. Shape the pizza dough into one large pizza or 4 individual pizzas. Cover with the radicchio leaves. Arrange the bacon slices on top and then cover with the onions. Season with salt and pepper. Transfer to the oven and bake for 10 minutes. Reduce the temperature to 400°F (200°C) and bake until the crust is golden, about 10 minutes longer. Serve immediately.

*Serves 4*

Basic Pizza Dough (page 318)

4 heads radicchio, cut in half lengthwise

3 tablespoons extra-virgin olive oil

2 yellow onions, thinly sliced

4 slices bacon

Salt and freshly ground pepper

# Spring Vegetable Calzone

Basic Pizza Dough (page 318)

4 tablespoons (2 fl oz/60 ml) extra-virgin olive oil

1 yellow onion, sliced

1 cup (5 oz/155 g) shelled English peas

1/4 lb (125 g) green beans, trimmed and cut into 1/2-inch (12-mm) pieces

1 carrot, peeled and cut into 1/2-inch (12-mm) pieces

3/4 lb (375 g) asparagus, top 2 inches (5 cm) of each spear cut on the diagonal into 1/2-inch (12-mm) pieces, bottoms discarded or reserved for another use.

10 oz (315 g) canned plum (Roma) tomatoes, drained and chopped

Salt and freshly ground pepper

1 tablespoon minced fresh flat-leaf (Italian) parsley

Make the pizza dough. Preheat the oven to 450°F (230°C). If using a baking stone or tiles, place in the oven now.

In a frying pan over medium heat, warm 3 tablespoons of the olive oil. Add the onion and sauté, stirring constantly, until golden, about 5 minutes. Add the peas, green beans, carrot, asparagus, and tomatoes and continue cooking until tender-crisp, about 5 minutes longer. Season to taste with salt and pepper and stir in the parsley.

Divide the pizza dough into 4 equal pieces. On a lightly floured work surface, shape each piece into a round about 6 inches (15 cm) in diameter. Arrange one-fourth of the vegetable mixture atop half of each round, leaving a 1/2-inch (12-mm) border uncovered. Brush the edges of each round with a little water and fold over the uncovered half to enclose the filling completely. Press the edges together to seal. Transfer the calzones to the oven and bake for about 10 minutes. Reduce the oven temperature to 400°F (200°C) and bake until the crust is golden, about 10 minutes longer. Drizzle the remaining 1 tablespoon oil over the tops and serve immediately.

*Serves 4*

# Two-Cheese and Garlic Calzone

From northwestern Italy's Piedmont region, this aromatic calzone is filled with sautéed garlic and Gorgonzola and fontina cheeses. Swiss cheese makes a good substitute for the fontina. Instead of the Gorgonzola, you might try a creamy Camembert or Brie pared of the white rind.

Make the pizza dough. Preheat the oven to 450°F (230°C). If using a baking stone or tiles, place in the oven now.

In a frying pan over low heat, warm 3 tablespoons of the olive oil. Add the garlic cloves and sauté until very soft and golden, about 5 minutes. Remove from the heat.

In a bowl, combine the Gorgonzola and lemon juice. Using a wooden spoon, work them together until soft and smooth. Stir in the garlic and fontina.

Divide the pizza dough into 4 equal pieces. On a lightly floured work surface, shape each piece into a round about 6 inches (15 cm) in diameter. Arrange one-fourth of the garlic-cheese mixture atop half of each round, leaving a $^1$/2-inch (12-mm) border uncovered. Brush the edges of each round with a little water and fold over the uncovered half to enclose the filling completely. Press the edges together to seal. Transfer the calzones to the oven and bake for 10 minutes. Reduce the temperature to 400°F (200°C) and bake until the crust is golden, about 10 minutes longer. Drizzle the remaining 1 tablespoon olive oil over the tops and serve immediately.

*Serves 4*

Whole-Wheat Pizza Dough (page 319)

4 tablespoons (2 fl oz/60 ml) extra-virgin olive oil

12 cloves garlic

6 oz (185 g) Gorgonzola cheese

1 tablespoon fresh lemon juice

6 oz (185 g) fontina cheese, diced

# Fresh Tuna Calzone

Piquant Mediterranean flavors abound here: olive oil, garlic, lemon, and black olives. In this recipe, the fish stays moist and flavorful because it spends only a short amount of time cooking in the pan. Salmon or sole makes a good alternative to the tuna.

Herb Pizza Dough (page 319)

1 lemon

4 tablespoons (2 fl oz/60 ml) extra-virgin olive oil

3 cloves garlic, chopped

1¼ lb (625 g) fresh tuna fillet, thinly sliced against the grain

½ (3 oz /90 g) Gaeta or Greek black olives, pitted

Salt and freshly ground pepper

Make the pizza dough. Preheat the oven to 450°F (230°C). If using a baking stone or tiles, place in the oven now.

Grate the zest from the lemon and set aside. Remove all the white pith from the lemon, then thinly slice the lemon. Cut the slices into ½-inch (12-mm) pieces.

In a frying pan over low heat, warm 3 tablespoons of the olive oil. Add the garlic and sauté, stirring constantly, until golden, about 5 minutes. Add the tuna, lemon pieces, lemon zest, and olives and cook for another 2 minutes. Season to taste with salt and pepper.

Divide the pizza dough into 4 equal pieces. On a lightly floured work surface, shape each piece into a round about 6 inches (15 cm) in diameter. Arrange one-fourth of the tuna mixture atop half of each round, leaving a ½-inch (12-mm) border uncovered. Brush the edges of each round with a little water and fold over the uncovered half to enclose the filling completely. Press the edges together to seal. Transfer the calzones to the oven and bake for 10 minutes. Reduce the oven temperature to 400°F (200°C) and bake until the crust is golden, about 10 minutes longer. Drizzle the remaining 1 tablespoon olive oil over the tops and serve immediately.

*Serves 4*

# Eggplant and Goat Cheese Calzone

Eggplant and cheese is a classic combination and a classic filling for calzones in Italian cooking. This mixture is particularly delectable stuffed into miniature calzones. Garnish with flat-leaf (Italian) parsley and kale.

Herb Pizza Dough (page 319)

2 eggplants (aubergines), about 10 oz (315 g) total weight, thinly sliced crosswise

3 tablespoons extra-virgin olive oil

4 slices bacon

7 oz (220 g) fresh goat cheese

2 tablespoons minced fresh basil

Salt and freshly ground pepper

Make the pizza dough. Preheat the broiler (grill).

Brush the eggplant slices on both sides with 1 tablespoon of the olive oil and arrange them on a baking sheet. Broil (grill), turning once, until tender, about 2 minutes per side. Season with salt and pepper. Set aside. Broil the bacon until crisp, 2 minutes per side. Drain on paper towels and crumble. In a small bowl crumble the cheese and stir in the basil and 1 tablespoon of the olive oil.

Preheat the oven to 450°F (230°C). If using a baking stone, place in the oven now.

Divide the pizza dough into 4 equal pieces (or more for miniature calzones). On a lightly floured work surface, shape each piece into a round. Arrange an equal amount of the eggplant atop half of each round, leaving a small border uncovered. Top with the cheese mixture and sprinkle with some bacon. Brush the edges of each round with a little water and fold over the uncovered half to enclose the filling completely. Press the edges together to seal. Transfer the calzones to the oven and bake for 10 minutes. Reduce the oven temperature to 400°F (200°C) and bake until the crust is golden, about 10 minutes longer. Drizzle the remaining 1 tablespoon olive oil over the tops and serve immediately.

*Serves 4*

# Braised Chicken Calzone

The chicken filling for this calzone is cooked *cacciatora*, or "huntsman," style, braised with onion, wine, and herbs. In Italy, rabbit is a favorite meat and is often prepared this same way.

Make the pizza dough. Preheat the oven to 450°F (230°C). If using a baking stone or tiles, place in the oven now.

In a large, heavy saucepan over low heat, warm 3 tablespoons of the olive oil. Add the carrot, chopped onion, and parsley. Sauté until the onions are lightly golden, about 10 minutes. Add the chicken, raise the heat to medium, and cook, stirring, until the chicken is golden. Add the wine, pearl onions, juniper berries, and thyme. Season with salt and pepper to taste, reduce the heat, cover, and cook until the juices evaporate and the chicken is tender, 1 hour. Let cool, then remove the meat from the bones. Cut the meat into large pieces, return it to the pan, and mix well.

Divide the dough into 4 equal pieces. On a lightly floured work surface, shape each piece into a round about 6 inches (15 cm) in diameter. Arrange one-fourth of the chicken mixture on top of half of each round, leaving a $^1/_2$-inch (12-mm) border uncovered. Brush the edges of each round with a little water and fold over the uncovered half to enclose the filling completely. Press the edges together to seal. Transfer the calzones to the oven and bake for 10 minutes. Reduce the oven temperature to 400°F (200°C) and bake until the crust is golden, about 10 minutes longer. Drizzle the remaining 1 tablespoon olive oil over the top and serve.

*Serves 4*

Basic Pizza Dough (page 318)

4 tablespoons (2 fl oz/60 ml) extra-virgin olive oil

1 small carrot, peeled and chopped

1 small yellow onion, chopped

1 tablespoon minced fresh flat-leaf (Italian) parsley

$^1/_2$ chicken, about 2 lb (1 kg), cut into 3 or 4 pieces

$1^1/_4$ cups (10 fl oz/310 ml) red wine

10 oz (315 g) pearl onions

1 tablespoon juniper berries

1 tablespoon fresh thyme leaves

Salt and freshly ground pepper

# Braised Pork Calzone

The pork filling for this calzone is cooked in the Neapolitan style — braised in white wine with oregano. Cubes of boned lamb or chicken breast can be prepared in the same way.

Herb Pizza Dough (page 319)

4 tablespoons (2 fl oz/60 ml) extra-virgin olive oil

1 small yellow onion, thinly sliced

3/4 lb (375 g) lean pork meat, cut into 1-inch (2.5-cm) dice

1 red or yellow bell pepper (capsicum), seeded, deribbed, and cut into 1/2-inch (12-mm) dice

1/2 cup (4 fl oz/125 ml) dry white wine

1 tablespoon dried oregano

Salt and freshly ground pepper

Make the pizza dough. Preheat the oven to 450°F (230°C). If using a baking stone or tiles, place in the oven now.

In a frying pan over medium heat, warm 3 tablespoons of the olive oil. Add the onion and sauté, stirring constantly, until golden, about 5 minutes. Add the pork and bell pepper and sauté until the pork begins to brown, about 10 minutes. Stir in the wine, oregano, and salt and pepper to taste. Cover and cook, stirring occasionally, until the wine evaporates, about 30 minutes.

Divide the pizza dough into 4 equal pieces. On a lightly floured work surface, shape each piece into a round about 6 inches (15 cm) in diameter. Arrange one-fourth of the pork mixture on top of half of each round, leaving a 1/2-inch (12-mm) border uncovered. Brush the edges of each round with a little water and fold over the uncovered half to enclose the filling completely. Press the edges together to seal. Transfer the calzones to the oven and bake for 10 minutes. Reduce the oven temperature to 400°F (200°C) and bake until the crust is golden, about 10 minutes longer. Drizzle the remaining 1 tablespoon olive oil over the tops and serve immediately.

*Serves 4*

# Sausage Calzone with Fennel Seeds

This calzone features hot Neapolitan sausage, which mellows when it is cooked in red wine. Substitute any hot or sweet Italian sausage, or Spanish or Mexican chorizo.

Make the pizza dough. Preheat the oven to 450°F (230°C). If using a baking stone or tiles, place in the oven now.

In a frying pan over low heat, warm 3 tablespoons of the olive oil. Add the garlic and sausage and sauté until the garlic begins to turn golden, about 5 minutes.

Add the fennel seeds and vinegar and cook until the vinegar evaporates, about 2 minutes. Add the wine, cover partially, and cook until the wine evaporates, about 10 minutes longer.

Divide the pizza dough into 4 equal pieces. On a lightly floured work surface, shape each piece into a round about 6 inches (15 cm) in diameter. Arrange one-fourth of the sausage mixture atop half of each round, leaving a 1/2-inch (12-mm) border uncovered. Brush the edges of each round with a little water and fold over the uncovered half to enclose the filling completely. Press the edges together to seal. Transfer the calzones to the oven and bake for 10 minutes. Reduce the temperature to 400°F (200°C) and bake until the crust is golden, about 10 minutes longer. Drizzle the remaining 1 tablespoon olive oil over the tops and serve immediately.

*Serves 4*

Whole-Wheat Pizza Dough
(page 319)

4 tablespoons (2 fl oz/60 ml) extra-virgin olive oil

3 cloves garlic, chopped

3/4 lb (375 g) hot Neapolitan sausage, cut into slices 1/2 inch (12 mm) thick

1 tablespoon fennel seeds

2 tablespoons red wine vinegar

1/2 cup (4 fl oz/125 ml) red wine

# Herb, Cheese & Vegetable Pasta

# Gemelli with Four Cheeses

Parmesan is an essential ingredient for this irresistibly rich pasta dish, but there are many substitutions for the other three cheeses. Try Camembert for the fontina; Roquefort for the Gorgonzola; and mozzarella for the Swiss.

2 oz (60 g) fontina cheese, cut into julienne

2 oz (60 g) Gorgonzola cheese, crumbled

2 oz (60 g) Swiss cheese, cut into julienne

1/2 cup (4 fl oz/120 ml) heavy (double) cream

1¼ lb (625 g) dried gemelli

Salt and freshly ground pepper

1/2 cup (2 oz/60 g) grated Parmesan cheese

Bring a large pot three-fourths full of salted water to a boil.

Meanwhile, combine the fontina, Gorgonzola, and Swiss cheeses and the cream in a saucepan over low heat. Cook gently until the cheeses have almost completely melted, about 5 minutes. Stir well. Set aside and keep warm.

Meanwhile, add the gemelli to the boiling water and cook until al dente, 10–12 minutes.

Drain the pasta and arrange it on a warmed platter. Spoon the cheese sauce over the pasta, season to taste with salt and pepper, and toss well. Sprinkle the Parmesan over the top and serve immediately.

*Serves 6*

# Fusilli with Goat Cheese, Celery, and Black Olives

Tossed together in just a few minutes, this pasta dish may be made with eye-catching shapes such as fusilli or conchiglie, or simply with penne. Add tiny cherry tomatoes to enliven the recipe further.

1 lb (500 g) fusilli

8 tablespoons (4 fl oz/ 125 ml) extra-virgin olive oil

3 stalks celery, thinly sliced

6 oz (185 g) fresh goat cheese, crumbled

Salt and freshly ground pepper

16 black olives such as Kalamata, pitted

Handful of tiny fresh basil leaves

Bring a large pot three-fourths full of salted water to a boil. Add the pasta and cook until al dente, 10–12 minutes.

Drain and transfer to a bowl. Add 2 tablespoons of the olive oil and toss well. Let cool to room temperature, stirring occasionally.

Transfer the cooled pasta to a serving dish and add the remaining 6 tablespoons (3 fl oz/90 ml) oil, the celery, goat cheese, and salt and pepper to taste. Toss well. Sprinkle with the olives and garnish with the basil leaves. Serve at once. Or, if you like, cover and refrigerate until well-chilled before serving.

*Serves 4*

# Macaroni with Eggs, Pecorino, and Black Pepper

Creamy scrambled eggs with cheese form a luscious, rustic sauce for pasta such as elbow macaroni, penne, or farfalle, which will hold their shape well during the final stage of cooking in a frying pan.

Bring a large pot three-fourths full of salted water to a boil.

In a bowl, beat the eggs until well blended. Add the cheese, milk, and a generous amount of pepper and mix together well.

Add the pasta to the boiling water and cook until al dente, 10–12 minutes. Meanwhile, in a large, wide frying pan over low heat, melt the butter.

When the pasta is barely al dente, drain and add to the frying pan along with the egg mixture and salt to taste. Finish cooking over medium heat, stirring constantly, until the eggs are firm but not dry, 1–2 minutes.

Transfer to a warmed serving bowl and serve at once.

*Serves 4*

3 eggs

¼ cup (1 oz/30 g) grated pecorino cheese, such as romano or sardo

6 tablespoons (3 fl oz/90 ml) milk

Salt and freshly ground pepper

1 lb (500 g) macaroni or other dried shaped pasta (see note)

½ cup (4 oz/125 g) unsalted butter

# Ruote with Ricotta, Pistachio, and Mint

Great for a summertime meal, this light, delicious, and refreshing topping for cold pasta pairs well with ruote or other round pasta shapes. Substitute hazelnuts (filberts) for the pistachio nuts, if you prefer.

Bring a large pot three-fourths full of salted water to a boil. Add the pasta and cook until al dente, 10–12 minutes. Drain the pasta, reserving about $1/4$ cup (2 fl oz/ 60 ml) of the cooking water. Transfer the pasta to a bowl. Add the olive oil and toss well. Let cool to room temperature, stirring occasionally.

Meanwhile, in a bowl, combine the ricotta, the reserved hot cooking water, and salt and green pepper to taste. Stir until the cheese is smooth and creamy.

When the pasta has cooled, add the ricotta and stir again to coat evenly. Transfer to a serving bowl and sprinkle with the nuts and mint. Serve at once.

*Serves 4*

1 lb (500 g) ruote or other dried shaped pasta (see note)

$1/4$ cup (2 fl oz/60 ml) extra-virgin olive oil

$3/4$ cup (6 oz/185 g) ricotta cheese

Salt and freshly ground green pepper

$2/3$ cup (3 oz/90 g) pistachios, coarsely chopped

2 tablespoons chopped fresh mint leaves

# Gemelli with Gorgonzola and Parmesan Cream

Sharp and tangy, melted Gorgonzola cheese imparts great character to baked pasta dishes featuring rigatoni, gemelli, or penne. Take care to season this dish sparingly, as both cheeses are naturally quite salty.

2 cups (16 fl oz/500 ml) milk

2½ tablespoons unsalted butter, plus extra for greasing

3½ tablespoons all-purpose (plain) flour

Pinch of ground nutmeg

Salt and freshly ground pepper

4 oz (125 g) Gorgonzola cheese, crumbled

1 lb (500 g) dried gemelli or other shaped pasta (see note)

½ cup (2 oz/60 g) grated Parmesan cheese

Pour the milk into a saucepan over medium-low heat. When the milk is little more than warm, turn off the heat.

In another saucepan over low heat, combine the butter and flour, vigorously stirring them together with a wooden spoon until the butter melts and the flour is incorporated. Once the butter is fully melted, cook and stir for 2 minutes longer. Then gradually add the warm milk, a little at a time, stirring constantly. Add more milk only after the previously added milk is fully incorporated. When all of the milk has been added, cook, stirring often, until nicely thickened, 3–4 minutes longer. Add the nutmeg and salt and pepper to taste and stir for a few seconds. Remove from the heat, cover, and keep warm.

Bring a large pot of water three-fourths full of salted water to a boil. Preheat the oven to 350°F (180°C). Lightly grease a 6-by-12-inch (15-by-30-cm) baking dish or 4 individual baking dishes with butter.

Add the pasta to the boiling water and cook only until half-cooked, 5 minutes. Drain the pasta and transfer to the prepared dish. Add the warm sauce and the Gorgonzola and stir gently. Sprinkle with the Parmesan cheese.

Bake until the top is golden, about 20 minutes. Serve immediately.

*Serves 4*

# Pasta with Emmentaler Cheese and Onion

Lightly spiced with bay leaves, this sauce is ideal for preparing a broiler-browned gratin with pasta ribbons of any size. Other Swiss-type cheeses such as Gruyère or Jarlsberg may replace the Emmentaler, or use slices of mozzarella.

In a saucepan over medium heat, melt the butter. Add the onions and sauté until translucent, about 2 minutes. Stir in salt and pepper to taste and the bay leaves. Add the milk and stock, reduce the heat to low, and simmer, uncovered, stirring occasionally, until the liquids are absorbed, about 30 minutes. Discard the bay leaves.

Meanwhile, bring a large pot three-fourths full of salted water to a boil. Preheat the broiler (grill). Grease a 6-by-12-inch (15-by-30-cm) flameproof dish.

Add the pasta to the boiling water and cook until al dente, about 8 minutes. Drain and immediately place in the prepared dish. Spoon the hot onion mixture evenly over the top, then cover withthe cheese. Broil (grill) until the top is golden, about 5 minutes. Serve immediately.

*Serves 4*

4 tablespoons (2 oz/60 g) unsalted butter, plus extra for greasing

1¼ lb (625 g) white onions, very thinly sliced

Salt and freshly ground pepper

2 bay leaves

½ cup (4 fl oz/125 ml) milk

½ cup (4 fl oz/125 ml) Vegetable Stock (page 321)

1 lb (500 g) dried ribbon pasta (see note)

1 cup (4 oz/120 g) grated Emmentaler cheese

# Linguine with Basil Sauce

You can also use this sauce on room-temperature pasta, taking care to toss the pasta with 2 tablespoons extra-virgin olive oil immediately after cooking, to prevent it from sticking together as it cools.

1 cup (1 oz/30 g) firmly packed fresh basil leaves

Salt

3 tablespoons grated Parmesan cheese

2 tablespoons grated Romano cheese

3 tablespoons pine nuts

2 cloves garlic

$1/2$ cup (4 fl oz/120 ml) extra-virgin olive oil

$1^1/_4$ lb (625 g) fresh (page 322) or dried linguine

Bring a large pot three-fourths full of salted water to a boil.

Meanwhile, in a blender or food processor fitted with the metal blade, combine the basil with $^1/_2$ teaspoon salt, or to taste. Process until coarsely chopped, just a few seconds. Add the cheeses, pine nuts, garlic, and olive oil. Process to form a smooth, creamy sauce. Set aside in the blender.

Add the linguine to the boiling water and cook until al dente, about 2 minutes for fresh pasta or 8 minutes for dried. Add 1 tablespoon of the pasta cooking water to the basil mixture and process briefly, just to blend.

Drain the pasta and arrange it on a warmed platter. Spoon the sauce over the linguine and toss well. Serve immediately.

*Serves 6*

# Tagliatelle with Vegetable Ragout

This ingredients called for in this recipe bring together both sweet and savory components to the finished dish. You may substitute spaghetti or another thin ribbon pasta for the tagliatelle.

Prepare the tagliatelle accroding to the directions for Fresh Egg Pasta (page 322).

Meanwhile, in a small bowl, soak the raisins in lukewarm water to cover for about 30 minutes. Drain and set aside.

Bring a large pot three-fourths full of salted water to a boil. Add the celery stalk and cook for 2 minutes. Remove with a slotted spoon and reserve the cooking water in the pot. Chop the celery into a $^{1}/_{2}$-inch (12-mm) dice and set aside.

In a large frying pan, warm the olive oil over medium heat. Add the onions and sauté until lightly golden, about 3 minutes. Add the eggplant and celery and cook, stirring occasionally, until softened, about 5 minutes. Add the tomatoes, raisins, pine nuts, capers, and olives. Stir well, season to taste with salt and pepper and cook for 5 minutes to allow the flavors to blend. Remove from the heat and set aside.

In a small, heavy saucepan, melt the sugar over medium heat, stirring only when the sugar starts melting at the edge of the pan. Continue heating until the sugar is a deep golden color and foams on top, about 3 minutes. Add the vinegar and mix well. Pour over the vegetables.

Return the water to a boil. Return the vegetables to medium heat and stir well. Add the tagliatelle to the boiling water and cook until they rise to the surface, about 2 minutes. Drain the pasta and transfer to the frying pan with the vegetables. Cook over medium heat, stirring gently, for 1 minute. Arrange the pasta on a warmed platter and serve immediately.

*Serves 6*

1 lb (500 g) fresh tagliatelle (page 322)

$^{1}/_{4}$ cup (1 oz/30 g) raisins

1 stalk celery

3 tablespoons extra-virgin olive oil

2 yellow onions, coarsely chopped

2 Asian eggplants (slender aubergines), cut into $^{1}/_{2}$-inch (12-mm) dice

10 oz (300 g) ripe plum (Roma) tomatoes, peeled (page 329) and chopped

$^{1}/_{4}$ cup (1 oz/30 g) pine nuts

2 tablespoons capers, rinsed and well drained

$^{1}/_{2}$ cup (3 oz/90 g) black olives, pitted and coarsely chopped

Salt and freshly ground pepper

2 tablespoons sugar

2 tablespoons white wine vinegar

# Tortelloni Stuffed with Herbs and Potato

8 tablespoons (4 fl oz/ 120 ml) extra-virgin olive oil

1 small yellow onion, finely chopped

3 russet or Yukon gold potatoes, peeled and cut crosswise into slices 1 inch (2.5 cm) thick

1 tablespoon chopped fresh rosemary

1 tablespoon chopped fresh oregano

1 tablespoon chopped fresh marjoram

3/4 cup (6 oz/180 g) ricotta cheese

2 egg yolks

Salt and freshly ground pepper

12 oz (375 g) Fresh Egg Pasta dough (page 322)

2 tablespoons chopped fresh flat-leaf (Italian) parsley

In a frying pan, warm 2 tablespoons of the olive oil over low heat. Add the onion and sauté until translucent, about 3 minutes. Add the potatoes, raise the heat to medium, and sauté, stirring often, until the potatoes are tender, about 15 minutes. Add the rosemary, oregano, and marjoram and stir for 1 minute. Remove from the heat and let cool.

In a large bowl, combine the ricotta and potato mixture. With a fork, mash the ingredients together well. Add the egg yolks and salt and pepper to taste. Stir until smooth. Set aside.

Prepare the pasta dough according to the directions for Fresh Egg Pasta (page 322). Roll out the dough into a very thin sheet. Cut into strips 3 inches (7.5 cm) wide and 12 inches (30 cm) long. On half of the strips, place small mounds of the filling at 3-inch (7.5-cm) intervals. Moisten the edges of the strips and in between the mounds with cold water. Cover the filled strips with the remaining strips. To seal, press along the edges and all around the stuffing. Using a pastry wheel with a fluted edge, cut into 2 1/2-inch (6-cm) squares. Using a spatula, set the tortelloni aside on a lightly floured work surface.

Bring a large pot three-fourths full of salted water to a boil. Add the tortelloni and cook until they rise to the surface, about 2 minutes. Drain well and arrange on a warmed platter. Sprinkle with the parsley and the remaining 6 tablespoons (3 fl oz/ 90 ml) olive oil. Serve at once.

*Serves 6*

# Fresh Basil Pappardelle

Mixing fresh basil into pasta dough results in attractively flecked noodles with a subtle herb flavor. If pecorino (sheep's milk cheese) is difficult to find, Parmesan may be substituted. For an even more colorful presentation, scatter a few extra herb leaves over the finished dish.

Combine the flour, basil, and pecorino in a blender or food processor. Process until the basil is pulverized and thoroughly mixed with the flour and cheese.

If using a blender, turn the mixture out onto a board. If using a food processor, leave it in the work bowl. Make the pappardelle (by hand or in the processor) using the flour-cheese mixture, whole eggs, and egg yolk and following the directions for Fresh Egg Pasta (page 322).

In a large pot bring 5 qt (5 l) salted water to a boil. Add the pappardelle and cook until they rise to the surface, about 2 minutes.

Drain the pasta and arrange it on a warm platter. Pour the olive oil over the top and season to taste with salt and pepper. Toss well and serve immediately.

*Serves 6*

2 cups (92 oz/300 g) all-purpose (plain) flour

1½ cups (12 oz/45 g) fresh basil leaves, well dried after washing

¼ cup (1 oz/30 g) grated pecorino cheese, such as Romano or Sardo

3 whole eggs plus 1 egg yolk

6 tablespoons (3 fl oz/90 ml) extra-virgin olive oil

Salt and freshly ground pepper

# Penne with Artichokes, Mint, and Parsley

Because the pasta in this recipe is cooked twice — once in boiling water and then briefly in oil — you need a fairly robust shape that will hold up well. Penne and radiatori are good choices.

Juice of 1 lemon

8 small artichokes, about
3 oz (90 g) each

1/4 cup (2 fl oz/60 ml)
extra-virgin olive oil

2 cloves garlic, thinly sliced

1 lb (500 g) penne or other
dried shaped pasta (see note)

1 tablespoon chopped
fresh mint

1 tablespoon chopped fresh
flat-leaf (Italian) parsley

Salt and freshly ground white
pepper

1/2 cup (2 oz/60 g) grated
Parmesan cheese

Fill a large bowl three-fourths full of water and add the lemon juice. Remove the stems and tough outer leaves from the artichokes until you reach the pale green hearts. Cut each artichoke in half lengthwise. Scoop out the prickly choke from the center and discard. Cut the artichokes lengthwise into thin slices. As each slice is cut, place it in the bowl of water.

Bring a large pot three-fourths full of salted water to a boil.

In a large frying pan over medium heat, warm the olive oil. Add the garlic and sauté, stirring often, until golden, about 3 minutes. Drain the artichokes, pat dry, and add to the pan. Raise the heat to high and sauté for a few minutes. Add 1/4 cup (2 fl oz/60 ml) water and cook over high heat until the water is absorbed and the artichokes are tender, 6–7 minutes.

Meanwhile, add the pasta to the boiling water and cook until almost al dente, 8–10 minutes. Drain the pasta, reserving about 1/4 cup (2 fl oz/60 ml) of the cooking water. Add the pasta and the reserved hot cooking water to the artichokes in the frying pan along with the mint, parsley, and salt and white pepper to taste. Finish cooking over high heat, stirring constantly, for 1–2 minutes.

Transfer to a warmed serving bowl or individual plates, top with the Parmesan, and toss well. Serve immediately.

*Serves 4*

# Pasta with Tomatoes and White Wine

So pure are the flavors of this sauce for strand pasta, such as spaghetti or fedelini, that they're at their tastiest without the addition of cheese. When adding the wine to the hot oil, do so carefully, as it will splatter.

In a frying pan over medium heat, warm the olive oil. Add the garlic, reduce the heat to very low, and cook very slowly, stirring occasionally, until lightly golden, about 5 minutes.

Bring a large pot three-fourths full of salted water to a boil.

Add the white wine, raise the heat to high, and cook until the wine evaporates, 2–3 minutes. Add the tomatoes, salt to taste, and plenty of white pepper. Cook uncovered, stirring often, until light and slightly thickened, about 5 minutes.

Meanwhile, add the pasta to the boiling water and cook until al dente; the timing will depend on the type of pasta. Drain and transfer to a warmed serving bowl. Immediately pour the sauce over the pasta and serve at once.

*Serves 4*

6 tablespoons (3 fl oz/90 ml) extra-virgin olive oil

3 or 4 cloves garlic, finely chopped

1 1/2 cup (4 fl oz/125 ml) dry white wine

1/2 lb (750 g) fresh plum (Roma) tomatoes, peeled (page 329) and chopped, or canned plum tomatoes, drained and chopped

Salt and freshly ground white pepper

1 lb (500 g) fresh (page 322) or dried strand pasta (see note)

# Tagliatelle with Butter and Sage

A classic of northern Italy, this sauce of sage and butter complements the delicate flavor of freshly made pasta. Extra-virgin olive oil may be substituted for the butter: Warm the oil and sage over medium-low heat, just until the leaves begin to darken.

1 lb (500 g) fresh tagliatelle (page 322)

1/2 cup (4 oz/120 g) unsalted butter

20 fresh sage leaves

3/4 cup (3 oz/90 g) grated Parmesan cheese

Salt

Prepare the tagliatelle according to the directions for Fresh Egg Pasta (page 322).

Bring a large pot three-fourths full of water to a boil.

Meanwhile, in a small saucepan, melt the butter over medium heat. Add the sage and cook, stirring occasionally, until the butter begins to turn golden and the sage darkens, about 5 minutes.

Add the tagliatelle to the boiling water and cook until they rise to the surface, about 2 minutes.

Drain the pasta and arrange it on a warmed platter. Pour the sage-butter mixture over the top. Sprinkle with half of the Parmesan and salt to taste and toss gently. Sprinkle with the remaining cheese and serve at once.

*Serves 6*

# Rigatoni with White Beans and Tomatoes

Simmered together, tomatoes and cannellini beans, the ubiquitous white beans
of Tuscany, take on a satisfying, porridgelike consistency. Canned cannellini may be
substituted; drain 2 cups (15 oz/470 g) canned beans and rinse with cold running water.

1 cup (7 oz/220 g) dried
cannellini beans

6 tablespoons (3 fl oz/90 ml)
extra-virgin olive oil

3 cloves garlic, chopped

20 fresh sage leaves

1¼ lb (625 g) fresh plum
(Roma) tomatoes, peeled
(page 329) and chopped, or
canned plum tomatoes,
drained and chopped

Salt and freshly ground pepper

1 lb (500 g) rigatoni

Pick over the beans, discarding any stones or misshapen beans. Rinse the beans.
Place in a bowl, add cold water to cover, and soak for about 12 hours.

Drain the beans and place in a saucepan with water to cover by about 1 inch (2.5 cm).
Bring to a boil, reduce the heat to low, and simmer gently, uncovered, until the beans
are tender and most of the liquid is absorbed, about 1½ hours.

When the beans have been cooking for about 1 hour, warm the olive oil in a large,
wide, shallow saucepan over low heat. Add the garlic and sage and sauté, stirring
often, until the garlic is translucent, about 2 minutes. Add the tomatoes and salt and
pepper to taste. Simmer for about 20 minutes. Add the beans, cover partially, and simmer for another 15 minutes.

Meanwhile, bring a large pot three-fourths full of salted water to a boil. Add the
rigatoni and cook until almost al dente, 8–10 minutes. Drain and transfer to the
saucepan with the beans. Finishing cooking over medium heat, stirring often, for
about 1 minute. Arrange the pasta on a warmed platter and serve at once.

*Serves 6*

# Penne with Cauliflower, Pine Nuts, and Raisins

The Arabic influence on this Italian pasta is evident in the use of raisins, pine nuts, and fragrant saffron. Toasted fresh bread crumbs (page 324) can be used in place of the pecorino cheese, if you like.

Bring a large pot three-fourths full of salted water to a boil.

Cut the cauliflower florets off the stalks. Cut any large florets in half. Discard the stalks or reserve for another use. Add the florets to the boiling water and cook until tender but not falling apart, 5–7 minutes. Using a slotted spoon, transfer to a bowl and set aside. Reserve the cooking water.

In a large frying pan over medium heat, warm the olive oil. Add the onion and the garlic, if using, and sauté, stirring often, until lightly golden, about 10 minutes. Add the saffron and its soaking liquid and the anchovies and cook for 3 minutes to allow the flavors to blend.

Meanwhile return the reserved cooking water to a boil. Add the penne and cook until al dente, about 10–12 minutes.

Add the cauliflower, raisins, and pine nuts to the onions in the frying pan along with a ladleful of the pasta water. Simmer over low heat until the florets are very soft, about 3–4 minutes.

Scoop out a little more pasta water and set aside. Drain the pasta and transfer to a warmed serving bowl. Add the sauce and toss well. If the mixture seems a little dry, add some of the reserved pasta water and toss again. Serve at once with the grated pecorino cheese, if desired.

*Serves 4–6*

1 small head cauliflower, about 1 lb (500 g)

1/4 cup (2 fl oz/60 ml) olive oil

1 yellow onion, chopped

2 cloves garlic, finely minced (optional)

1/2 teaspoon saffron threads, crushed and steeped in 1/2 cup (4 fl oz/125 ml) dry white wine

6 anchovy fillets, finely chopped

1 lb (500 g) dried penne or rigatoni

1/3 cup (2 oz/60 g) raisins, soaked in lukewarm water to cover for about 30 minutes and drained

1/3 cup (2 oz/60 g) pine nuts, toasted (page 329)

Freshly grated pecorino cheese, such as romano or sardo, for serving

# Penne with Asparagus

Each spring, Italians anxiously await the appearance of the first asparagus in the markets and on the hillsides where the plants grow wild. This easy presentation plays off the distinctive taste of asparagus against the sharp, briny flavor of anchovies.

3 lb (1.5 kg) asparagus

1 lb (500 g) dried penne

6 tablespoons (3 fl oz/90 ml) extra-virgin olive oil

6 anchovy fillets

Salt and freshly ground pepper

Bring a large pot three-fourths full of salted water to a boil.

Break off the tough end of each asparagus spear by bending it gently until it snaps. Discard the bottoms or reserve for another use. Cut the tender tops on the diagonal into 1-inch (2.5-cm) pieces.

Add the penne and asparagus to the boiling water and cook until the pasta is almost al dente, about 8–10 minutes.

Meanwhile, in a large frying pan, warm the olive oil over low heat. Add the anchovies and, with the back of a wooden spoon, mash them into the oil for about 1 minute. Drain the penne and asparagus and transfer to the frying pan with the anchovies. Finish cooking over medium heat, stirring often, for about 2 minutes. Season with salt and pepper to taste.

Arrange the pasta on a warmed platter and serve hot.

*Serves 6*

# Spaghetti with Escarole, Pine Nuts, and Raisins

The Sicilians add raisins and pine nuts to many of their pasta sauces, especially those in which vegetables or fish are the dominant ingredients. This bittersweet combination is also good with radicchio substituted for the escarole.

In a small bowl, soak the raisins in lukewarm water to cover for about 30 minutes. Drain and set aside.

Bring a large pot three-fourths full of salted water to a boil.

In a large frying pan, warm the olive oil over low heat. Add the garlic and sauté, stirring often, until translucent, about 2 minutes. Add the escarole, stir to coat well, and season to taste with salt and pepper. Cover the pan and continue to cook over low heat, stirring occasionally, until wilted, about 10 minutes.

Meanwhile, add the spaghetti to the boiling water and cook until almost al dente, about 1 minute for fresh pasta or 7 minutes for dried.

Drain the pasta and transfer to the frying pan with the escarole. Add the raisins and finish cooking over low heat, stirring often, for about 2 minutes.

Arrange the pasta on a warmed serving platter or individual bowls. Sprinkle with the pine nuts and serve immediately.

*Serves 6*

1/3 cup (2 oz/60 g) raisins

6 tablespoons (3 fl oz/90 ml) extra-virgin olive oil

3 cloves garlic, chopped

10 oz (300 g) escarole, shredded

Salt and freshly ground pepper

1 1/4 lb (625 g) fresh (page 322) or dried spaghetti

6 tablespoons (2 oz/60 g) pine nuts

# Fedelini with Bread Crumbs, Garlic, and Olive Oil

The Apulians sometimes add anchovies to this old-fashioned sauce. If you wish to include some, mash 3 anchovy fillets into the oil at the same time you are sautéing the garlic.

1¼ lb (600 g) dried fedelini

½ cup (4 fl oz/120 ml) extra-virgin olive oil

3 cloves garlic, finely chopped

6 oz (180 g) fairly stale coarse country bread, crusts discarded and bread crumbled

Salt and freshly ground pepper

Bring a large pot three-fourths full of salted water to a boil. Add the fedelini and cook until al dente, 3–4 minutes.

Meanwhile, in a frying pan, warm the olive oil over medium heat. Add the garlic and sauté, stirring often, until it begins to turn golden, about 3 minutes. Add the bread crumbs and continue stirring until the crumbs turn golden, about 2 minutes.

Drain the pasta and arrange it on a warmed platter. Pour the bread crumb mixture over the top and season to taste with salt and pepper. Toss well and serve immediately.

*Serves 6*

# Angel Hair with Eggs, Leeks, and Cream

This delicate sauce is best served with delicate pasta such as angel hair, and is also good with penne or gemelli. Cook the pasta only until almost al dente, since it will continue cooking with the sauce in the frying pan.

Trim the leeks, discarding the root ends and the tough green tops. Slit the leeks lengthwise three-fourths of the way down to the root ends. Wash under cold running water to remove all dirt. Cut the white portions and the tender green tops crosswise into very thin slices.

In a large frying pan over medium heat, melt the butter. Add the leeks and sauté, stirring occasionally, until tender, about 5 minutes. Set aside and keep warm.

In a bowl, beat together the eggs, 1/4 cup (1 oz/30 g) of the Parmesan, the cream, and salt and pepper to taste. Set aside.

Add the pasta to the boiling water and cook until almost al dente; the timing will depend on the type of pasta used.

Drain the pasta and transfer to the frying pan with the leeks. Raise the heat to high. Pour in the egg mixture and stir vigorously until the eggs are firm but not dry, about 1–2 minutes.

Transfer to a warmed serving bowl and serve immediately. Pass the remaining Parmesan at the table.

*Serves 4*

2 leeks

1/4 cup (2 oz/60 g) unsalted butter

4 eggs

1 cup (4 oz/120 g) grated Parmesan cheese

1/4 cup (2 fl oz/60 ml) light (single) cream

Salt and freshly ground pepper

1 lb (500 g) dried fine-strand or shaped pasta (see note)

# Farfalle with Walnuts and Lemon Zest

In Italy, lemons from sun-baked Sicily are paired with Cognac from neighboring France to produce this international sauce. Almonds, hazelnuts (filberts), or pine nuts can stand in for the walnuts.

1¼ lb (600 g) dried farfalle

⅓ cup (3 oz/90 g) unsalted butter

½ cup (2 oz/60 g) walnuts, very finely chopped

1 tablespoon grated lemon zest

2 tablespoons Cognac or other brandy

Salt and freshly ground pepper

Bring a large pot three-fourths full of salted water to a boil. Add the farfalle and cook until al dente, 10–12 minutes.

Meanwhile, in the top pan of a double boiler placed over simmering water (or in a saucepan set in a larger pan halfway filled with barely simmering water), melt the butter. Stir in the walnuts, lemon zest, and Cognac and keep warm over low heat.

Drain the pasta and arrange it on a warmed platter. Add the walnut-butter mixture and sprinkle to taste with salt and pepper. Toss well and serve hot.

*Serves 6*

# Pappardelle with Stuffed Tomatoes

This Tuscan dish may be prepared up to 6 hours in advance and refrigerated until ready to warm in the oven. When reheating, increase the baking time to 20 minutes.

6 ripe tomatoes, halved and seeded

8 tablespoons (4 fl oz/ 120 ml) extra-virgin olive oil

½ cup (2 oz/60 g) grated Parmesan cheese

½ cup (2 oz/60 g) fine dried bread crumbs (page 324)

2 tablespoons dried oregano

Salt and freshly ground pepper

1 lb (500 g) fresh pappardelle (page 322)

Preheat the oven to 350°F (180°C).

In a bowl, combine 3 tablespoons of the olive oil, the Parmesan, bread crumbs, and oregano. Season with salt and pepper to taste and stir until blended. Divide the mixture evenly among the tomato halves, spooning it into the hollows. Arrange, stuffing side up, on a damp baking sheet. Bake, occasionally sprinkling the sheet with a little water to keep it damp, until lightly golden on top, about 40 minutes.

Meanwhile, prepare the pappardelle according to the directions for Fresh Egg Pasta (page 322). Bring a large pot three-fourths full of salted water to a boil.

When the tomatoes are cooked, remove from the oven and leave the temperature set at 350°F (180°C).

Add the pappardelle to the boiling water and cook until they rise to the surface, about 2 minutes. Drain the pasta and transfer it to a large bowl. Pour 3 tablespoons of the olive oil over the pasta and toss well.

In an 8-by-12-inch (20-by-30-cm) baking dish brushed with the remaining 2 tablespoons olive oil, arrange the pasta. Cover it with the tomatoes, stuffing side up. Bake for 10 minutes. Serve hot.

*Serves 6*

# Tagliatelle with Zucchini

This is a versatile Tuscan sauce. A number of other vegetables — diced eggplant (aubergine) or slices of fennel bulb or artichoke heart — are good substitutes for the zucchini.

Prepare the tagliatelle according to the directions for Fresh Egg Pasta (page 322).

Bring a large pot three-fourths full of salted water to a boil.

In a frying pan, melt $^1/_4$ cup (2 oz/60 g) of the butter over medium heat. Add the zucchini and sauté, stirring occasionally, until tender-crisp, about 5 minutes. Sprinkle with the thyme and salt and pepper to taste.

Add the tagliatelle to the boiling water and cook until they rise to the surface, about 2 minutes.

Drain the pasta and arrange it on a warmed platter. Pour the zucchini mixture over the pasta, then add the remaining $^1/_4$ cup (2 oz/60 g) butter and the Parmesan. Toss well and serve immediately.

*Serves 6*

1 lb (500 g) fresh tagliatelle
(page 322)

$^1/_2$ cup (4 oz/120 g) unsalted
butter, at room temperature

6 small zucchini (courgettes),
cut into $^1/_2$-inch (12-mm) dice

1 tablespoon fresh thyme leaves

Salt and freshly ground pepper

$^3/_4$ cup (3 oz/90 g) grated
Parmesan cheese

# Mezzelune Stuffed with Eggplant

8 tablespoons (4 fl oz/ 120 ml) extra-virgin olive oil

1 clove garlic, chopped

2 large Asian eggplants (slender aubergines), about 13 oz (410 g) total weight, trimmed and diced

1 tablespoon fresh marjoram, mint, thyme, or oregano leaves

3 tablespoons grated Swiss cheese

2 egg yolks

1/2 cup (4 oz/120 g) ricotta cheese

Salt and freshly ground pepper

12 oz (375 g) Fresh Egg Pasta dough (page 322)

In a frying pan, warm 3 tablespoons of the olive oil over low heat. Add the garlic and sauté, until translucent, about 2 minutes. Add the eggplant and sprinkle with the herbs. Cover and cook, stirring occasionally, until tender, about 10 minutes. Remove from the heat, let cool, and chop finely.

In a bowl, combine the cooled eggplant mixture, Swiss cheese, egg yolks, ricotta, and salt and pepper to taste and stir until well mixed.

Prepare the pasta dough according to the directions for Fresh Egg Pasta (page 322). Roll out the dough into a very thin sheet and, using a pastry cutter, cut it into 2-inch (5-cm) rounds. On the center of each round, place a small spoonful of filling. Moisten the edges with cold water and fold in half to form half-moons. Pinch to seal. Using a spatula, set the mezzelune aside on a lightly floured work surface.

Bring a large pot three-fourths full of salted water to a boil. Add the mezzelune and cook until they rise to the surface, about 2 minutes.

Drain well and arrange on a warmed platter. Drizzle the remaining 5 tablespoons (3 fl oz/80 ml) olive oil over the top and serve immediately.

*Serves 6*

# Fusilli with Sweet Corn

This is an especially good way to show off the fresh, tender corn of summer, but frozen or canned corn kernels can be used when the days turn cold. The butter is a northern Italian touch; if you like, substitute extra-virgin olive oil.

Bring a large pot three-fourths full of salted water to a boil. Add the corn. As soon as the water returns to a boil, remove from the heat, cover, and let stand for about 5 minutes. Remove the corn from the water and set aside until cool enough to handle. Then, using a sharp knife, cut off the kernels and place in a warmed serving bowl. Set aside.

Return the water to a boil. Add the fusilli and cook until al dente, 8–11 minutes.

Drain the pasta and transfer to the bowl with the corn kernels. Add the butter, chives, and salt and pepper to taste. Toss well and serve at once.

*Serves 6*

3 ears white or yellow corn, husks and silk removed, or 1½ cups thawed frozen or drained canned corn kernels

1 lb (500 g) dried fusilli

⅓ cup (3 oz/90 g) unsalted butter, at room temperature

2 tablespoons finely chopped fresh chives

Salt and freshly ground pepper

# Broccoli and Tomato Lasagne

In a small bowl, soak the raisins in lukewarm water to cover for about 30 minutes. Drain and set aside.

Bring a large pot three-fourths full of salted water to a boil.

Cut the broccoli florets off the stalks. Cut any large florets in half. Peel the stalks and cut them into slices $1/3$ inch (12mm) thick. Add the florets and stalks to the boiling water and boil for 2 minutes. Using a slotted spoon, transfer to a bowl and set aside. Reserve the cooking water.

In a frying pan, warm the 7 tablespoons olive oil over low heat. Add the garlic and anchovies and sauté until the garlic is translucent, about 2 minutes. Add the broccoli and cook for about 2 minutes. Add the tomatoes and chile powder, stir well and season with salt and pepper to taste. Cook over low heat until the liquid evaporates, about 30 minutes. Meanwhile, prepare the lasagne according to the directions for Fresh Egg Pasta (page 322).

Return the water to a boil. Have a bowl of cold water ready. A few at a time, add the lasagne to the boiling water and cook until they rise to the surface, about 2 minutes. Remove with tongs and drop into the bowl of cold water. Remove from the cold water and spread flat on a kitchen towel to drain.

Preheat the oven to 350°F (180°C). Brush an 8-by-12-inch (20-by-30-cm) ovenproof dish with olive oil. Arrange a layer of lasagne on the bottom. Spoon a little of the sauce on top and sprinkle with some of the raisins and pine nuts. Continue making layers, ending with sauce, raisins, and pine nuts.

Bake until lightly golden on top, about 20 minutes. Serve immediately.

*Serves 6*

1/3 cup (2 oz/60 g) raisins, soaked in warm water and drained

2 lb (1 kg) broccoli

7 tablespoons (32 fl oz/ 110 ml) extra-virgin olive oil, plus extra for brushing

3 cloves garlic, chopped

3 anchovy fillets, chopped

1 1/4 lb (625 g) ripe plum (Roma) tomatoes, peeled (page 329) and chopped, or canned tomatoes, drained and chopped

Pinch of chile powder

Salt and freshly ground black pepper

1 lb (500 g) fresh lasagne (page 322)

6 tablespoons (2 oz/60 g) pine nuts

# Baked Spaghetti with Eggplant

In a saucepan, warm the 6 tablespoons olive oil over low heat. Add the garlic and sauté, stirring often, until translucent, about 2 minutes. Add the tomatoes and chile powder, stir well, and season with salt to taste. Cook over low heat until the liquid evaporates, about 30 minutes.

Pour the 5 cups oil into a deep frying pan and heat to 350°F (180°C) on a deep-frying thermometer. Slip the eggplant into the hot oil, a few slices at a time, and deep-fry until golden, about 3 minutes. Transfer with a slotted spoon to paper towels to drain. Season with salt to taste.

Preheat the oven to 350°F (180°C). Grease a 9-inch (23-cm) springform pan with butter and then coat the bottom and sides evenly with the bread crumbs. Line the pan bottom and sides with the eggplant slices, overlapping them slightly. Reserve any leftover slices.

Bring a large pot three-fourths full of water to a boil. Add the spaghetti and cook only until half-cooked, about 4 minutes. Drain the spaghetti and transfer it to a bowl. Pour the tomato sauce over the top and add any leftover eggplant slices. Toss well. Pile the spaghetti mixture in the prepared pan and press the top to pack it lightly. Bake until lightly browned on top, about 20 minutes. Invert onto a warm platter and serve at once.

*Serves 6*

6 tablespoons (3 fl oz/90 ml) extra-virgin olive oil, plus 5 cups (40 fl oz/ 1.2 l) for deep-frying

3 cloves garlic, chopped

1¼ lb (625 g) ripe plum (Roma) tomatoes, peeled (page 329) and chopped, or canned plum tomatoes, drained and chopped

Pinch of chile powder

Salt

3 large Asian eggplants (slender aubergines), about 1¼ lb (625 g) total weight, trimmed and cut crosswise into slices about ¼ inch (6 mm) thick

Unsalted butter for greasing

¾ cup (3 oz/90 g) fine dried bread crumbs (page 324)

1 lb (500 g) dried spaghetti

# Linguine with Potatoes and Rosemary

A native of the Mediterranean, rosemary flourishes along much of the Italian seashore. Here, in a Genoese dish, its aromatic leaves are used to flavor a simple sauce of potato strips and fruity olive oil.

1 lb (500 g) dried linguine

3 boiling potatoes, peeled and cut into julienne

6 tablespoons (3 fl oz/90 ml) extra-virgin olive oil

1 small yellow onion, finely chopped

2 tablespoons finely chopped fresh rosemary

Salt and freshly ground pepper

Bring a large pot three-fourths full of salted water to a boil. Add the linguini and potatoes and cook until the pasta is al dente, about 8 minutes.

Meanwhile, in a frying pan, warm 3 tablespoons of the olive oil over medium heat. Add the onion and rosemary and sauté until the onion is golden, about 5 minutes.

Drain the linguine and potatoes and arrange them on a warmed serving platter. Pour the onion mixture and the remaining 3 tablespoons olive oil over the top. Season to taste with salt and pepper. Toss well and serve at once.

*Serves 6*

# Pasta with Red and Green Sauce

Red tomatoes and green herbs combine to make a vibrantly perfumed sauce that is ideal on fresh or dried tagliatelle or fettuccine. For an additional touch of color, use green spinach pasta. Replace the carrots with zucchini (courgettes), if you wish.

Bring a large pot three-fourths full of salted water to a boil.

In a large frying pan over high heat, warm 2 tablespoons of the olive oil. Add the onion and garlic and sauté until translucent, 3–4 minutes. Add the carrot and bell pepper strips and continue cooking over high heat a few minutes longer. Add the tomatoes, oregano, and salt to taste and reduce the heat to low. Cook uncovered, stirring occasionally, until the liquid evaporates and the vegetables are tender, about 10 minutes longer.

Meanwhile, add the pasta to the boiling water and cook until almost al dente, about 1 minute for fresh pasta or 7 minutes for dried.

Drain the pasta and add to the sauce in the frying pan. Finish cooking over high heat, stirring constantly, for 1–2 minutes. Remove from the heat and stir in the remaining 2 tablespoons olive oil.

Transfer to a warmed serving bowl. Sprinkle with the parsley and basil and serve at once. Pass the Parmesan at the table, if desired.

*Serves 4*

4 tablespoons (2 fl oz/60 ml) extra-virgin olive oil

1 white onion, sliced

1 clove garlic, sliced

2 carrots, peeled and cut into julienne

1 red bell pepper (capsicum), seeded, deribbed, and cut into thin strips

10 oz (300 g) fresh plum (Roma) tomatoes, peeled (page 329) and chopped, or canned plum tomatoes, drained and chopped

1 tablespoon dried oregano

Salt

1 lb (500 g) fresh (page 322) or dried ribbon pasta (see note)

2 tablespoons chopped flat-leaf (Italian) parsley

1 tablespoon chopped fresh basil

3/4 cup (3 oz/90 g) grated Parmesan cheese, optional

# Cannelloni Stuffed with Spinach and Ricotta

12 oz (375 g) Fresh Egg Pasta dough (page 322)

2 lb (1 kg) spinach leaves, tough stems removed, boiled until tender, and drained

1¼ cups (10 oz/300 g) ricotta cheese

2 egg yolks

¾ cup (3 oz/90 g) grated Parmesan cheese

Pinch of ground nutmeg

Salt and freshly ground pepper

Unsalted butter for greasing

1 cup (8 fl oz/350 ml) heavy (double) cream

Prepare the pasta dough according to the directions for Fresh Egg Pasta (page 322). Roll out the dough into a very thin sheet and cut into 3-inch (7.5-cm) squares.

Bring a large pot three-fourths full of salted water to a boil.

Meanwhile, squeeze any excess water out of the cooked spinach, then chop finely. In a bowl, combine the spinach, ricotta, egg yolks, ¼ cup (1 oz/30 g) of the Parmesan, the nutmeg, and salt and pepper to taste. Blend well with a fork.

Have a large bowl of cold water ready. A few at a time, add the pasta squares to the boiling water and cook until they rise to the surface, about 2 minutes. Remove with tongs and drop into the bowl of cold water. Remove from the cold water and spread flat on a kitchen towel to drain.

Preheat the oven to 350°F (180°C). Lightly grease an 8-by-12-inch (20-by-30-cm) baking dish with butter.

Spread a little of the spinach-ricotta mixture onto one half of each pasta square, leaving the edges of the square uncovered. Beginning at the edge nearest the filling, roll up the square to form a cylinder. Arrange the cannelloni, seam side down and side by side, in a single layer in the prepared dish. Sprinkle with the remaining ½ cup (2 oz/60 g) Parmesan and pour the cream evenly over the top.

Bake the cannelloni until the top begins to turn golden, about 20 minutes. Serve immediately.

*Serves 6*

# Farfalle with Sun-Dried Tomatoes and Olives

So intense are the flavors of sun-dried tomatoes and green olives that this sauce requires little if any additional seasoning. This recipe is particularly good with such pasta shapes as farfalle and conchiglie, because they trap the sauce in their hollows.

1 lb (500 g) farfalle or other dried shaped pasta (see note)

3/4 cup (6 fl oz/180 ml) heavy (double) cream

12 green olives, pitted and finely chopped

1/2 cup (2 1/2 oz/ 75 g) drained, oil-packed, sun-dried tomatoes, finely chopped

Salt and freshly ground pepper

3/4 cup (3 oz/90 g) grated Parmesan cheese

Bring a large pot three-fourths full of salted water to a boil. Add the pasta and cook until al dente, 10–12 minutes. Drain the pasta, reserving 1/4 cup (2 fl oz/60 ml) of the cooking water.

Meanwhile, combine the cream, olives, and sun-dried tomatoes in a frying pan over very low heat. Heat just until the cream is lukewarm and slightly pink. Stir in the reserved hot cooking water.

Transfer the pasta to a warmed serving bowl. Immediately pour the sauce over the pasta. Add salt and pepper to taste and the Parmesan. Toss well. Serve at once.

*Serves 4*

# Spaghetti with Red Bell Pepper Purée

The naturally sweet flavor of roasted red bell peppers comes through in this easy preparation, ideal on spaghetti. The dish is also wonderful served chilled: Purée 1 celery stalk with the sauce ingredients, toss with the pasta, and chill.

Bring a large pot three-fourths full of salted water to a boil.

Preheat the broiler (grill). Cut the bell peppers in half lengthwise and remove the stems, seeds, and ribs. Arrange cut sides down on a baking sheet. Broil (grill) until the skins blacken and blister, about 10 minutes. Transfer to a paper or plastic bag and let stand until the peppers cool and the skins loosen, about 10 minutes. Using your fingers or a small knife, peel off the skins. Cut lengthwise into strips about 3/8 inch (1 cm) wide. Set aside.

In a blender or food processor, combine the roasted bell pepper strips, garlic, olive oil, and salt to taste. Process until smooth.

Add the pasta to the boiling water and cook until al dente, about 8 minutes. Drain and transfer to a warmed serving bowl. Immediately pour the purée over the top and toss well. Sprinkle with the parsley and serve at once.

*Serves 4*

3 red bell peppers (capsicums)

1 clove garlic

1/4 cup (2 fl oz/60 ml) extra-virgin olive oil

Salt

2 tablespoons chopped fresh flat-leaf (Italian) parsley

1 lb (500 g) dried spaghetti

# Spaghetti with Cherry Tomatoes and Basil

The success of this quick recipe—a classic topping for spaghetti—depends upon finding sun-ripened, sweet, and flavorful cherry tomatoes. For a more substantial dish, add 4 ounces (125 g) mozzarella cheese, cut into 1-inch (2.5-cm) cubes and tossed into the pasta with the tomatoes.

3 cups (1 lb/500 g) cherry tomatoes

Coarse salt

6 tablespoons (3 fl oz/90 ml) extra-virgin olive oil

5 cloves garlic, thinly sliced

Pinch of cayenne pepper

1 lb (500 g) spaghetti or other dried strand pasta

12 fresh basil leaves, torn into small pieces

Bring a large saucepan half full of water to a boil. Drop the tomatoes into the boiling water and cook for 1 minute. Drain and peel while still hot. Cut the tomatoes in half and place in a fine-mesh sieve. Sprinkle with coarse salt and let stand for 30 minutes to drain.

Bring a large pot three-fourths full of salted water to a boil.

In a frying pan over medium heat, warm the olive oil. Add the garlic and cayenne, reduce the heat to very low, and cook, stirring occasionally, until the garlic is lightly golden, about 5 minutes.

Meanwhile, add the pasta to the boiling water and cook until is al dente, about 8 minutes. Drain and transfer to a warmed serving bowl. Immediately add the tomatoes and basil to the dish. Raise the heat under the garlic sauce for a few seconds to heat it as much as possible without further coloring the garlic, then pour it over the pasta and toss well. Serve at once.

*Serves 4*

# Spinach Tagliatelle with Pumpkin and Sage

With its mild, slightly sweet flavor and vibrant color, pumpkin is a perfect match for tagliatelle, and is also lovely with spinach pastas. For a more exotic flavor, add grated nutmeg and a crumbled amaretto cookie.

1 piece baking pumpkin, about 1 lb (500 g)

6 tablespoons (3 oz/90 g) unsalted butter

1 white onion, sliced paper-thin

8 fresh sage leaves

1 lb (500 g) fresh (page 322) or dried ribbon pasta (see note)

3/4 cup (3 oz/90 g) grated Parmesan cheese

Salt and freshly ground white pepper

Peel the piece of pumpkin; remove any seeds and strings and discard. Cut the pumpkin into small cubes and set aside.

In a large frying pan over medium heat, melt 3 tablespoons of the butter. Add the onion and sauté until it is translucent, about 10 minutes. Add the pumpkin, raise the heat to medium-high and cook, stirring often, until the pumpkin is tender, about 20 minutes longer.

When the pumpkin is almost ready, melt the remaining 3 tablespoons butter in another frying pan over medium-high heat. Add the sage leaves and fry until they are slightly crisp, about 3 minutes.

Meanwhile, bring a large pot three-fourths full of salted water to a boil. Add the pasta and cook until al dente; the timing will depend on the type of pasta used. Drain and transfer to a warmed serving bowl. Immediately pour the pumpkin sauce over the pasta. Add the Parmesan and salt and white pepper to taste and toss well. Pour the sage and butter over the top and serve at once.

*Serves 4*

# Rigatoni with Cauliflower and Gruyère

This favorite vegetable-and-cheese combination is excellent with a pasta shape such as rigatoni. Try substituting other types of Swiss cheese or adding some finely chopped ham.

Pour the milk into a saucepan placed over medium-low heat. When the milk is little more than warm, turn off the heat.

In another saucepan over low heat, add the butter and flour, vigorously stirring them together with a wooden spoon until the butter melts and the flour is incorporated. Once the butter is fully melted, cook and stir for 2 minutes longer. Then gradually add the warm milk, a little at a time, stirring constantly. Add more milk only after the previously added milk has been fully incorporated. When all the milk has been added, add salt to taste and the nutmeg and cook, stirring often, until thickened, 3–4 minutes longer. Remove from the heat, cover, and keep warm.

Meanwhile, cut the cauliflower florets off the stalks. Cut any large florets in half. Discard the stalks or reserve for another use. Arrange the cauliflower in a steamer basket and place over gently boiling water. Cover and steam just until barely tender, about 10 minutes. Set aside.

Meanwhile, preheat the oven to 350°F (180°C). Grease a 6-by-12-inch (15-by-30-cm) oval baking dish.

Bring a large pot three-fourths full of salted water to a boil. Add the pasta and cook until almost al dente, 8–10 minutes, then drain.

Pour a few spoonfuls of the white sauce into the prepared baking dish. Top with the pasta, the cauliflower, and the remaining sauce. Sprinkle with the cheese. Bake until the top is golden, about 20 minutes. Serve immediately.

*Serves 4*

2 cups (16 fl oz/500 ml) milk

2½ tablespoons unsalted butter, plus extra for greasing

3½ tablespoons all-purpose (plain) flour

Salt

Pinch of ground nutmeg

1 small head cauliflower, about 1 lb (500 g)

1 lb (500 g) rigatoni or other dried shaped pasta (see note)

½ cup (2 oz/60 g) shredded Gruyère cheese

# Radiatori with Potatoes and Arugula

Use plain or spinach radiatori. For a richer version, add 2 or 3 ripe peeled plum (Roma) tomatoes, 2 anchovy fillets, and 2 tablespoons drained capers, all finely chopped together, to the garlic and oil.

1 large russet potato, peeled and cut into ³/₈-inch (1-cm) cubes

³/₄ lb (375 g) arugula (rocket), tough stems removed, cut into long, thin strips

1 lb (500 g) radiatori or other dried shaped pasta (see note)

6 tablespoons (3 fl oz/90 ml) extra-virgin olive oil

1 clove garlic

Pinch of cayenne pepper

Bring a large saucepan three-fourths full of salted water to a boil. Add the potatoes and the arugula. When the water returns to a boil, add the pasta and cook until al dente, 10–12 minutes.

Meanwhile, in a saucepan over medium heat, warm the olive oil. Add the garlic and cayenne, reduce the heat to very low, and cook very slowly, stirring occasionally, until the garlic is lightly golden, about 5 minutes.

Drain the pasta and vegetables and transfer to a warmed serving bowl. Raise the heat under the garlic sauce for a few seconds to heat it as much as possible without further coloring the garlic. Discard the garlic. Immediately pour the oil over the pasta and toss well. Serve at once.

*Serves 4*

# Garganelli with Green Beans and Saffron

This colorful green–and–yellow topping pairs well with garganelli (shown here) or regular or spinach penne. Italian beans, sometimes called romano beans, are flat, flavorful green beans.

Slice the beans on the diagonal into diamond-shaped pieces about 3/8 inch (1 cm) long. Set aside.

In a large frying pan over medium heat, warm the olive oil. Add the onions and the saffron and its soaking water and sauté until the onions begin to soften, about 5 minutes. Add the beans and sauté over high heat, stirring constantly, for 2 minutes.

Meanwhile, bring a large pot three-fourths full of salted water to a boil. Add the pasta and cook until almost al dente, 8–10 minutes. Drain, reserving about 1/2 cup (4 fl oz/125 ml) of the cooking water. Add the pasta to the sauce in the frying pan, along with the egg yolks, salt and pepper to taste, and the reserved hot cooking water. Raise the heat to high and cook, stirring vigorously, until the pasta is al dente and the beans are tender, 1–2 minutes.

Remove from the heat, add the cheese, and toss well. Transfer to a warmed platter, sprinkle with the parsley, and serve immediately.

*Serves 4*

7 oz (220 g) Italian (romano) beans, trimmed

1/4 cup (2 fl oz/60 ml) extra-virgin olive oil

2 white onions, thinly sliced

2 pinches of saffron threads, soaked in 1 tablespoon hot water

1 lb (500 g) dried shaped pasta (see note)

2 egg yolks, lightly beaten

Salt and freshly ground pepper

3/4 cup (3 oz/90 g) grated pecorino romano cheese

2 tablespoons chopped fresh flat-leaf (Italian) parsley

# Spaghetti with Eggplant and Bread Crumbs

In a popular Sicilian version of this recipe, the eggplant (aubergine) is fried until golden in an abundance of extra-virgin olive oil and then patted dry with paper towels.

3/4 cup (6 fl oz/180 ml) extra-virgin olive oil

2 cloves garlic, thinly sliced

3/4 lb (375 g) fresh plum (Roma) tomatoes, peeled (page 329) and chopped, or canned plum tomatoes, drained and chopped

2 tablespoons chopped fresh basil

Pinch of cayenne pepper

Salt

2 Asian eggplants (slender aubergines), about 3/4 lb (375 g) total weight, trimmed and cut crosswise into slices about 1/4 inch (6 mm) thick

6 oz (185 g) somewhat stale coarse country bread, crusts discarded and bread crumbled

1 lb (500 g) fresh (page 322) or dried spaghetti

In a frying pan over medium heat, warm 1/4 cup (2 fl oz/60 ml) of the olive oil. Add the garlic, raise the heat to high, and sauté until golden, about 2 minutes. Add the tomatoes, basil, cayenne, and salt to taste. Cook, uncovered, over medium heat, stirring occasionally, until thickened, about 15 minutes.

Meanwhile, in another frying pan over medium heat, warm 1/4 cup (2 fl oz/60 ml) of the olive oil. Add the eggplant and sauté, stirring often, until tender, about 15 minutes.

In another frying pan over medium heat, warm the remaining 1/4 cup (2 fl oz/60 ml) olive oil. Add the bread crumbs and toast, stirring often, until they turn golden, about 7 minutes.

Meanwhile, bring a large pot three-fourths full of salted water to a boil. Add the pasta and cook until al dente, about 2 minutes for fresh pasta or 8 minutes for dried. Drain and transfer to a warmed serving bowl. Immediately pour the eggplant and tomato mixtures over the pasta and toss well. Sprinkle with the hot bread crumbs and serve at once.

*Serves 4*

# Rigatoni with Chickpeas and Cabbage

This robust combination turns a simple bowl of rigatoni into a complete, healthful meal. Substitute dried lentils, cranberry (borlotti) beans, or fava (broad) beans for the chickpeas, or use a mixture.

Place the chickpeas in a bowl, add water to cover, and soak for 12 hours at room temperature, changing the water a few times.

Drain the chickpeas and transfer to a saucepan. Add the celery, olive oil, onion, cabbage, and water to cover by several inches. Bring to a boil, reduce the heat to low, cover partially, and simmer until the chickpeas are very tender, about 3 hours. If the chickpeas begin to dry out before they are tender, add a little lukewarm water to the pan.

When the chickpeas are nearly ready, drain the mushrooms and remove their stems and discard. Slice the mushrooms and add to the chickpeas. Then, using a fork, mash a few of the chickpeas to thicken the sauce. Season to taste with salt and pepper.

Meanwhile, bring a large pot three-fourths full of salted water to a boil. Add the pasta and cook until al dente, 12–14 minutes. Drain and transfer to a warmed serving bowl. Immediately add the sauce and cheese and toss well. Serve at once.

*Serves 4*

2/3 cup (5 oz/150 g) dried chickpeas (garbanzo beans)

1 celery stalk, sliced

1/4 cup (2 fl oz/60 ml) olive oil

1 red onion, sliced

1 head savoy cabbage, about 3/4 lb (375 g), cored and chopped

5 or 6 dried shiitake mushrooms, soaked in warm water to cover until softened, about 30 minutes

Salt and freshly ground pepper

1 lb (500 g) rigatoni or other dried shaped pasta

3/4 cup (3 oz/90 g) grated pecorino romano cheese

# Seafood, Poultry & Meat Pasta

# Conchiglie Salad with Tuna and Lettuce

For added color, substitute marbled red radicchio or deep scarlet cabbage leaves for the lettuce in this light Genoese pasta salad. Accompany with lemon wedges and garnish with fresh dill. Serve at a picnic or buffet lunch.

Bring a large pot bring three-fourths full of salted water to a boil. Add the conchiglie and cook until al dente, 10–12 minutes.

Drain the pasta and transfer to a serving bowl. Add the oil and toss well. Let the pasta cool for about 5 minutes.

Add the lettuce and tuna to the pasta and season to taste with salt and pepper. Toss well and serve slightly warm or at room temperature.

*Serves 6*

1 lb (500 g) dried conchiglie

6 tablespoons (3 fl oz/90 ml) extra-virgin olive oil

1 small head butter (Boston) lettuce, leaves separated and torn into bite-sized pieces

7 oz (220 g) canned tuna, packed in water or olive oil, drained and flaked

Salt and freshly ground pepper

# Tagliatelle with Smoked Salmon and Fennel

Strips of silky smoked salmon and crisp, anise-flavored fennel bulb make this
a refreshing, light dinner dish. To serve it cold, toss the pasta with the olive oil
immediately after cooking and refrigerate for up to 6 hours.

1 lb (500 g) fresh tagliatelle
(page 322)

1 fennel bulb, trimmed
and cut crosswise into
paper-thin slices

Juice of 1/2 lemon

Freshly ground pepper

6 oz (185 g) smoked salmon,
cut into thin strips

6 tablespoons (3 fl oz/90 ml)
extra-virgin olive oil

Salt

Prepare the tagliatelle according to the directions for Fresh Egg Pasta (page 322).

Bring a large pot of salted water to a boil.

Meanwhile, place the fennel in a bowl, sprinkle with the lemon juice, and season to
taste with pepper. Toss well and set aside.

Add the tagliatelle to the boiling water and cook until the pasta rises to the surface,
about 2 minutes.

Drain the pasta and transfer to a warmed platter. Scatter the salmon and fennel
over the pasta, then sprinkle with the oil. Season to taste with salt and pepper and
toss gently. Serve immediately.

*Serves 6*

# Linguine and Shrimp Tart

Preheat the oven to 350°F (180°C).

In a bowl, combine the flour and butter. Using a pastry blender or 2 knives, work the butter into the flour until the mixture resembles coarse cornmeal. In a small bowl, beat the water with the egg yolk. Add the egg mixture to the flour mixture and work them together until a soft, smooth dough forms. Pat the dough into a ball, wrap in plastic, and refrigerate for about 2 hours.

On a lightly floured work surface, roll out the dough into a round about 11 inches (28 cm) in diameter. Transfer to a 9-inch (23-cm) tart pan with a removable bottom. Press the dough onto the bottom and sides. Trim off the top even with the rim. Prick the bottom of the crust all over with a fork.

Bake the tart shell for 30 minutes. If the pastry puffs up during baking, press it down with the palm of your hand. Remove from the oven and let cool on a wire rack. Leave the oven temperature set at 350°F (180°C).

While the crust is baking, in a heavy saucepan, bring the cream to a boil over medium heat. Add the shrimp and cook until barely opaque, about 2 minutes. Season to taste with salt and pepper and stir in the curry powder.

Meanwhile, bring a large pot three-fourths full of salted water to a boil. Add the linguine and cook until al dente, about 8 minutes. Drain and transfer to a large bowl. Add the shrimp mixture and the cheese and toss well. Fill the cooled tart shell with the linguine mixture. Place in the oven until hot, about 5 minutes. Serve at once.

*Serves 6*

1⅓ cups (7 oz/220 g) all-purpose (plain) flour

⅓ cup (3 oz/90 g) unsalted butter, chilled and cut into small pieces

2 tablespoons water

1 egg yolk

1 cup (8 fl oz/250 ml) heavy (double) cream

6 oz (185 g) shrimp (prawns), peeled

Salt and freshly ground pepper

1 tablespoon curry powder

10 oz (315 g) dried linguine

2 tablespoons shredded Swiss cheese

# Pappardelle with Fresh Marinated Salmon

Arrange the salmon slices in a single layer in a shallow glass dish.

Pour the lemon juice over the top and marinate at room temperature, turning occasionally, for about 1 hour.

Prepare the pappardelle according to the directions for Fresh Egg Pasta (page 322).

Drain the salmon and arrange it in a shallow soup plate that is large enough to span the rim of the large pot in which you will cook the pasta. Distribute the coriander seeds, parsley, and olive oil evenly over the top. Season to taste with salt and pepper. Let stand, turning occasionally, for about 10 minutes, to allow the flavors to blend.

Bring a large pot three-fourths full of salted water to a boil. Meanwhile, place the plate of salmon on top of the pot and cover the plate with a lid. This will warm the salmon without cooking it. When the water boils, remove the salmon plate, add the pappardelle, and cook until the pasta rises to the surface, 2 minutes. Drain the pasta and transfer to a warmed platter. Add the salmon and toss gently. Sprinkle with the lemon zest and serve at once.

*Serves 6*

6 oz (185 g) salmon fillet, cut on the diagonal into paper-thin slices

Juice of 3 lemons

1 lb (500 g) fresh pappardelle (page 322)

1 tablespoon coriander seeds

1 tablespoon chopped fresh flat-leaf (Italian) parsley

6 tablespoons (3 fl oz/90 ml) extra-virgin olive oil

Salt and freshly ground pepper

Grated zest of 1 lemon

# Linguine with Clams

When you order pasta with clams in Italy, the clams are usually tiny and served in the shell. Here, small or large clams can be used and are removed from their shells. For a "red" clam sauce, add the tomatoes; for a "white" clam sauce, leave them out.

6 dozen Manila clams or 3–4 dozen larger clams, well scrubbed

1 cup (8 fl oz/250 ml) dry white wine

1 lb (500 g) fresh (page 322) or dried linguine

1/2 cup (4 fl oz/125 ml) extra-virgin olive oil

4 cloves garlic, minced

2 teaspoons dried oregano (optional)

Pinch of red pepper flakes (optional)

2 cups (12 oz/375 g) peeled (page 329), seeded, and diced tomatoes (optional)

1/2 cup (3/4 oz/20 g) chopped fresh flat-leaf (Italian) parsley

Salt and freshly ground pepper

3 tablespoons extra-virgin olive oil or 3–4 tablespoons unsalted butter (optional)

Place the clams in a large, wide saucepan, discarding any that do not close to the touch. Add the wine, cover, and place over high heat. Cook, shaking the pan occasionally, until the clams open and release their juices, about 5 minutes. Discard any clams that do not open. Using a slotted spoon, transfer the clams to a bowl. Reserve the cooking liquid. When cool enough to handle, remove the clams from their shells. If they are small, place in a small bowl; if they are large, chop into bite-sized pieces and place in the bowl. Strain the clam broth through a fine-mesh sieve lined with cheesecloth (muslin) into a bowl.

Bring a large pot three-fourths full of salted water to a boil. Add the linguine and cook until al dente, about 2 minutes for fresh pasta or 8 minutes for dried.

Meanwhile, in a frying pan over medium-low heat, warm the 1/2 cup (4 fl oz/125 ml) olive oil. Add the garlic and the oregano and red pepper flakes, if using. Cook until fragrant, about 2 minutes. Add the clams, the strained broth, and the tomatoes, if using. Heat through gently; do not overcook or the clams will toughen. Add the parsley and season with salt, if needed, and a generous amount of black pepper. Add in the 3 tablespoons oil or 3–4 tablespoons butter, if using.

Drain the pasta and transfer to a warmed serving bowl. Add the sauce, toss well, and serve at once.

*Serves 4–6*

# Pasta with Mussels and Cannellini Purée

This sauce is ideal for wide pasta ribbons such as pappardelle. For the best results, buy mussels only from the most reputable fishmongers, and only at their peak of season; do not make this during warmer months, when mussels are chancy.

Pick over the beans, discarding any stones or misshapen beans. Rinse the beans. Place the beans in a bowl, add cold water to cover, and soak for about 12 hours. Drain the beans and place in a saucepan with water to cover by about 1 inch (2.5 cm). Bring to a boil, reduce the heat to low, cover partially, and cook until tender, about 1 1/2 hours. Drain the beans, reserving the cooking liquid. Transfer to a blender or food processor. Process until smooth, adding a little cooking liquid if needed. Set aside.

Discard any mussels with opened or cracked shells. Place the mussels in a saucepan. Cover and place over medium heat, shaking occasionally, until the mussels open, about 5 minutes. Discard any that do not open. Using a slotted spoon, transfer the mussels to a bowl. If the mussels released any liquid during cooking, strain it through a fine-mesh sieve lined with cheesecloth (muslin) into a bowl; set aside. Remove the mussels from their shells. In a frying pan over medium heat, combine the mussels, puréed beans, and salt and pepper to taste. Stir to prevent sticking and add the mussel liquid as needed for moisture. Keep hot.

In a saucepan over medium heat, warm the oil. Add the garlic and sage, reduce the heat to very low, and cook until the leaves are crisp and the garlic is golden, about 5 minutes. Using a slotted spoon, transfer the sage to a small dish. Meanwhile, bring a large pot three-fourths full of salted water to a boil. Add the pasta and cook until al dente, about 2 minutes for fresh or 8 minutes for dried. Drain and transfer to a warmed serving bowl. Pour on the hot garlic and oil and toss well. Top with the bean-mussel mixture and garnish with the sage. Sprinkle with pepper and serve.

*Serves 4*

2/3 cup (5 oz/155 g) dried cannellini, small white (navy), or Great Northern beans

2 lb (1 kg) mussels, well scrubbed and debearded

Salt and freshly ground pepper

6 tablespoons (3 fl oz/90 ml) extra-virgin olive oil

2 cloves garlic, sliced

10 fresh sage leaves

1 lb (500 g) fresh (page 322) or dried ribbon pasta (see note)

# Spaghetti with Shrimp Sauce

Sautéed tomato and dry white wine intensify the sweet flavor of fresh shrimp (prawns) in this Venetian dish. For a special occasion, substitute freshly boiled lobster, shelled and coarsely chopped.

3 tablespoons extra-virgin olive oil

1 small onion, chopped

1 lb (500 g) shrimp (prawns), peeled and deveined

⅓ cup (3 fl oz/90 ml) dry white wine

10 oz (315 g) ripe plum (Roma) tomatoes, peeled (page 329) and chopped, or canned plum tomatoes, drained and chopped

Salt and freshly ground pepper

1 lb (500 g) dried spaghetti

1 tablespoon chopped fresh flat-leaf (Italian) parsley

Bring a large pot three-fourths full of salted water to a boil.

In a large frying pan, warm the olive oil over low heat. Add the onion and sauté, stirring often, until translucent, about 3 minutes. Add the shrimp, raise the heat to medium, and sauté, stirring constantly, for 2 minutes. Add the wine and cook, stirring often, until it evaporates, about 2 minutes. Add the tomatoes and salt and pepper to taste and cook for 2 minutes longer.

Meanwhile, add the spaghetti to the boiling water and cook until almost al dente, about 7 minutes.

Drain the pasta and transfer to the frying pan with the tomato sauce. Add the parsley and finish cooking over medium heat, stirring often, for 2 minutes.

Arrange the pasta on a warmed platter and serve hot.

*Serves 6*

# Linguine with Sole, Tomatoes, and Bacon

Strips of delicate white fish and chunks of tomato are tossed with linguine ("little tongues") in this easily prepared dish. Fresh cod fillets or whole peeled shrimp (prawns) may be used instead of the sole.

Bring a large pot three-fourths full of salted water to a boil.

Cut the sole fillets into pieces 2 inches (5 cm) long and $1/2$ inch (12 mm) wide. Set aside.

In a large frying pan, warm the olive oil over medium heat. Add the bacon and cook, stirring occasionally, until crisp, about 5 minutes. Add the fish to the frying pan and cook for 2 minutes. Add the tomatoes and cook, stirring occasionally for 5 minutes. Season to taste with salt and pepper.

Meanwhile, add the linguine to the boiling water and cook until almost al dente, about 1 minute for fresh pasta or 7 minutes for dried.

Drain the pasta and transfer to the frying pan with the tomato sauce. Finish cooking over medium heat, stirring gently, for 2 minutes.

Arrange the pasta on a warmed platter and serve at once.

*Serves 6*

1 lb (500 g) sole fillets

3 tablespoons extra-virgin olive oil

2 oz (60 g) bacon, cut into thin strips

10 oz (315 g) ripe plum (Roma) tomatoes, peeled (page 329) and chopped, or canned plum tomatoes, drained and chopped

Salt and freshly ground pepper

1 lb (500 g) dried linguine

# Pasta with Scallops and Tomatoes

Select the fullest-flavored vine-ripened plum (Roma) tomatoes in the market. Buy the freshest scallops you can find; their sweet, mild flavor will be highlighted by the ripe, barely cooked tomatoes.

12 sea scallops

1 lb (500 g) dried shaped pasta

6 tablespoons (3 fl oz/90 ml) extra-virgin olive oil

2 cloves garlic, thinly sliced

3–4 plum (Roma) tomatoes, peeled (page 329) and chopped

Salt and freshly ground pepper

3 tablespoons chopped fresh basil

Cut the scallops into rounds $^{1}/_{4}$ inch (6 mm) thick. Set aside.

Bring a large pot three-fourths full of salted water to a boil. Add the pasta and cook until al dente, about 10–12 minutes, depending on the type of pasta.

Meanwhile, warm the oil in a large frying pan over medium heat. Add the garlic and sauté until lightly golden, about 2 minutes. Raise the heat to high and add the scallops and tomatoes. Cook, stirring gently, until the scallops are opaque, 1–2 minutes. Season to taste with salt and pepper.

Drain the pasta and transfer to a warmed serving bowl. Pour the scallop sauce over the pasta and toss well. Sprinkle with the basil and serve immediately.

*Serves 4*

# Taglierini with Sautéed Scallops

Quick sautéing with olive oil and garlic transforms sweet, fresh scallops into a delectable topping for pasta. If fresh scallops in their shells are available, they are preferred for this dish. Or try peeled shrimp (prawns) or shelled fresh mussels or clams.

1 lb (520 g) taglierini
(page 322)

12 sea scallops

6 tablespoons (3 fl oz/90 ml)
extra-virgin olive oil

1 clove garlic, chopped

Salt and freshly ground pepper

l tablespoon chopped flat-leaf
(Italian) parsley

Prepare the taglierini according to the directions for basic egg pasta (page 322).

Cut the scallops crosswise into slices 4 inch (6 mm) thick.

In a large pot bring 5 qt (5 l) salted water to a boil.

Meanwhile, in a large frying pan heat 3 tablespoons of the olive oil over low heat. Add the garlic and sauté, stirring frequently, until translucent, about 2 minutes. Raise the heat to medium, add the sliced scallops and cook, turning once, until tender, about 3 minutes. Season to taste with salt and pepper. When the scallops are almost tender, add the taglierini to the boiling water and cook until they rise to the surface, about 2 minutes.

Drain the pasta and transfer it to the frying pan containing the scallops. Sprinkle with the parsley and cook over medium heat, stirring gently, for 2 minutes.

Arrange the pasta on a warm platter and sprinkle with the remaining 3 tablespoons olive oil. Serve at once.

*Serves 6*

# Pasta with Smoked Salmon and Radicchio

Salmon is a versatile fish whose rich flavor is not overpowered by the bitterness of radicchio. This combination goes best with a pasta that will cling to the sauce, such as fusilli, linguine, taglierini, or fresh tagliatelle.

1/4 cup (2 oz/60 g) unsalted butter

1/2 white onion, thinly sliced

2 small heads (about 1/2 lb/ 250 g) radicchio, cored and thinly sliced

1/4 cup (2 fl oz/60 ml) dry white wine

Salt and freshly ground white pepper

3 1/2 oz (105 g) smoked salmon, cut into thin strips

1 lb (500 g) fresh (page 322) or dried pasta (see note)

2 tablespoons chopped fresh flat-leaf (Italian) parsley

In a large frying pan over medium heat, melt the butter. Add the onion and 3 tablespoons water, cover, and cook gently, stirring occasionally, until the onion is tender and translucent, about 10 minutes.

Add the radicchio, wine, and salt and white pepper to taste. Stir well, raise the heat to high, and cook, stirring often, until the wine evaporates, about 2 minutes.

When the wine has evaporated, add the salmon and continue sautéing until heated through.

Meanwhile, bring a large pot three-fourths full of salted water to a boil. Add the pasta and cook until almost al dente; the timing will depend on the type of pasta used. Drain, reserving about 1/4 cup (2 fl oz/60 ml) of the cooking water. Add the pasta and the reserved hot cooking water to the frying pan with the radicchio and finish cooking over high heat, stirring constantly, for 1–2 minutes.

Transfer to a warmed serving bowl, sprinkle with the parsley, and serve immediately.

*Serves 4*

# Pasta with Tuna, Tomatoes, and Mushrooms

This meaty-tasting dish combines two sauces that are cooked separately. It marries well with long, flattened strands like fettucini, linguine, or pappardelle. A more traditional alternative to the steaklike shiitake mushrooms would be fresh porcini.

8 tablespoons (4 fl oz/125 ml) extra-virgin olive oil

2 cloves garlic

1 small dried red chile

4 plum (Roma) tomatoes, peeled (page 329) and chopped

2 tablespoons minced fresh basil

Salt and freshly ground pepper

4 oz (125 g) canned Italian tuna packed in olive oil, drained and flaked

2 anchovy fillets, chopped

3 oz (90 g) fresh shiitake mushrooms, stems removed and caps cut into 3/4-inch (2-cm) pieces

1 lb (500 g) fresh (page 322) or dried ribbon pasta (see note)

In a large frying pan over medium heat, warm 3 tablespoons of the oil. Add the garlic cloves and chile and sauté, stirring often, for 2 minutes. Add the tomatoes, basil, and salt to taste and cook uncovered, stirring often, until the sauce is thickened but not too dry, about 15 minutes. Discard the garlic cloves and chile.

Meanwhile, warm 3 tablespoons of the olive oil in another frying pan over medium heat. Add the tuna, anchovies, and mushrooms. Raise the heat to high and cook, stirring often, for 2 minutes.

Bring a large pot three-fourths full of salted water to a boil. Add the pasta and cook until al dente, 2 minutes for fresh pasta or 8 minutes for dried. Drain and transfer to a warmed platter. Toss with the remaining 2 tablespoons oil and pepper to taste. Spoon the two sauces in alternating vertical stripes atop the pasta. Serve at once.

*Serves 4*

# Fettuccine with Shrimp and Broccoli

Broccoli's assertive flavor and bright green color combine well with shrimp (prawns) and freshly made pasta. If fresh artichokes are available, use the hearts in place of the broccoli.

Prepare the fettuccine according to the directions for Fresh Egg Pasta (page 322).

In a large frying pan, heat the olive oil over low heat. Add the garlic and sauté, stirring often, until translucent, about 2 minutes. Add the broccoli, cover, and cook, stirring occasionally, until tender, about 5 minutes.

Raise the heat to medium, add the shrimp, and sauté for 2 minutes. Add the wine and salt and pepper to taste. Cook for 2 minutes longer. Remove the pan from the heat and set aside.

Bring a large pot three-fourths full of salted water to a boil. Add the fettuccine and cook until the pasta rises to the surface, about 2 minutes.

Drain the pasta and transfer to the frying pan with the broccoli and shrimp. Add the parsley and finish cooking over medium heat, stirring often, for 2 minutes.

Arrange the pasta on a warmed platter and serve immediately.

*Serves 6*

1 lb (500 g) fresh fettuccine (page 322)

6 tablespoons (3 fl oz/90 ml) extra-virgin olive oil

3 cloves garlic, chopped

1 lb (500 g) broccoli

18 large shrimp (prawns), peeled and deveined

1/2 cup (4 fl oz/125 ml) dry white wine

Salt and freshly ground pepper

1 tablespoon chopped fresh flat-leaf (Italian) parsley

# Pasta with Clams, Garlic, and Parsley

Always use fresh clams, still in the shell, for the most traditional rendition of this favorite sauce for spaghetti or bucatini. Place one or more plates on the dining table for collecting the discarded shells.

Place the clams in a large, wide saucepan, discarding any that do not close to the touch. Cover and place over medium heat. Cook, shaking the pan occasionally, until the clams open and release their juices, about 2–3 minutes. Discard any clams that do not open. Remove from the heat. Using a slotted spoon, transfer the clams to a bowl. Strain the liquid in the pan through a fine-mesh sieve lined with cheese cloth (muslin). Set aside.

Bring a large pot three-fourths full of salted water to a boil. Add the pasta and cook until almost al dente, about 1 minute for fresh pasta or 7 minutes for dried. Meanwhile, warm the olive oil in a large frying pan over medium heat. Add the garlic and sauté, stirring often, until golden, about 3 minutes.

Drain the pasta and transfer to the frying pan with the garlic. Add the clams, the strained clam liquid, and the parsley and finish cooking over medium heat, stirring constantly, for 1–2 minutes; do not overcook or the clams will toughen.

Transfer to a warmed serving bowl and serve immediately.

*Serves 4*

1½ lb (750 g) small clams, well scrubbed

1 lb (500 g) fresh (page 322) or dried strand pasta (see note)

6 tablespoons (3 fl oz/90 ml) extra-virgin olive oil

3 cloves garlic, sliced

3 tablespoons minced fresh flat-leaf (Italian) parsley

# Pasta with Prosciutto, Porcini, and Red Wine

This sauce goes well with robust pasta shapes such as plain or spinach rigatoni. An even heartier version calls for adding 3 oz (90 g) chicken livers, coarsely chopped, and browning them with the mushrooms.

3 oz (90 g) prosciutto, thinly sliced

5 tablespoons (2¹/₂ oz/75 g) unsalted butter, at room temperature

2 tablespoons chopped white onion

3 oz (90 g) fresh porcini mushrooms, sliced

4 ripe plum (Roma) tomatoes, peeled (page 329) and chopped

6 fresh basil leaves, coarsely chopped

Salt and freshly ground pepper

²/₃ cup (5 fl oz/160 ml) dry red wine

1 lb (500 g) dried shaped pasta

³/₄ cup (3 oz/90 g) grated Parmesan cheese

Trim the fat from the prosciutto and reserve. Cut the lean portion into thin strips.

In a frying pan over low heat, combine the prosciutto fat, 1 tablespoon of the butter, and the onion. Sauté slowly, stirring occasionally, until the onion is golden, about 10 minutes. Add the lean prosciutto and porcini and continue to sauté, stirring often, for 2 minutes. Add the tomatoes, basil, and salt and pepper to taste and simmer uncovered, stirring occasionally, until the liquid evaporates and the sauce is slightly thickened and creamy, about 15 minutes longer.

Meanwhile, in a small saucepan over medium heat, simmer the wine until reduced by half. Add the wine to the tomato mixture. Simmer until the wine is almost evaporated, then remove from the heat, cover, and keep warm.

When the sauce is nearly ready, bring a large pot three-fourths full of salted water to a boil. Add the pasta and cook until al dente, 10–12 minutes. Drain and transfer to a warmed serving bowl. Immediately add the remaining 4 tablespoons (2 oz/60 g) butter and toss well. Top the pasta with the sauce and serve at once. Pass the Parmesan at the table.

*Serves 4*

# Conchiglie with Trout and Tomatoes

This topping for cold pasta is ideal with large shells, which not only look attractive but also stay al dente once they have cooled. If you'd like the pasta chilled, place in the refrigerator for up to 1 hour before serving.

Cut the tomatoes into small cubes. Place in a fine-mesh sieve, sprinkle with coarse salt, and let stand for 30 minutes to drain.

Meanwhile, bring a saucepan three-fourths full of salted water to a boil. Have a bowl of ice water ready. Add the green beans to the boiling water and boil until tender, about 5 minutes. Drain, immediately immerse in the ice water, and drain again. Set aside.

Bring a pot three-fourths full of salted water to a boil. Add the conchiglie and cook until al dente, about 10–12 minutes. Drain and transfer to a serving bowl. Add 2 tablespoons of the olive oil and toss well to mix. Let cool to room temperature, stirring occasionally.

Add the trout, tomatoes, green beans, capers, basil, and remaining 2 tablespoons olive oil to the cooled pasta. Toss well. Garnish with the egg slices and olives and serve.

*Serves 4*

3 ripe plum (Roma) tomatoes

Coarse salt

1/2 lb (250 g) green beans, trimmed and cut on the diagonal into 3/4-inch (2-cm) pieces

1 lb (500 g) large dried conchiglie

4 tablespoons (2 fl oz/60 ml) extra-virgin olive oil

1/2 lb (250 g) smoked trout fillet, skinned and broken into small pieces

2 tablespoons capers, rinsed and well-drained

8 fresh basil leaves, torn into small pieces

2 peeled hard-boiled eggs, thinly sliced crosswise

12 black olives, such as Niçoise

# Chicken Ravioli with Parmesan

In a frying pan, melt 2 tablespoons of the butter over low heat. Add the celery, carrot, and onion and sauté, stirring often, until the onion is translucent, about 3 minutes. Add the chicken, raise the heat to medium-low, and sauté, stirring often, until the chicken is golden, about 10 minutes. Add the Marsala, return the heat to low, cover, and cook until the liquid is absorbed, about 5 minutes.

Remove the pan from the heat, turn out the contents onto a cutting board, and chop very finely. Transfer to a bowl and add the egg yolks and half of the Parmesan. Mix thoroughly and season to taste with salt and pepper. Set aside.

Prepare the pasta dough according to the directions for Fresh Egg Pasta (page 322). Roll out the dough into a very thin sheet. Cut into strips 2 1/2 inches (6 cm) wide and 12 inches (30 cm) long. On half of the strips, place small mounds of the filling at 2 1/2-inch (6-cm) intervals. Moisten the edges of the strips and in between the mounds with cold water. Cover the filled strips with the remaining strips. To seal, press along the edges and all around the stuffing. Using a pastry wheel with a fluted edge, cut the strips into 2-inch (5-cm) squares. Using a spatula, set the ravioli aside on a lightly floured work surface.

Bring a large pot three-fourths full of salted water to a boil. In a saucepan, melt the remaining 6 tablespoons (3 oz/90 g) butter over low heat. Keep warm.

Add the ravioli to the boiling water and cook until they rise to the surface, about 2 minutes. Drain well and arrange on a platter or individual plates. Sprinkle with the remaining Parmesan and drizzle with the melted butter. Serve hot.

*Serves 6*

8 tablespoons (4 oz/125 g) unsalted butter

1 stalk celery, finely chopped

1 carrot, peeled and finely chopped

1 small yellow onion, finely chopped

10 oz (315 g) skinless, boneless chicken breast, cut into 1-inch (2.5-cm) pieces

1/4 cup (2 fl oz/60 ml) dry Marsala wine

2 egg yolks

3/4 cup (3 oz/90 g) grated Parmesan cheese

Salt and freshly ground pepper

12 oz (375 g) Fresh Egg Pasta dough (page 322)

# Manicotti with Chicken and Spinach

In a frying pan over medium heat, warm the olive oil. Add the chicken and onion and cook, breaking up the meat with a spatula, until the meat is opaque throughout, about 10 minutes. Transfer to a large bowl and let cool for 10 minutes.

Put the spinach in a fine-mesh sieve and press against it firmly with the back of a spoon to remove any excess liquid. Add to the chicken along with the cottage cheese, thyme, egg, Parmesan, 1/2 teaspoon salt, and 1/4 teaspoon pepper. Using a wooden spoon, beat vigorously to blend.

Preheat the oven to 325°F (165°C). Spread 1/2 cup (4 fl oz/125 ml) of the tomato sauce over the bottom of an 8-by-12-inch (20-by-30-cm) baking dish.

Bring a large pot three-fourths full of salted water to a boil. Add the manicotti tubes and cook until almost al dente, about 8 minutes. Drain them, rinse under cold running water, and drain again.

Using a small spoon, stuff each tube with about 1/3 cup (3 oz/90 g) of the filling. Arrange in a single layer in the baking dish and spoon the remaining sauce over the top. Cover with aluminum foil and bake until the sauce is bubbling a little around the edges of the dish and the filling is heated through, about 40 minutes.

Remove from the oven and uncover the dish. Let stand for 5 minutes before serving.

*Serves 4*

Olive oil

1/2 lb (250 g) ground (minced) white chicken or turkey meat

1/2 cup (2 1/2 oz/75 g) yellow onion, finely chopped

1 cup (7 oz/220 g) spinach cooked, drained, and chopped

1 1/2 cups (12 oz/375 g) nonfat small-curd cottage cheese

1 teaspoon dried thyme or basil

1 egg

1/4 cup (1 oz/30 g) grated Parmesan cheese

Salt and freshly ground pepper

2 1/2 cups (20 fl oz/625 ml) Simple Tomato Sauce (page 323)

8 dried manicotti tubes

# Chicken and Pistachios
# with Marsala and Lemon Zest

Thin strips of chicken breast take on great delicacy when combined with the other ingredients in this wonderful topping for ribbon pasta such as pappardelle or linguine. If you like, substitute walnuts and Cognac for the pistachios and Marsala.

In a frying pan over low heat, melt 3 tablespoons of the butter. Add the onion and 2 tablespoons water, cover, and cook gently, stirring occasionally, until the onion is tender and translucent, about 10 minutes. Add the chicken, raise the heat to high, and sauté, stirring often, until almost cooked through, 7–8 minutes.

Reduce the heat, add the Marsala, 2 tablespoons of the butter, the lemon zest, and pistachios. Stir well and simmer, stirring occasionally, for about 2 minutes. Remove from the heat, cover, and keep warm.

In a small frying pan over medium heat, melt the remaining 3 tablespoons butter. Add the bread crumbs and salt to taste, raise the heat to high, and toast, stirring often, until the crumbs turn golden, about 2 minutes.

Meanwhile, bring a large pot three-fourths full of salted water to a boil. Add the pasta and cook until al dente, about 2 minutes for fresh pasta or 8 minutes for dried. Drain and transfer to a warmed serving bowl. Immediately pour the sauce over the pasta and toss well. Sprinkle with the hot bread crumbs and serve at once.

*Serves 4*

8 tablespoons (4 oz/125 g) unsalted butter

3 tablespoons chopped white onion

6 oz (185 g) skinless, boneless chicken breast, cut into thin strips

2 tablespoons dry Marsala

2 tablespoons grated lemon zest

3/4 cup (3 oz/90 g) pistachios, coarsely chopped

5 oz (155 g) fairly stale coarse country bread, crusts discarded and bread crumbled

Salt

1 lb (500 g) fresh (page 322) or dried ribbon pasta (see note)

# Fettuccine with Fresh Peas and Ham

Springtime peas are best for this classic recipe of the Emilia–Romagna region, but you can also use frozen peas. Add them to the boiling water first and return to a boil before adding the pasta.

2 tablespoons unsalted butter

1 small yellow onion, finely chopped

3 oz (90 g) cooked ham, cut into julienne

1 cup (8 fl oz/250 ml) heavy (double) cream

Salt

2 cups (10 oz/315 g) shelled English peas

1 lb (500 g) fresh (page 322) fettuccine

Bring a large pot three-fourths full of salted water to a boil.

Meanwhile, in a frying pan, melt the butter over low heat. Add the onion and sauté, stirring often, until translucent, about 3 minutes. Add the ham and cream. Simmer, stirring often, for 5 minutes. Season to taste with salt. Remove from the heat, cover, and keep warm.

Prepare the fettucine according to the dirctions for Fresh Egg Pasta (page 322). Add the peas and fettuccine to the boiling water and cook until the pasta is al dente, about 2 minutes.

Drain the pasta and peas and transfer to a warmed platter. Pour the cream mixture over the top and toss well. Serve at once.

*Serves 6*

# Bucatini with Chicken, Eggplant, and Mushrooms

This rapid sauté of autumnal ingredients makes an ideal quick topping for bucatini. If you can't find slender Asian eggplants, substitute the smallest globe eggplants available.

In a frying pan over low heat, warm the olive oil. Add the garlic and sauté, stirring, until browned, about 3 minutes.

Add the eggplant, chicken, and mushrooms. Raise the heat to medium and cook, stirring often, until the vegetables are tender and the chicken is opaque throughout, about 10 minutes. Add the oregano and season to taste with salt and pepper. Remove from the heat, cover, and keep warm.

Meanwhile, bring a large pot three-fourths full of salted water to a boil. Add the pasta and cook until al dente; the timing will depend on the type of pasta used. Drain and transfer to a warmed serving bowl. Immediately pour the sauce over the pasta, toss well, and serve at once. Pass the Parmesan at the table.

*Serves 4*

6 tablespoons (3 fl oz/90 ml) extra-virgin olive oil

3 cloves garlic, sliced

2 small Asian eggplants (slender aubergines), about $1/2$ lb (250 g) total weight, cut into $1/4$-inch (6-mm) dice

$3/4$ lb (375 g) skinless, boneless chicken breast, cut into $3/4$-inch (2-cm) dice

6 oz (185 g) very small fresh button mushrooms

$1^1/2$ tablespoons dried oregano

Salt and freshly ground pepper

1 lb (500 g) dried bucatini

1 cup (4 oz/125 g) grated Parmesan cheese

# Pasta with Sausage and Swiss Chard

The flavor of the Swiss chard nicely counterbalances the richness of the sausage in this quick sauté for tossing with pappardelle or linguine. For a sweet-and-sour accent, add 2 tablespoons raisins soaked in warm water to cover until soft.

In a large frying pan over medium heat, warm 2 tablespoons of the olive oil. Add the garlic, reduce the heat to very low, and cook, stirring occasionally, until the garlic is lightly golden, about 5 minutes. Add the sausage and continue to cook, stirring occasionally, until cooked but not browned, 2 minutes. Remove from the heat, cover, and keep warm.

Bring a large pot three-fourths full of salted water to a boil. Add the Swiss chard. When the water returns to a boil, add the pasta and cook until almost al dente, about 7 minutes. Drain the pasta and Swiss chard and add to the frying pan with the sausage. Finish cooking over high heat, stirring constantly, for 1–2 minutes.

Transfer to a warmed serving bowl. Immediately add the cheese and the remaining 4 tablespoons (2 fl oz/60 ml) olive oil and toss well. Serve at once.

*Serves 4*

6 tablespoons (3 fl oz/90 ml) extra-virgin olive oil

2 cloves garlic, minced

6 oz (185 g) sweet Italian sausage, casings removed and meat crumbled

1 lb (500 g) bunch Swiss chard, stalks removed and leaves thinly sliced

1 lb (500 g) fresh (page 322) or dried ribbon pasta (see note)

1/2 cup (2 oz/60 g) grated pecorino romano cheese

# Spaghetti alla Puttanesca

A specialty of the Campania region, this pasta probably appears on every restaurant menu in Naples. *Puttana* is Italian slang for "harlot," and this pasta dish is said to be as spicy as a lady of the evening.

6 anchovy fillets

3 tablespoons extra-virgin olive oil

3 cloves garlic, minced

1–2 teaspoons red pepper flakes

2 cups (16 fl oz/500 ml) Simple Tomato Sauce (page 323)

2 tablespoons capers, well-drained, rinsed, and coarsely chopped

1/4 cup (1/3 oz/10 g) fresh basil, cut into julienne

20 Mediterranean-style black olives, preferably Gaeta, pitted and quartered or sliced

Salt and freshly ground black pepper

1 lb (500 g) dried spaghetti

In a food processor, process the anchovy fillets to a purée. (Alternatively, pound in a mortar with a pestle or crush in a small bowl using a fork.)

In a frying pan over low heat, warm the olive oil. Add the 1 tablespoon garlic and the anchovy purée and cook until the garlic is softened, about 3 minutes. Add 1 teaspoon of the red pepper flakes. Stir in the tomato sauce and simmer, uncovered, until slightly thickened, about 5 minutes. Add the capers, basil, and olives and simmer until slightly thickened, about 5 minutes longer. Season to taste with salt and black pepper and more red pepper flakes, if desired.

Meanwhile, bring a large pot three-fourths full of salted water to a boil. Add the spaghetti and cook until al dente, about 8 minutes.

Drain the pasta and transfer to a warmed serving bowl. Add the sauce, toss well, and serve at once.

*Serves 4–6*

# Macaroni with Salami, Mozzarella, and Tomatoes

In this cold, uncooked topping for elbow macaroni, the powerful flavor of Italian salami is tamed by bell peppers (capsicums), celery, and perfectly ripe cherry tomatoes. Serve on a bed of tender young lettuces for an attractive presentation.

1 lb (500 g) dried elbow macaroni

6 tablespoons (3 fl oz/90 ml) extra-virgin olive oil

8 small cherry tomatoes, cut in half

4 oz (125 g) salami, cut into small cubes

2 celery stalks, thinly sliced

1 yellow, red, or green bell pepper (capsicum), seeded, deribbed, and cut into long, thin strips

4 oz (125 g) mozzarella cheese, diced

Salt and freshly ground white pepper

2 tablespoons minced fresh oregano

Bring a large pot three-fourths full of salted water to a boil. Add the macaroni and cook until al dente, 10–12 minutes. Drain and transfer to a bowl. Add 2 tablespoons of the oil and toss well. Let the pasta cool to room temperature, stirring occasionally.

Add the remaining 4 tablespoons (2 fl oz/60 ml) olive oil, the cherry tomatoes, salami, celery, bell pepper, mozzarella, and salt and white pepper to taste. Toss well, sprinkle with the oregano, and toss again. Transfer to a serving bowl and serve at once. Or, if you like, cover and refrigerate until well chilled before serving.

*Serves 4*

# Pasta with Ham, Spinach, and Cream

The simple union of fresh spinach, ham, and a splash of cream makes an excellent topping for regular or green taglierini or tagliatelle. Steaming rather than boiling the spinach gives it more flavor and a better texture.

1 lb (500 g) spinach, tough stems removed, leaves well rinsed and torn into pieces

1/4 cup (2 oz/60 g) unsalted butter

3 oz (90 g) cooked ham, cut into thin strips

6 tablespoons (3 fl oz/90 ml) heavy (double) cream

Generous pinch of ground nutmeg

Salt

1 lb (500 g) fresh (page 322) or dried ribbon pasta (see note)

3/4 cup (3 oz/90 g) grated Parmesan cheese

Bring a saucepan three-fourths full of water to a boil. Add the spinach and boil for 2 minutes. Alternatively, place the spinach in a steamer rack over gently boiling water, cover, and steam until tender, 3–4 minutes. Drain well, squeeze the spinach dry, and then chop.

In a large frying pan over medium heat, melt the butter. Add the spinach and sauté until all moisture evaporates, about 3–4 minutes. Add the ham, cream, and nutmeg and cook until heated throughout, stirring constantly, about 2 minutes. Season to taste with salt.

Meanwhile, bring a large pot three-fourths full of salted water to a boil. Add the pasta and cook until al dente, about 2 minutes for fresh pasta or 8 minutes for dried. Drain and transfer to a warmed serving bowl. Immediately pour the sauce over the pasta and toss very gently. Sprinkle with 1/4 cup (1 oz/30 g) of the Parmesan and serve at once. Pass the remaining Parmesan at the table.

*Serves 4*

# Fusilli with Onion and Bacon

For this recipe from northeastern Italy, you can substitute dried or fresh chanterelles for the porcini. Or you can omit the mushrooms and add 1 tablespoon fennel seeds with the wine.

⅓ oz (10 g) dried porcini mushrooms or 6 oz (185 g) fresh button mushrooms, stems removed, caps brushed clean, and sliced

6 tablespoons (3 fl oz/90 ml) extra-virgin olive oil

2 yellow onions, thinly sliced

½ cup (4 fl oz/125 ml) dry white wine

Salt and freshly ground pepper

3 oz (90 g) smoked bacon or smoked pancetta, cut into julienne

1¼ lb (625 g) dried fusilli

½ cup (2 oz/60 g) grated Parmesan cheese

If using porcini, place in a bowl of lukewarm water to cover and soak until softened, about 30 minutes. Drain, squeeze out excess water, chop finely, and set aside.

In a large frying pan, warm 4 tablespoons (2 fl oz/60 ml) of the olive oil over medium heat. Add the onions and sauté, stirring occasionally, until golden, about 5 minutes. (If using fresh mushrooms, sauté them with the onions.) Add the wine, porcini, and salt and pepper to taste. Reduce the heat, cover, and simmer gently, 40 minutes.

Meanwhile, in a small frying pan, heat the remaining 2 tablespoons oil over medium heat. Add the bacon and sauté, stirring occasionally, until golden, about 5 minutes. Set aside.

Bring a large pot three-fourths full of salted water to a boil. Add the fusilli and cook until almost al dente, about 7 minutes. Drain and transfer to the pan with the onions. Add the contents of the bacon pan and finish cooking over medium heat, stirring often, for 1–2 minutes.

Arrange the pasta on a warmed platter and sprinkle with the Parmesan. Serve hot.

*Serves 6*

# Spaghetti with Pancetta and Provolone

A classic *all'amatriciana* sauce for spaghetti is altered here by substituting rich provolone for the traditional pecorino romano cheese. For a lighter version, omit the cheese, and add more cayenne for extra flavor.

In a frying pan over medium heat, warm the olive oil. Add the pancetta and cook until crisp, 5 minutes. Using a slotted spoon, transfer to a bowl and set aside.

Add the onion to the same pan and sauté, stirring occasionally, until softened, 3–5 minutes. Add the tomatoes and salt and cayenne pepper to taste. Cook uncovered, stirring occasionally, until the liquid evaporates and the sauce is slightly thickened and creamy, about 10 minutes.

Meanwhile, bring a large pot three-fourths full of salted water to a boil. Add the spaghetti and cook until al dente, about 8 minutes. Drain and transfer to a warmed serving bowl. Immediately pour the hot sauce over the pasta, add the cheese and pancetta, and toss well. Serve at once.

*Serves 4*

2 tablespoons extra-virgin olive oil

6 oz (185 g) pancetta or bacon, cut into thin strips

3 tablespoons finely chopped white onion

5 very ripe plum (Roma) tomatoes, peeled (page 329) and coarsely chopped

Salt

Cayenne pepper

1 lb (500 g) dried spaghetti

3/4 cup (3 oz/90 g) shredded provolone cheese

# Pasta with Tomatoes and Bacon

This popular combination of bacon and tomatoes can be spiced with as much (or as little) cayenne papper as you like. Eat it hot when the weather is cold, or at room temperature when the sun is hot. Feel free to use any pasta shape that you want.

In a frying pan over medium heat, warm the olive oil. Add the bacon and cook until crisp, about 5 minutes. Add the tomatoes, cayenne, and salt to taste. Raise the heat to high and sauté, stirring occasionally, until the sauce thickens, about 10 minutes.

Meanwhile, bring a large pot three-fourths full of salted water to a boil. Add the pasta and cook until al dente; the timing will depend on the type of pasta used. Drain and transfer to a warmed serving bowl. Immediately pour the sauce over the pasta and toss well. Serve at once.

*Serves 4*

2 tablespoons extra-virgin olive oil

4 strips bacon, cut into $1/2$-inch (12-mm) pieces

10 oz (315 g) fresh plum (Roma) tomatoes, peeled (page 329), seeded, and chopped, or canned plum tomatoes, seeded, drained and chopped

2 pinches of cayenne pepper

Salt

1 lb (500 g) fresh (page 322) or dried shaped pasta

# Pasta with Bolognese Meat Sauce

The product of slow, patient simmering for at least an hour, this well-known meat sauce from Bologna has a rich, full flavor that complements any fresh or dried pasta.

2 oz (60 g) dried porcini mushrooms

3 tablespoons unsalted butter

2 tablespoons extra-virgin olive oil

1 small carrot, peeled and finely chopped

1 celery stalk, finely chopped

1 small white onion, finely chopped

1/2 lb (250 g) ground (minced) beef

1 tablespoon fresh flat-leaf (Italian) parsley

1/4 cup (2 fl oz/60 ml) dry white wine

3 ripe plum (Roma) tomatoes, peeled (page 329), seeded, and chopped

Pinch of ground nutmeg

Salt and freshly ground pepper

1 lb (500 g) fresh (page 322) or dried pasta (see note)

3/4 cup (3 oz/90 g) grated Parmesan cheese

Place the porcini in a bowl of lukewarm water to cover and soak until softened, about 30 minutes. Drain, squeeze out the excess water, slice, and set aside.

In a large frying pan over medium heat, melt the butter with the oil. Add the carrot, celery, and onion and cook, stirring, until very tender, 20 minutes or longer.

Add the beef and parsley and raise the heat to high. Cook, stirring occasionally, for 3–4 minutes. Add the porcini and wine and cook, stirring often, until the wine evaporates, about 2 minutes. Add the tomatoes and reduce the heat to low. Stir in the nutmeg and salt and pepper to taste. Pour in 1 cup water, stir well, cover, and simmer until the the sauce reduces considerably and is very thick, at least 1 hour.

When the sauce is nearly ready, bring a large pot three-fourths full of salted water to a boil. Add the pasta and cook until al dente; the timing will depend on the type of pasta used. Drain and transfer to a warmed serving bowl. Immediately pour the sauce over the pasta, toss well, and serve at once. Pass the Parmesan at the table.

*Serves 4*

# Farfalle with Ricotta, Ham, and Corn

During summer's heat, try serving this satisfying dish lukewarm. Farfalle is the ideal pasta for this creamy sauce; other shapes of similar size will work well, too.

Bring a large saucepan three-fourths full of water to a boil. Add the corn. As soon as the water returns to a boil, remove from the heat, cover, and let stand for about 5 minutes. Remove the corn from the water and set aside until cool enough to handle. Then, using a sharp knife, cut off the kernels. Set aside.

Bring a large pot three-fourths full of salted water to a boil. Add the pasta and cook until al dente, 10–12 minutes.

Meanwhile, place the ricotta in a bowl, add a few tablespoons of hot pasta cooking water, and stir until the cheese is smooth and creamy.

Drain the pasta and transfer to a warmed serving bowl. Immediately add the butter, ham, ricotta, and salt and white pepper to taste. Toss well, scatter the corn on top, and serve immediately. Pass the Parmesan at the table.

*Serves 4*

2 ears white or yellow corn, husks and silk removed, or 1 cup thawed frozen or drained canned corn

1 lb (500 g) dried farfalle

3/4 cup (6 oz/185 g) ricotta cheese

1/4 cup (2 oz/60 g) unsalted butter, at room temperature

3 oz (90 g) cooked ham, cut into thin strips

Salt and freshly ground white pepper

3/4 cup (3 oz/90 g) grated Parmesan cheese

# Baked Pappardelle with Ham and Cheese

If you wish to make this Bolognese dish in advance, substitute a dried pasta shape such as rigatoni or penne, as reheating would overcook the fresh pappardelle.

1 lb (500 g) fresh pappardelle (page 322)

1¼ cups (10 fl oz/310 ml) milk

8 tablespoons (4 oz/125 g) unsalted butter, plus extra for greasing

3 tablespoons all-purpose (plain) flour

8 oz (250 g) cooked ham, cut into julienne

¾ cup (3 oz/90 g) grated Parmesan cheese

Pinch of ground nutmeg

Salt and freshly ground pepper

Prepare the pappardelle according to the directions for Fresh Egg Pasta (page 322). Bring a large pot three-fourths full of salted water to a boil. Preheat a broiler (grill).

Pour the milk into a saucepan over medium-low heat. When the milk is a little more than warm, turn off the heat.

In another saucepan over low heat, combine 2 tablespoons of the butter and the flour, vigorously stirring them together with a wooden spoon until the butter melts and the flour is incorporated. Once the butter is fully melted, cook and stir for 2 minutes longer. Then gradually add the warm milk, a little at a time, stirring constantly. Add more milk only after the previously added milk is fully incorporated. When all of the milk has been added, cook, stirring often, until nicely thickened, 3–4 minutes longer. Add the ham, half of the Parmesan, the nutmeg, and salt and pepper to taste. Continue stirring until the butter melts.

Add the pappardelle to the boiling water and cook until the pasta rises to the surface, about 2 minutes.

Grease an 8-by-12-inch (20-by-30-cm) flameproof baking dish. Drain the pasta and transfer to the prepared dish. Pour the warm sauce over the top and toss well. Sprinkle evenly with the remaining Parmesan. Broil (grill) until the top is golden, about 3 minutes. Serve at once.

*Serves 6*

# Baked Penne with Ham and Peas

Dotted with cubes of ham and fresh green peas, a flour-and-butter-thickened sauce binds this baked pasta dish. Penne or rigatoni are ideal pasta shapes to use.

Pour the milk into a saucepan over medium-low heat. When the milk is little more than warm, turn off the heat.

In another saucepan over low heat, combine the butter and the flour, vigorously stirring them together with a wooden spoon until the butter melts and the flour is incorporated. Once the butter is fully melted, cook and stir for 2 minutes longer. Then gradually add the warm milk, a little at a time, stirring constantly. Add more milk only after the previously added milk is fully incorporated. When all the milk has been added, cook, stirring often, until thickened, 3–4 minutes longer. Add the tarragon, ham, and salt to taste and stir for a few seconds. Remove from the heat, cover, and keep warm.

Preheat the broiler (grill). Grease a 6-by-12-inch (15-by-30-cm) flameproof baking dish with butter.

Bring a large pot three-fourths full of salted water to a boil and add the peas. When the water returns to the boil, add the pasta. Cook until al dente, 10–12 minutes. Drain the pasta and peas and transfer to the prepared dish. Pour the warm sauce over the top and sprinkle with the Parmesan.

Broil (grill) until the top is golden, about 3 minutes. Serve immediately.

*Serves 4*

2 cups (16 fl oz/500 ml) milk

2½ tablespoons unsalted butter, plus extra for greasing

3½ tablespoons all-purpose (plain) flour

1 tablespoon chopped fresh tarragon

¼ lb (120 g) cooked ham, cut into ⅓-inch (9-mm) dice

Salt

1¼ cups (6½ oz/200 g) shelled English peas

1 lb (500 g) dried penne

½ cup (2 oz/60 g) grated Parmesan cheese

# Main Courses

# Italian Fish Stew

Called *zuppa di pesce*, this is a typical Italian tomato-and-wine-based fish stew. The stew can be prepared several hours ahead of serving, up to the point where the fish is added; at mealtime, reheat the base and add the fish.

Cut the fish into 2-inch (5-cm) chunks. Place in a shallow glass dish and sprinkle with salt and pepper to taste. Cover and refrigerate while making the broth.

In a large, heavy saucepan over medium heat, warm the olive oil. Add the onions and bell peppers and cook, stirring often, until tender, about 10 minutes.

Add the garlic, red pepper flakes (if using), fennel seeds, oregano, and bay leaf and cook for 2 minutes. Add the tomatoes and simmer for 3 minutes. Add the wine and stock and simmer, uncovered, about 10 minutes longer.

Season to taste with salt and pepper. Add the fish and simmer, uncovered, until opaque throughout when pierced with the tip of a knife, 5–8 minutes. If desired, stir in the parsley and basil. Serve at once.

*Serves 4–6*

2–3 lb (1–1.5 kg) firm white fish fillets such as rockfish, sea bass, monkfish, or halibut

Salt and freshly ground pepper

1/4 cup (2 fl oz/60 ml) extra-virgin olive oil

3 yellow onions, chopped

2 green bell peppers (capsicums), seeded, deribbed, and chopped

3–6 cloves garlic, minced

1/2–2 teaspoons red pepper flakes (optional)

2 *each* teaspoons fennel seeds and dried oregano

1 bay leaf

4 or 5 large, ripe plum (Roma) tomatoes, peeled (page 329), seeded, and coarsely chopped

2 cups (16 fl oz/500 ml) dry white or red wine

2 cups (16 fl oz/500 ml) fish stock (page 321) or bottled clam juice

4 tablespoons (1/3 oz/10 g) chopped fresh flat-leaf (Italian) parsley

4 tablespoons (1/3 oz/10 g) chopped fresh basil (optional)

# Swordfish with Lemon, Garlic, and Olive Oil

In Sicily, swordfish is greatly prized. While it is prepared in innumerable ways, grilling it on skewers is among the most popular. Serve with rice pilaf or roasted potatoes, and broccoli, cauliflower, zucchini (courgettes), or eggplant (aubergine).

In a bowl, combine the lemon juice and olive oil. Place the swordfish cubes in a shallow glass dish and sprinkle with salt and pepper to taste. Pour about $^{1}/_{3}$ cup (3 fl oz/80 ml) of the olive oil and lemon mixture over the fish and toss to coat evenly. Cover and refrigerate for 2–4 hours. Add the garlic and the oregano, if using, to the remaining olive oil and lemon mixture. Set aside to use as a sauce.

Preheat the broiler (grill) or prepare a fire in a charcoal grill.

Cut the onion through the stem end into quarters and separate each quarter into individual "leaves" or thin pieces. Alternate the swordfish cubes with the onion pieces and 18 lemon slices and/or bay leaves on the skewers. Arrange the skewers on a broiler pan or the grill rack. Broil or grill, turning once, until the fish is opaque throughout when pierced with the tip of a knife, about 3 minutes on each side. Serve hot, garnished with lemon slices and accompanied by the reserved sauce.

*Serves 6*

$^{1}/_{3}$ cup (3 fl oz/80 ml) fresh lemon juice

$^{2}/_{3}$ cup (5 fl oz/160 ml) extra-virgin olive oil

$2^{1}/_{4}$ lb (1.1 kg) swordfish fillets, cut into $1^{1}/_{2}$-inch (4-cm) cubes

Salt and freshly ground pepper

1 tablespoon minced garlic

2 teaspoons dried oregano (optional)

1 red onion

18 lemon slices and/or 18 bay leaves, plus lemon slices for garnish

6 wooden skewers, soaked for 30 minutes, or metal skewers

# Trout with Prosciutto and Sage

This northern Italian recipe couldn't be simpler, and it looks pretty, too. Ask your fishmonger to prepare the trout for cooking. Serve with fried potatoes and spinach, asparagus, or green beans.

4 trout or Coho salmon, cleaned and boned with heads intact, about 10 oz (315 g) each

Salt and freshly ground pepper

12 fresh sage leaves

4 large, thin slices prosciutto

Olive oil for brushing

5 tablespoons (2½ oz/75 g) unsalted butter

Grated zest of 1 lemon

2 tablespoons fresh lemon juice

1 teaspoon freshly ground pepper

Preheat the broiler (grill) or prepare a fire in a charcoal grill.

Using a sharp knife, cut a few shallow diagonal slashes in the fleshiest part of each side of each fish. Sprinkle with a little salt and pepper to taste. Place 3 sage leaves in the cavity of each fish and then wrap each fish in a slice of prosciutto.

Brush each fish on both sides with olive oil. Arrange on a broiler pan or the grill rack. Broil or grill, turning once, until the prosciutto is browned and the fish is opaque throughout when pierced with the tip of a knife, 4–5 minutes on each side.

Meanwhile, in a small saucepan, melt the butter and stir in the lemon zest and juice and 1 teaspoon pepper.

Transfer the fish to warmed individual plates and spoon a little of the butter sauce over each fish. Serve immediately.

*Serves 4*

# Mediterranean Fish Stew

In Italy, seafood stews like this one are traditionally ladled into shallow bowls atop thick slices of toasted bread that have been rubbed with fresh garlic and drizzled with oil.

Cut the fish steaks into 1-inch (2.5-cm) cubes. Spread the flour on a plate, dredge the fish pieces in the flour, and shake off any excess.

In a large heavy pot over medium-high heat, melt the butter with 2 tablespoons of the oil. Add the fish and sauté, stirring occasionally, until lightly browned on all sides, about 5 minutes.

Transfer the fish and any pan juices to a large bowl. Add 2–3 tablespoons of the fish stock to the pot and, using a wooden spoon, deglaze the pot over medium-high heat by stirring to scrape up any browned bits from the pot bottom. Pour the liquid over the fish.

Reduce the heat to medium and add the remaining 1 tablespoon oil to the pot. Add the onions and bell pepper and sauté, stirring often, until the onions are translucent, 3–4 minutes. Return the fish and juices to the pot and add the tomatoes, bouquet garni, basil, 1/4 teaspoon pepper, and the remaining stock. Reduce heat to very low, cover, and simmer until the fish flakes when pierced with the tip of a knife and is opaque throughout, about 15 minutes. The stew will form more liquid as it cooks.

Remove from the heat and add the olives, stirring them in gently. Let stand, covered, for 5 minutes. Discard the bouquet garni. Spoon into warmed bowls and serve.

*Serves 4*

1 1/2 lb (750 g) tuna or sword-fish steaks, each 3/4–1 inch (2–2.5 cm) thick

1/2 cup (2 1/2 oz/75 g) all-purpose (plain) flour

2 tablespoons unsalted butter

3 tablespoons olive oil

1 cup (8 fl oz/250 ml) Fish Stock (page 321)

2 large sweet onions, halved lengthwise and then cut crosswise into slices 1/2 inch (12 mm) thick

1 green bell pepper (capsicum), seeded, deribbed, and cut into strips about 1/2 inch (12 mm) wide

2 large tomatoes, cut into wedges 3/4 inch (2 cm) thick

Bouquet garni (page 320)

1/2 teaspoon dried basil

Freshly ground pepper

1/2 cup (2 1/2 oz/75 g) pitted small green or black olives

# Roast Fish with Mediterranean Herbed Tomato Sauce

You can vary the taste of this dish by changing the herbs. For example, omit the thyme and use only parsley and basil, or omit the basil and add 1 tablespoon dried oregano or 2 tablespoons chopped fresh oregano or marjoram.

Preheat the oven to 450°F (230°C). Grease a baking dish large enough to fit the fish fillets in a single layer.

In a saucepan over medium heat, warm the olive oil. Add the onion and sauté, stirring often, until tender and translucent, about 10 minutes. Add the garlic and sauté for 1–2 minutes. Stir in the tomatoes and cook over low heat until the sauce thickens, 15–20 minutes. Season to taste with salt and pepper. Taste the sauce; if the tomatoes are too sour, add the sugar. Stir in half of the parsley, half of the basil, and half of the thyme and simmer for 2 minutes to allow the flavors to blend.

Place the fillets in the prepared baking dish. Spoon the tomato sauce evenly over the top. Bake until the fish is opaque when pierced with the tip of a knife, 8–10 minutes. Sprinkle with the remaining herbs and serve at once.

*Serves 4*

2–3 tablespoons olive oil, plus extra for greasing

1 yellow onion, finely chopped

2 cloves garlic, minced

8 plum (Roma) tomatoes, peeled (page 329), seeded, and chopped

Salt and freshly ground pepper

Pinch of sugar, if needed

6 tablespoons (1/2 oz/15 g) chopped fresh flat-leaf (Italian) parsley

1/4 cup (1/3 oz/10 g) chopped fresh basil

2 tablespoons chopped fresh thyme

4 flaky white fish fillets such as cod, snapper, flounder, or sea bass, 5–6 oz (155–185 g) each

# Sautéed Fish with Garlic, Rosemary, and Red Pepper Flakes

This fish dish from Italy's Abruzzi region is fast and easy. Traditionally prepared with monkfish, it is equally good with another firm, meaty fish such as tuna or swordfish. Serve with orecchiette or another favorite pasta, or with broccoli or sautéed greens such as Swiss chard.

1½ lb (750 g) monkfish fillets, cut on the diagonal into slices 1 inch (2.5 cm) thick, or swordfish or tuna fillets, about 1 inch (2.5 cm) thick

Salt and freshly ground pepper

¼ cup (2 fl oz/60 ml) extra-virgin olive oil

1 tablespoon red pepper flakes

2 tablespoons chopped fresh rosemary

1 tablespoon minced garlic

1 cup (8 fl oz/250 ml) dry white wine

Sprinkle the monkfish fillets with salt and pepper to taste. In a large frying pan over medium-high heat, warm the olive oil. Working in batches, add the fish and sauté on both sides, turning once, until golden brown and almost cooked through, about 3 minutes on each side. (If using tuna fillets, they may be cooked less, to your taste.) Transfer the fish to a warmed platter.

Reduce the heat to medium and add the red pepper flakes, rosemary, garlic, and wine to the pan. Simmer, uncovered, stirring occasionally, until the wine is reduced by half and becomes somewhat syrupy, about 5 minutes.

Return the fish to the pan for 1–2 minutes and stir to coat evenly with the sauce, then serve at once.

*Serves 4*

# Salmon Risotto

Risotto is extremely popular in Italy's Veneto region. For this salmon version, you can add texture with the addition of 1 cup (5 oz/155 g) diced fennel with the last ladleful of stock and ½ cup (2½ oz/75 g) toasted pine nuts with the chives.

5 cups (40 fl oz/1.25 l) Chicken Stock (page 320), or half chicken stock and half fish stock

¼ cup (2 fl oz/60 ml) olive oil

1 lb (500 g) salmon fillets, cut into pieces 1 inch (2.5 cm) wide by 2 inches (5 cm) long

Salt and freshly ground pepper

4 tablespoons (2 oz/60 g) unsalted butter

1 yellow onion, chopped

1½ cups (10½ oz/330 g) Arborio rice

1 cup (5 oz/155 g) shelled English peas

6 cups (6 oz/185 g) spinach leaves, or a combination of spinach and watercress leaves, cut into thin strips

2 teaspoons grated lemon zest

2 tablespoons minced fresh chives

Pour the stock into a saucepan and bring to a boil. Reduce the heat to achieve a gentle simmer and maintain over low heat.

In a large frying pan over medium-high heat, warm the olive oil. Sprinkle the salmon strips with salt and pepper to taste and add to the pan. Sauté quickly, turning once, until lightly browned, about 3 minutes. The fish will not be fully cooked. Set aside.

In a large, heavy saucepan over medium heat, melt the butter. Add the onion and sauté, stirring occasionally, until translucent, about 10 minutes. Reduce the heat to low, add the rice, and stir to coat with the butter. Cook, stirring occasionally, until the rice is translucent, 3–5 minutes.

Add ½ cup (4 fl oz/125 ml) of the hot stock. Cook, stirring often, until most of the stock is absorbed, about 5 minutes. Continue adding stock, ½ cup (4 fl oz/125 ml) at a time and allowing it to be fully absorbed before adding more, until the grains are tender but slightly al dente, about 20 minutes. Stir often to prevent sticking.

Meanwhile, bring a saucepan three-fourths full of water to a boil. Add the peas and cook until tender-crisp, 1–4 minutes depending on their age and size. Drain well.

During the last addition of stock to the rice, add the spinach and lemon zest and cook, stirring constantly, until the spinach wilts. Add the salmon, peas, and chives and stir until heated through. Season with salt and pepper to taste and serve at once.

*Serves 4*

# Chicken with Wine and Grapes

In late summer, when grapes mature and hang from the vines in plump bunches of green, amber, deep red, and black, cooks in the Chianti region of northern Italy bake chicken with grapes and wine. Look for fresh sage to add as a garnish.

1 chicken, about 3½ lb (1.75 kg), quartered

1 lemon, cut in half

2 teaspoons dried sage

3 tablespoons olive oil

4 shallots, cut in half lengthwise

½ cup (4 fl oz/125 ml) Chicken Stock (page 320)

½ cup (4 fl oz/125 ml) dry white wine

3 small bunches grapes (a mixture of green and red)

Salt and freshly ground pepper

2 tablespoons Cognac or other brandy

Preheat the oven to 375°F (190°C).

Trim any excess fat from the chicken. Rub with the cut side of a lemon half and sprinkle the sage on both sides of the chicken pieces.

Place the chicken in a shallow baking dish, skin side down, and drizzle with the olive oil. Place 2 shallot halves in the hollow of each chicken quarter.

Bake for 20 minutes. In a small saucepan over medium-low heat, gently heat the stock and wine. Stir ½ cup (4 fl oz/125 ml) of the mixture into the bottom of the baking dish. Baste the chicken with the pan juices. Turn the pieces skin side up and arrange the grapes around the chicken. Bake for 30 minutes longer, basting a few times with the remaining stock mixture. Season to taste with salt and pepper.

Pour the brandy into a small saucepan and warm gently over medium-low heat. Using a long-handled match, ignite the brandy. When the flame dies, pour the brandy evenly over the chicken and grapes. Baste the chicken and grapes with the pan juices. Bake until the chicken is golden brown, 15–20 minutes.

Transfer the chicken to a warmed platter with the grapes arranged around the sides. Strain the pan juices and serve in a bowl alongside.

*Serves 4*

# Chicken Breasts, Italian Style

Chicken breasts cooked in this manner are a light main course. Green peas alongside make a winning final touch. For added flavor, serve with a slice of lemon to squeeze over the chicken.

4 boneless, skinless chicken breast halves, about 1¹/₂ lb (750 g) total weight

2 eggs

1 teaspoon salt

2 tablespoons all-purpose (plain) flour

¹/₂ cup (2 oz/60 g) dried bread crumbs

¹/₂ cup (4 fl oz/125 ml) vegetable oil

Salt and freshly ground pepper

2 lemons, cut in half

2 tablespoons capers, rinsed and well-drained (optional)

Trim off any excess fat from the chicken breasts. Place the breasts between 2 sheets of plastic wrap and pound gently with a meat pounder until they are an even ¹/₂ inch (12 mm) thick. Trim the breast pieces into uniform ovals.

In a bowl, beat the eggs with the 1 teaspoon salt and 2 tablespoons water. Dip the chicken breasts, one at a time, into the egg mixture. Dust each breast lightly with flour and then roll in the bread crumbs to coat.

Warm the oil in a deep, heavy frying pan over medium heat. Place the breasts in the oil and cook, turning once, until golden on both sides, 3–4 minutes on each side. Transfer to paper towels to drain. Season to taste with salt and pepper.

Serve on individual plates, garnished with a lemon half and capers, if desired.

*Serves 4*

# Chicken Marsala

This stew combines tender pieces of herb-crusted chicken and a rich wine-mushroom sauce. You can serve it over an herbed rice pilaf or steamed white rice studded with toasted blanched almonds.

In a large lock-top plastic bag, combine the flour, basil, and 1 teaspoon salt. Fold the top over tightly and shake to mix. In batches of 3 or 4 at a time, add the chicken pieces to the bag and shake until well coated.

Preheat the oven to 350°F (180°C). Brush a 9-by-13-inch (23-by-33-cm) rectangular or oval baking dish with olive oil.

In a large, heavy frying pan over medium-high heat, warm the olive oil. Add the garlic and the chicken pieces and sauté until the chicken is golden, about 8 minutes. Scrape the bottom of the pan often to dislodge any browned bits. Remove from the heat and transfer the chicken and garlic to the prepared baking dish.

Return the frying pan to medium-high heat and add the butter. When it melts, add the mushrooms and sauté, stirring gently, for 2–3 minutes. Pour in the Marsala or sherry and, using a wooden spoon, deglaze the pan by stirring to scrape up any browned bits from the pan bottom. Pour the liquid and mushrooms over the chicken.

Cover the baking dish with aluminum foil and bake until the chicken is opaque throughout, about 20 minutes.

Spoon into warmed individual bowls and serve.

*Serves 4*

1 cup (5 oz/155 g) all-purpose (plain) flour

1 teaspoon dried basil

Salt

4 boneless, skinless chicken breast halves, about 1½ lb (750 g) total weight, cut crosswise into thirds

¼ cup (2 fl oz/60 ml) extra-virgin olive oil, plus extra for brushing

2 cloves garlic, chopped

2 tablespoons unsalted butter

10 oz (315 g) small white mushroom caps (about 3 cups)

½ cup (4 fl oz/125 ml) sweet Marsala or sweet sherry

# Cornish Hens Stuffed with Ricotta Cheese and Pesto

For this recipe, use moist, "fresh" ricotta. If you can find only dense prepackaged ricotta, pass it through a sieve or whip it with a little milk in a food processor. Accompany the hens, if desired, with baked tomatoes stuffed with garlic, parsley, and bread crumbs (page 324).

3 cups (1¹/₂ lb/750 g) ricotta cheese (see note)

¹/₂ cup (4 fl oz/125 ml) pesto (page 71) made with cheese and walnuts

2 tablespoons chopped fresh flat-leaf (Italian) parsley

Salt and freshly ground pepper

6 Cornish hens, about 1¹/₄ lb (625 g) each, or poussins, about 1 lb (500 g) each

¹/₂ cup (4 oz/125 g) unsalted butter, melted, or ¹/₂ cup (4 fl oz/125 ml) olive oil, or equal amounts butter and olive oil (optional)

3 cloves garlic, chopped (optional)

Preheat the oven to 400° F (200°C).

In a large bowl, combine the ricotta, pesto, parsley, and salt and pepper to taste. Stir to mix well. Using your fingers and starting at the cavity opening, loosen the skin from the meat of each bird. Be careful not to puncture the skin. Spoon the ricotta mixture into a pastry bag fitted with the wide tip and pipe the stuffing under the breast skin and the thigh skin. (Alternatively, use a lock-top plastic bag with one of the corners cut away.)

Place the birds breast side up on a rack in a large, shallow baking pan. Sprinkle with salt and pepper to taste. If you wish to baste the birds, stir together the butter and/or olive oil, garlic, and salt and pepper to taste in a bowl. Roast, basting every 10 minutes with the butter and/or oil mixture, until an instant-read thermometer inserted into the thickest part of a thigh away from the bone registers 170°F (77°C), 50–60 minutes for game hens and 45 minutes for poussins. (Alternatively, pierce a thigh joint with the tip of a knife; the juices should run clear.)

Transfer the birds to a cutting board. Cut each bird in half along the backbone with a sharp knife or poultry shears. Place 2 halves on each of 6 warmed individual plates and serve at once.

*Serves 6*

# Chicken and Vegetables with Pesto

This Italian-inspired, brightly colored stir-fry tastes wonderful spooned over pasta or rice. It is easy to prepare and can be served as a first or main course. Use your own favorite recipe for pesto, or purchase a high-quality product at a specialty food store.

In a wok or deep frying pan over high heat, warm 2 tablespoons of the oil, swirling to coat the bottom and sides of the pan. When the oil is very hot but not quite smoking, add the chicken pieces and stir and toss every 15–20 seconds until lightly browned and opaque throughout, 4–6 minutes. Be sure to distribute the chicken evenly in the pan so it comes into maximum contact with the heat and cooks evenly. Transfer to a dish and set aside.

Add the remaining 1 tablespoon oil to the same pan over medium-high heat, again swirling to coat the pan. When the oil is hot, add the onion and stir and toss every 15–20 seconds until it begins to soften, about 2 minutes. Add the bell pepper, zucchini, and mushrooms and stir and toss every 15–20 seconds until the onion is tender, 3–4 minutes longer. Return the chicken to the pan, add the stock, and stir and toss just until the chicken and stock are heated through, 2–3 minutes.

Remove from the heat, add the pesto, $^1/_2$ teaspoon salt, and $^1/_4$ teaspoon pepper and toss until the chicken and vegetables are nicely coated with the sauce. Taste and adjust the seasoning. Serve immediately.

*Serves 4*

3 tablespoons peanut oil or vegetable oil

1 lb (500 g) boneless, skinless chicken breasts, cut into 1 $^1/_2$-inch (4-cm) chunks

1 yellow onion, thinly sliced

1 red bell pepper (capsicum), seeded, deribbed, and thinly sliced

2 small zucchini (courgettes), cut into pieces 2 inches (5 cm) long, $^3/_4$ inch (2 cm) wide and $^1/_2$ inch (12 mm) thick

$^1/_2$ lb (250 g) fresh button mushrooms, sliced $^1/_4$ inch (6 mm) thick

$^1/_4$ cup (2 fl oz/60 ml) Chicken Stock (page 320)

$^1/_2$ cup (4 fl oz/125 ml) basil pesto (page 71)

Salt and freshly ground pepper

# Mediterranean Chicken

This interesting mix of aromatic flavors—basil, garlic, orange zest, olives, and fennel—bring to mind the warm Mediterranean sun. Serve with room-temperature broccoli or green beans with vinaigrette.

1 chicken, about 3¹/₂ lb (1.75 kg)

1 tablespoon dried basil

2 tablespoons olive oil

1 clove garlic, halved

1 red bell pepper (capsicum), seeded, deribbed, and chopped

Grated zest of 1 orange

¹/₄ cup (2 fl oz/60 ml) Chicken Stock (page 320)

Salt and freshly ground pepper

¹/₂ cup (3 oz/90 g) thinly sliced fennel

¹/₄ cup (2 fl oz/60 ml) dry white wine

16 small black olives, preferably Greek or Italian

Cut the chicken into 8 pieces. Trim off any excess fat. Sprinkle with the basil.

Warm the olive oil in a frying pan over medium heat. Add the garlic and chicken and sauté, turning the pieces as they become golden, 3–4 minutes on each side. Remove the garlic and discard. Add the bell pepper and orange zest and cook for about 2 minutes.

Stir in the chicken stock and salt and pepper to taste. Add the fennel and white wine, cover, and simmer gently until the chicken is tender, 30–40 minutes. During the last 10 minutes of cooking, uncover the pan and add the olives.

Transfer the chicken to a warmed platter and surround with the vegetables and pan juices. Serve immediately.

*Serves 4*

# Sicilian Stuffed Steak Rolls

In Sicily, this dish is served on special occasions and may be prepared with beef or veal. Marjoram may be replaced for the Oregano. Serve the steak rolls with broccoli or Swiss chard for a colorful and festive dinner.

To make the filling, soak the bread in water, squeeze dry and crumble. Combine the ground beef or veal, bread, eggs, parsley, oregano, and Parmesan in a bowl and season to taste with salt and pepper. Mix well and set aside.

Place the round steaks between sheets of plastic wrap and pound gently with a meat pounder until they are $1/2$ inch (12 mm) thick. Spread half of the filling on top of each steak and press down in an even layer. Place the mortadella in a single layer on top of the filling. Cut the salami and provolone into strips. Place 2 or 3 hard-boiled eggs in a row down the center of each steak and surround them with the strips of salami and cheese. Carefully roll up each steak like a log and tie in several places with kitchen string.

Warm 3 tablespoons of the oil in a frying pan over high heat. Brown the steak rolls on all sides, 15–20 minutes. Set aside.

In a heavy pot large enough to hold the 2 steak rolls, warm the remaining 2 tablespoons oil over medium heat. Add the onion and cook until tender and translucent, 10–15 minutes. Add the garlic, wine, tomatoes, and tomato paste and bring to a simmer. Add the steak rolls, reduce the heat to low, cover, and simmer until the beef is tender, about $1 1/2$ hours.

Transfer the steak rolls to a warmed platter and let rest for a few minutes. Season the sauce to taste with salt and pepper. Snip the strings from the steak rolls and slice crosswise $1/2$ inch (12 mm) thick. Serve the sauce in a bowl alongside.

*Makes 2 steak rolls; serves 6–8*

3 slices bread

1 lb (500 g) ground (minced) beef or veal

3 eggs

4 tablespoons chopped parsley

2 tablespoons chopped oregano

$1/4$ cup (1 oz/30 g) grated Parmesan cheese

Salt and freshly ground pepper

2 round steaks, each about $1 1/2$ lb (750 g) and about 1 inch (2.5 cm) thick

8 slices mortadella

4–6 hard-boiled eggs

$1/4$ lb *each* (125 g) salami and provolone cheese, sliced

5 tablespoons (3 fl oz/80 ml) olive oil

2 cups (8 oz/250 g) diced onion

4 cloves garlic, finely minced

$1 1/2$ cups (12 fl oz/375 ml) dry red wine

4 cups (32 fl oz/1 l) puréed canned tomatoes

2 tablespoons tomato paste

# Italian Beef Stew

Long cooking at a low temperature makes chuck steak wonderfully tender. If you cannot find Italian green beans, substitute regular green beans, but reduce the cooking time to about 15 minutes.

3 tablespoons olive oil

1 beef chuck steak, 2 lb (1 kg), trimmed of fat

2 tablespoons red wine vinegar

2 large sweet onions, halved lengthwise and then cut crosswise into slices 1/2 inch (12 mm) thick

2 red bell peppers (capsicums), seeded, deribbed, and cut crosswise into strips 1/2 inch (12 mm) wide

2 green bell peppers (capsicums), seeded, deribbed, and cut lengthwise into strips 1 inch (2.5 cm) wide

2 cups (16 fl oz/500 ml) Beef Stock (page 320)

1/2 lb (250 g) Italian (romano) green beans, trimmed and cut into 2-inch (5-cm) pieces

8 oz (250 g) canned straw mushrooms, drained

Salt and freshly ground pepper

In a large heavy pot over medium-high heat, warm 1 tablespoon of the oil. Place the chuck steak in the pot and cook, turning once, until richly browned on both sides, 4–6 minutes. Transfer the chuck steak to a dish. Add the vinegar to the pot and, using a wooden spoon, deglaze the pot over medium-high heat by stirring to scrape up any browned bits from the pot bottom. Pour the liquid over the steak.

In the same pot over medium-high heat, warm the remaining 2 tablespoons oil. Add the onions and the bell peppers and sauté, stirring, until well browned, 10 minutes. Add 2–3 tablespoons water if necessary to keep the vegetables from sticking.

Slowly stir in the beef stock, scraping the pot bottom to scrape up any browned bits. Return the meat to the pot and bring to a simmer. Reduce the heat to medium-low, cover, and simmer gently until the meat is very tender, about 2 1/2 hours.

Add the beans, re-cover, and simmer gently until the beans are just tender, about 20–30 minutes longer. Transfer the meat to a cutting board and cut it into bite-sized pieces. Return the meat to the pot over medium heat. Add the mushrooms and simmer, stirring gently, until the mushrooms and meat are heated through, 2–3 minutes. Season to taste with salt and pepper.

Spoon into warmed individual bowls and serve.

*Serves 4*

# Italian Hamburgers or Meatballs alla Pizzaiola

This ground beef mixture makes great hamburgers or small tasty meatballs. Either spoon the pizzaiola (pizza maker's) sauce over the cooked burgers or brown the meatballs and then warm them in the sauce.

To make the sauce, in a small saucepan, warm the olive oil over low heat. Add the garlic and oregano and sauté until the garlic is translucent, about 4 minutes. Add the tomato sauce and simmer for 5 minutes to allow the flavors to blend. Season to taste with salt and pepper. Set aside and keep warm.

In a bowl, combine the beef, Parmesan, bread crumbs, egg, onion, parsley, oregano, and $1/2$ teaspoon pepper. Using your hands, mix well. Form into 4–6 patties or into meatballs about 1 inch (2.5 cm) in diameter.

Warm the olive oil in a heavy frying pan over high heat. If making burgers, add the patties to the pan and cook, turning once, until done to your liking. Transfer to individual plates, spoon the sauce over the tops, and serve. If making meatballs, add to the pan and cook beyond medium-rare or they will not hold together. Drain off the excess fat from the pan and add the sauce. Turn the meatballs in the sauce for 2 minutes, then serve.

*Serves 4–6*

FOR THE SAUCE:

2 tablespoons extra-virgin olive oil

2 cloves garlic, minced

2 teaspoons dried oregano

$1^1/2$ cups (12 fl oz/375 ml) Simple Tomato Sauce (page 323)

Salt and freshly ground pepper

$1^1/2$ lb (750 g) ground (minced) beef

$2/3$ cup ($2^1/2$ oz/75 g) grated Parmesan cheese

2 cups (4 oz/125 g) fresh bread crumbs (page 324)

1 egg, lightly beaten

$1/4$ cup (2 oz/60 g) grated yellow onion

5 tablespoons ($1/3$ oz/10 g) chopped fresh flat-leaf (Italian) parsley

3 tablespoons chopped fresh oregano

$1/2$ teaspoon ground pepper

$1/4$ cup (2 fl oz/60 ml) olive oil

# Veal Piccata

This is the simplest of veal scallop recipes. The veal should be cut from the leg and pounded gently. A simple deglazing of the pan with a little stock and lemon juice makes a tasty and light sauce.

Place the veal scallops between 2 sheets of plastic wrap and pound gently with a meat pounder until they are an even 1/4 inch (6 mm) thick. In a shallow bowl, combine the flour and salt and pepper to taste. Stir to blend. Dredge the veal slices in the seasoned flour and shake off any excess.

In a large frying pan over high heat, melt 2 tablespoons of the butter with the olive oil. Add the veal, in batches if necessary, and cook, turning once, until golden on both sides, 2–3 minutes on each side. Transfer to a warmed platter and keep warm.

Pour off the excess butter and oil from the pan. Pour in the stock and bring to a boil over high heat. Using a wooden spoon, deglaze the pan by stirring to scrape up any browned bits from the pan bottom. Boil until the stock is reduced by half. Add the lemon juice and capers and then stir in the remaining 2 tablespoons butter. Pour the sauce over the veal. Sprinkle with the parsley and serve at once.

*Serves 4*

1 lb (500 g) veal scallops, about 1/2 inch (12 mm) thick

3/4 cup (4 oz/125 g) all-purpose (plain) flour

Salt and freshly ground pepper

4 tablespoons (2 oz/60 g) unsalted butter

1 1/2 teaspoons extra-virgin olive oil

1 cup (8 fl oz/250 ml) veal stock or Beef Stock (page 320)

3 tablespoons fresh lemon juice

1/4 cup (2 1/2 oz/75 g) capers, rinsed and well drained

2 tablespoons chopped fresh flat-leaf (Italian) parsley

# Ossobuco alla Milanese

Ossobuco means "bone with a hole." In *ossobuco alla milanese*, veal shanks
are braised with aromatic vegetables, wine, stock, and occasionally a little tomato.
Use 1 tablespoon grated orange zest for more flavor in the gremolata, if you like.

1½ cups (7½ oz/235 g) all-purpose (plain) flour

Salt and freshly ground pepper

6 meaty veal shanks, each about 1½ lb (750 g), sawed crosswise into 2 pieces

½ cup (4 fl oz/125 ml) olive oil, or as needed

½ cup (4 oz/125 g) butter

3 large yellow onions, chopped

1½ cups (8 oz/250 g) peeled, diced carrots

1½ cups (8 oz/250 g) diced celery

1 cup (8 fl oz/250 ml) dry white wine

4 cups (2 lb/1 kg) diced plum (Roma) tomatoes

3–4 cups (24–32 fl oz/750 ml–1 l) Beef Stock (page 320)

Salt and freshly ground pepper

FOR THE GREMOLATA:

5 tablespoons (⅓ oz/10 g) chopped fresh parsley

2 tablespoons grated lemon zest

2 teaspoons finely minced garlic

In a shallow bowl, combine the flour and salt and pepper to taste. Stir to blend. Saw each veal shank crosswise into 2 pieces. Coat the veal shanks with the seasoned flour.

Warm ¼ cup (2 fl oz/60 ml) of the olive oil in a large, heavy frying pan over high heat. Add as many veal shanks as will fit without crowding and brown on all sides, 15–20 minutes. Transfer to a platter and add the remaining ¼ cup (2 fl oz/60 ml) olive oil to the pan. Brown the remaining shanks in the same way. Transfer to the platter and set aside.

In a large, heavy pot, melt the butter over medium heat. Add the onions, carrots, and celery and cook, stirring occasionally, until tender, about 15 minutes. Place the veal shanks on top of the vegetables and add the wine and tomatoes. Pour in enough stock to cover. Bring to a boil, reduce the heat to low, cover, and simmer until the veal is very tender, 1–1¼ hours. The meat should be almost falling off the bones. Season the vegetable sauce to taste with salt and pepper.

To make the gremolata, in a small bowl, combine the parsley, lemon zest, and garlic. Mix well and sprinkle over the shanks. Cook for 5 minutes longer and serve with the vegetable sauce.

*Serves 6*

# Pork Ragout with Polenta

For pork stews and ragouts, use shoulder, blade-end loin, or boneless country-style ribs, all of which become tender with long, gentle cooking. Garnish with chopped parsley, if you like.

2¹/₂ lb (1.25 kg) boneless pork (see note)

1–2 tablespoons olive oil

1 large yellow onion, halved and sliced

4 cloves garlic, chopped

¹/₄ cup (2 fl oz/60 ml) balsamic vinegar

Salt

2 carrots, peeled and diced

1 bay leaf

1¹/₂–2 cups (12–16 fl oz/ 375–500 ml) dry red wine

³/₄–1 cup (6–8 fl oz/180– 250 ml) Chicken Stock (page 320)

Hot, soft-cooked polenta (page 272)

¹/₂ cup (2¹/₂ oz/75 g) drained, oil-packed sun-dried tomatoes, chopped

Large handful of fresh flat-leaf (Italian) parsley leaves, chopped

Cut the pork into 1¹/₂-inch (4-cm) cubes, trimming off any excess fat. In a large frying pan over medium-high heat, warm 1 tablespoon of the olive oil. Add the pork and cook until evenly browned, about 6 minutes. Transfer the pork to a heavy saucepan.

Add the remaining 1 tablespoon olive oil, if needed, to the frying pan over medium heat. Add the onion and sauté, stirring often, until browned, about 5 minutes, adding the garlic during the last 30 seconds. Add the vinegar, and using a wooden spoon, deglaze the pan by stirring to scrape up any browned bits from the pan bottom. Pour the liquid over the pork and season to taste with salt. Add the carrots, bay leaf, and enough wine and stock almost to cover. Bring to a boil, reduce the heat to low, cover, and simmer until the meat is tender, about 1¹/₂ hours. About 30 minutes before the pork is done, cook the polenta.

About 15 minutes before the pork is done, stir in the tomatoes. Taste and adjust the seasoning. Spoon polenta onto warmed individual plates and top with ragout. Garnish with parsley. Serve immeditately.

*Serves 6*

# Calves' Liver with Onions, Lemon, and Sage

This is a Venetian dish of sautéed liver and onions, lightened with lemon juice and perfumed with fresh sage. In Venice, the liver is cut into tiny strips, but large slices are easier to cook and turn.

Warm ¹/₄ cup (2 fl oz/60 ml) of the olive oil in a large frying pan over medium heat. Add the onions and sauté until tender and translucent, 10–15 minutes. Using a slotted spoon, transfer to a bowl and set aside.

In a shallow bowl, combine the flour and salt and pepper to taste. Stir to blend. Dredge the liver in the seasoned flour and shake off any excess. Warm the remaining ¹/₄ cup (2 fl oz/60 ml) olive oil in the same pan over high heat. Add the liver and sear, turning once, 2–3 minutes on each side for medium-rare, or until done to your liking. Transfer the liver to a plate and keep warm.

Pour off the excess oil from the pan. Pour in the stock and, using a wooden spoon, deglaze the pan over high heat by stirring to scrape up any browned bits from the pan bottom. Boil until slightly thickened. Return the onions to the pan, add the sage leaves and lemon juice, and cook for 2 minutes to allow flavors to blend. Season to taste with salt and pepper.

Place the liver on warmed individual plates and spoon the onions over the top.

*Serves 4*

½ cup (4 fl oz/120 ml) extra-virgin olive oil

3 large red onions, sliced

³/₄ cup (4 oz/125 g) all-purpose (plain) flour

Salt and freshly ground pepper

1½ lb (750 g) calves' liver, trimmed of all gristle and cut into 8 slices, each about ¹/₃ inch (9 mm) thick

1 cup (8 fl oz/250 ml) Chicken Stock (page 320)

8 fresh sage leaves

¹/₄ cup (2 fl oz/60 ml) fresh lemon juice

# Veal alla Parmigiana

Despite its name, this classic veal dish is from the Italian south. Parmesan cheese does come from the north, but this mixture of mozzarella and tomato speaks of Naples. Serve with sautéed or broiled eggplant (aubergine).

1¹/₂ lb (750 g) veal scallops, about ¹/₂ inch (12 mm) thick

³/₄ cup (4 oz/125 g) all-purpose (plain) flour

Salt and freshly ground pepper

¹/₂ cup (2 oz/60 g) grated Parmesan cheese

¹/₄ cup (2 fl oz/60 ml) extra-virgin olive oil

8–12 thin slices fresh mozzarella

1 cup (8 fl oz/250 ml) Simple Tomato Sauce (page 323)

Place the veal scallops between 2 sheets of plastic wrap and pound gently with a meat pounder until they are an even ¹/₄ inch (6 mm) thick. In a shallow bowl, combine the flour, salt and pepper to taste, and a few tablespoons of the Parmesan. Stir to blend. Dredge the veal in the seasoned flour and shake off any excess.

Warm the olive oil in a large frying pan over medium-high heat. Add the veal, in batches if necessary, and brown lightly on one side, about 2 minutes. Turn the veal, brown on the second side for 1 minute, and top with the mozzarella slices. Reduce the heat to low, cover, and cook until the cheese softens, about 2 minutes.

Meanwhile, in a saucepan, warm the tomato sauce over medium-high heat.

Transfer the veal to warmed individual plates and spoon hot tomato sauce over the top. Sprinkle with the remaining Parmesan and serve.

*Serves 4*

# Beef with Tomatoes and Oregano

The name of this Neapolitan specialty, *bistecca alla pizzaiola*, refers to cooking slices of beef with a classic pizza-style sauce. The sauce is equally delicious with veal or pounded chicken or turkey breasts.

1½ lb (750 g) rib-eye steak or other tender cut, sliced ⅓ inch (9 mm) thick

Salt and freshly ground pepper

2 tablespoons extra-virgin olive oil

2 or 3 large plum (Roma) tomatoes, peeled (page 329), seeded, and diced, or 2 cups (12 oz/375 g) canned tomatoes, preferably in purée, diced

4 cloves garlic, minced

1 tablespoon dried oregano

1 anchovy fillet, minced (optional)

½ cup (4 fl oz/125 ml) dry white wine (optional)

Place the beef slices between 2 sheets of plastic wrap, and pound gently with a meat pounder until they are an even ¼ inch (6 mm) thickness. Using a sharp knife, cut away any sinews. Lay each slice flat and make small cuts around the edges, spaced about 1 inch (2.5 cm) apart, to prevent the slices from curling in the pan. Sprinkle with salt and pepper to taste.

In a large frying pan over high heat, warm the olive oil. Add the beef slices, in batches if necessary, and quickly sear on both sides, turning once, about 3 minutes on each side. Transfer the beef to a platter and set aside.

Add the tomatoes, garlic, and oregano to the oil remaining in the pan. If desired, add the anchovy and wine. Bring to a boil over high heat. Reduce the heat to low and simmer, uncovered, until the tomatoes are reduced to a chunky sauce, 8–10 minutes.

Return the beef to the pan and simmer briefly in the sauce to heat through. Spoon on to individual plates and serve immediately.

*Serves 4*

# Broiled Veal Chops alla Valdostana

This recipe comes from Val d'Aosta, a mountainous area that borders the Piedmont region of northern Italy and is known for its rustic cuisine. This veal recipe is delicious served with polenta and broccoli.

Cut a horizontal pocket in each veal chop. Insert 1 prosciutto slice, 1 cheese slice, and 2 sage leaves into each pocket. Alternatively, coarsely chop the prosciutto, cheese, and sage, mix together and spread inside each chop pocket.

Preheat the broiler (grill) or prepare a fire in a charcoal grill. Brush the chops with olive oil and sprinkle with salt and pepper to taste. Arrange on a rack in a broiler pan, or on the grill rack. Broil or grill, turning once, about 4 minutes on each side for rare, or until done to your liking.

Meanwhile, in a saucepan, warm the tomato sauce over medium-high heat.

Transfer the veal chops to warmed individual plates, spoon the hot tomato sauce over the top, and serve.

*Serves 6*

6 large bone-in veal chops, each about 3/4 lb (375 g) and 1 inch (2.5 cm) thick

6 thin slices prosciutto

6 thin slices fontina cheese

12 fresh sage leaves

Olive oil for brushing

Salt and freshly ground pepper

2 cups (16 fl oz/500 ml) Simple Tomato Sauce (page 323)

# Braised Lamb Shanks with White Beans

This dish is a modern adaptation of ossobuco, the classic northern Italian specialty of braised veal shanks. Here, it is served with white beans instead of the more traditional risotto. The lemon-and-parsley garnish is called gremolata.

1½ cups (10½ oz/330 g) dried cannellini beans

3 tablespoons olive oil

6 lamb shanks, ½–¾ lb (250–375 g) each

2 red onions, cut into ½-inch (12-mm) dice

2 large carrots, peeled and cut into ½-inch (12-mm) dice

6 cloves garlic, minced

1½ cups (12 fl oz/375 ml) dry red wine

1½ cups (12 fl oz/375 ml) Chicken Stock (page 320)

3 tablespoons tomato paste

1 cup (6 oz/185 g) peeled (page 329), seeded, and chopped fresh tomatoes or seeded, drained, and chopped canned tomatoes

1 teaspoon chopped fresh thyme

1 bay leaf

Salt and freshly ground pepper

1 tablespoon grated lemon zest

2 tablespoons chopped fresh flat-leaf (Italian) parsley

Pick over the beans, discarding any stones or misshapen beans. Rinse the beans. Place in a bowl, and add cold water to cover, and soak for about 12 hours.

Drain the beans and place in a saucepan with water to cover by 2 inches (5 cm). Bring to a boil, reduce the heat to low, and simmer, uncovered, until tender, 45–60 minutes. Drain the beans and set aside.

Meanwhile, in a large, heavy pot over medium heat, warm the olive oil. Add the lamb shanks and brown on all sides, 10–12 minutes. Remove from the pan and set aside. Add the onions and carrots to the pot and sauté, stirring occasionally, until the onions are soft, about 10 minutes. Add the garlic and sauté, stirring, for 1 minute. Add the wine, stock, tomato paste, tomatoes, thyme, and bay leaf and stir well. Return the lamb shanks to the pot. Raise the heat to high and bring to a boil. Reduce the heat to low, cover, and simmer until the shanks are very tender, 1½–2 hours.

Add the beans, stir well, cover, and simmer gently over low heat until the lamb begins to fall off the bones, about 30 minutes. Season to taste with salt and pepper.

In a bowl, stir together the lemon zest and parsley. Transfer the lamb and beans to individual plates and garnish with the lemon-parsley mixture. Serve immediately.

*Serves 6*

# Vegetables & Grains

# Italian Green Beans with Cannellini Beans

Canned white beans make this an especially quick recipe to prepare. If you can't find long Italian sweet peppers, use green bell peppers (capsicums) instead. Serve this savory ragout over bowls of creamy polenta or cooked linguine and garnish with fresh oregano or basil sprigs.

Using a sharp knife, trim off the root ends of the boiling onions. Cut a shallow X in each trimmed end (to keep the onions whole during cooking). Place in a saucepan three-fourths full of water and bring to a boil. Boil for about 2 minutes. Drain and, when cool enough to handle, slip off the skins. Set the onions aside.

In a large, heavy pot over medium heat, warm the olive oil. Add the chopped onion and garlic and sauté until the onion is translucent, about 5 minutes. Add the green beans, sweet peppers, and the reserved boiling onions. Continue to sauté until the peppers just start to soften, about 5 minutes longer.

Add the beans, tomatoes, olives, oregano, and basil. Cover and cook over medium-low heat until the green beans are tender, about 15 minutes. Season to taste with salt and pepper.

Spoon into warmed shallow bowls and serve.

*Serves 4–6*

1 lb (500 g) small white or yellow boiling onions

2 tablespoons extra-virgin olive oil

1 yellow onion, coarsely chopped

2 cloves garlic, finely chopped

1 lb (500 g) Italian (romano) green beans, trimmed and cut on the diagonal into 2-inch (5-cm) pieces

4 long Italian green sweet peppers (capsicums), seeded, deribbed, and cut lengthwise into strips 1/2 inch (12 mm) wide

1 can (20 oz/625 g) cannellini, Great Northern, or white kidney beans, drained

6 large plum (Roma) tomatoes, cut crosswise into quarters

1/2 cup (2 1/2 oz/75 g) pitted small black olives

1 tablespoon fresh oregano leaves

1 tablespoon thinly sliced fresh basil or 1 teaspoon dried basil

Salt and freshly ground pepper

# Asparagus with Prosciutto

The prosciutto and cheese heighten the flavor of the fresh asparagus in this classic Italian dish. For a creamier result, use thin slices of fontina in place of the Parmesan. The asparagus can be served as a first course followed by lightly sautéed chicken breasts or veal.

12 large asparagus spears

4 thin slices prosciutto

2 tablespoons unsalted butter, cut into small pieces, plus extra for greasing

Freshly ground pepper

1/2 cup (2 oz/60 g) grated Parmesan cheese

1/2 teaspoon paprika

1 lemon, quartered

Preheat the oven to 375°F (190°C). Grease a baking dish large enough to hold the asparagus and set aside.

Using a sharp knife, cut off the tough ends of the asparagus. Peel the stalks to within about 2 inches (5 cm) of the tips. Gather the stalks together and trim off the bottoms so all the asparagus are the same length.

Fill a frying pan with just enough water to cover the asparagus when it is added. Bring to a boil. Add the asparagus spears, overlapping them as little as possible, and cook, uncovered, over high heat until tender but still quite firm, 3–4 minutes (the timing will depend on the thickness of the stalks). Drain well.

Divide the asparagus into 4 bundles of 3 stalks each. Wrap 1 prosciutto slice around the center of each bundle. Place the 4 bundles in the prepared baking dish. Dot with butter, season to taste with pepper, and sprinkle evenly with the Parmesan. Bake for 5 minutes to brown the cheese. Remove from the oven, dust with the paprika, and serve hot with the lemon quarters.

*Serves 4*

# Eggplant Parmigiana

This version of eggplant parmigiana includes hard-boiled eggs. It is ideal for entertaining, as it can be assembled in advance and slipped into the oven just before serving. It reheats well, too.

3 eggplants (aubergines), about 1 lb (500 g) each

Salt

Olive oil for sautéing

1 yellow onion, thinly sliced

2 cups (12 oz/375 g) peeled (page 329), seeded, and diced tomatoes

2 cloves garlic, minced (optional)

Salt and freshly ground pepper

2 or 3 hard-boiled eggs, peeled and sliced

1/2 cup (2 oz/60 g) grated pecorino romano cheese

1/2 cup (2 oz/60 g) fine dried bread crumbs (page 324)

Peel the eggplants and cut crosswise into slices about 1/2 inch (12 mm) thick. Sprinkle the slices with salt and place in a colander. Let stand for 30 minutes to drain off the bitter juices. Rinse and pat dry with paper towels.

Preheat the oven to 400°F (200°C).

In a large frying pan, preferably nonstick, over medium heat, pour in oil to a depth of 1/4 inch (6 mm). Working in batches, add the eggplant slices and sauté, turning once, until very lightly browned and translucent, about 4 minutes on each side. Transfer to paper towels to drain. Add more oil to the pan only as needed to prevent sticking; the eggplant will "drink" more oil than it needs. Add the onion to the oil remaining in the pan and cook over medium heat, stirring, until softened, about 5 minutes. Add the tomatoes and the garlic, if using, and cook, stirring occasionally, until the tomatoes are reduced to a chunky sauce, about 10 minutes. Season to taste with salt and pepper.

Spread one-third of the tomato sauce on the bottom of an 8-by-12-inch (20-by-30-cm) baking dish with 2-inch (5-cm) sides. Top with half of the eggplant slices. Spread half of the remaining sauce over the eggplant. Layer on half of the eggs and then the remaining eggplant. Top with the remaining eggs and then the remaining sauce. Sprinkle on the cheese and bread crumbs. Bake until the top is lightly golden, about 20 minutes. Let stand for 15 minutes before serving.

*Serves 6*

# Grilled Fennel and Endive with Olive Vinaigrette

The olive vinaigrette is a good match for the strongly flavored vegetables used here. You can also serve them plain, drizzled with just a little lemon juice. Garnish with the feathery tops of the fennel bulbs, if you like.

Prepare a fire for indirect-heat cooking in a covered grill: Center the drip pan on the fire bed and use a pair of long-handed tongs to position the hot coals along the edges of the pan. Position the grill rack 4–6 inches (10–15 cm) above the fire.

Rinse the olives briefly in cold water. Drain and pat dry with paper towels. Chop finely and combine in a small bowl with $^1/_2$ cup (4 fl oz/125 ml) of the olive oil, garlic, $^1/_4$ teaspoon salt, and $^1/_4$ teaspoon pepper. Whisk briskly until smooth and blended, then whisk in the vinegar. Set aside.

Cut each fennel bulb and each endive in half lengthwise. In a large bowl, gently toss the fennel and the endive with the remaining $^1/_4$ cup (2 fl oz/60 ml) olive oil and salt and pepper to taste.

Place the fennel on the center of the grill rack over the drip pan, cover the grill, and open the vents halfway. Cook for 15 minutes, then turn the fennel and place the endives on the rack. Re-cover and continue to cook, turning the vegetables again after 10 minutes, until they are lightly browned and tender when pierced with the tip of a knife, 10–15 minutes longer.

Transfer the vegetables to a platter and spoon some of the vinaigrette over them. Serve hot, warm, or at room temperature. Pass the remaining vinaigrette at the table.

*Serves 6*

FOR THE VINAIGRETTE:

$^1/_2$ cup (3 oz/90 g) oil-cured black olives, pitted

$^3/_4$ cup (4 fl oz/125 ml) extra-virgin olive oil

1 clove garlic, minced

Salt and freshly ground pepper

2 tablespoons white or red wine vinegar

3 large fennel bulbs, trimmed

6 heads Belgian endive (chicory/witloof)

$^1/_4$ cup (2 fl oz/60 ml) extra-virgin olive oil

# Artichokes with Mint and Garlic

In this classic Roman dish, artichokes are stuffed with a savory mixture of garlic, parsley, mint, and bread crumbs and then cooked in olive oil. If you like, add a few teaspoons minced anchovy fillet to the stuffing mixture.

4 artichokes

3 cloves garlic, minced

¼ cup (⅓ oz/10 g) chopped fresh flat-leaf (Italian) parsley

⅓ cup (½ oz/15 g) chopped fresh mint, plus 2 fresh mint sprigs for garnish

1 cup (4 oz/125 g) dried bread crumbs (page 324)

Salt and freshly ground pepper

About ¼ cup (2 fl oz/60 ml) extra-virgin olive oil

Salt

Olive oil for cooking

Working with 1 artichoke at a time, cut off the stem even with the base. Break off all the tough outer leaves. Cut off the thorny leaf tops with a serrated knife. Pull the leaves apart to expose the center and, using a melon baller or a sharp spoon, scoop out the prickly choke.

Preheat the oven to 325°F (165°C).

In a small bowl, stir together the garlic, parsley, chopped mint, and bread crumbs. Season to taste with salt and pepper. Add a little of the extra-virgin olive oil and mix well to combine; the stuffing should be crumbly but moist. Tuck the stuffing into the center of the artichokes, dividing it evenly. Tightly close the leaves over the filling. Place the artichokes stem end down in a deep baking dish with a lid. Sprinkle with salt to taste. Add a mixture of 1 part water and 2 parts olive oil to the dish to reach two-thirds of the way up the sides of the artichokes. Cover and bake until the artichokes are tender when pierced with a knife, 45–60 minutes.

Transfer to a serving platter, drizzle with the remaining extra-virgin olive oil, and garnish with the mint sprigs. Serve warm or at room temperature.

*Serves 4*

# Salad of Warm Roasted Beets, Green Beans, and Olives

Tiny roasted potatoes make a great addition to this salad. To roast the potatoes, follow the procedure for the beets, but omit the water from the baking dish. Whole fresh basil leaves or thyme sprigs make a nice garnish.

8–10 beets, about 1½ lb (750 g) total weight, unpeeled and well scrubbed

1 tablespoon extra-virgin olive oil

½ lb (250 g) green beans, trimmed

1 cup (8 fl oz/250 ml) mayonnaise, preferably homemade (page 323)

2 cloves garlic, minced

2 tablespoons warm water

¼ red onion, thinly sliced

½ cup (2½ oz/75 g) well-drained Kalamata or Niçoise olives

Salt and freshly ground pepper

2 lemons, cut into wedges

Preheat the oven to 350°F (180°C).

Place the beets in a 9-by-13-inch (23-by-33-cm) baking dish. Drizzle evenly with olive oil and ¼ cup (2 fl oz/60 ml) water. Cover with aluminum foil and bake until the beets are easily pierced with a skewer, 1–1¼ hours.

About 15 minutes before the beets are done, bring a large saucepan three-fourths full of salted water to a boil over high heat. Add the beans and cook until tender when pierced with the tip of a knife, 10–12 minutes. Drain immediately and keep warm.

In a small bowl, whisk together the mayonnaise, garlic, and warm water to form a barely fluid sauce. Set aside.

When the beets are cooked, remove from the oven, remove the foil, and let the beets stand just until cool enough to handle. Then peel the beets and cut into slices ¼ inch (6 mm) thick.

To serve, place the warm beets on a large platter. Top with the warm green beans. Scatter the onion and olives on top and season to taste with salt and pepper. Drizzle the vegetables with the mayonnaise sauce and garnish with the lemon wedges. Serve at once.

*Serves 6*

# Wilted Greens with Garlic and Balsamic Vinegar

Many types of greens can be used for this dish, including Swiss chard, mustard greens, escarole, chicory, radicchio, turnip greens, and beet greens. Serve as an accompaniment to Polenta with Tomato Sauce (page 272) or Gemelli with Four Cheeses (page 92).

Cut the greens into strips 1 inch (2.5 cm) wide.

In a large sauté pan over medium-high heat, warm the olive oil. Add the greens and, using tongs, toss them until they are wilted but still retain their bright color, about 3–4 minutes.

Add the vinegar, garlic, red pepper flakes, and salt and black pepper to taste and toss well. Transfer to a warmed serving bowl and serve immediately.

*Serves 6*

10 cups (10 oz/315 g) assorted stemmed greens (see note)

3 tablespoons extra-virgin olive oil

2 tablespoons balsamic vinegar, or to taste

2 cloves garlic, minced

Pinch of red pepper flakes

Salt and freshly ground black pepper

# Risotto Primavera

3–3½ cups (24–28 fl oz/
750–875 ml) Vegetable Stock
(page 321) or Chicken Stock
(page 320)

2 tablespoons extra-virgin
olive oil

1 yellow onion

6 fresh white mushrooms,
brushed clean

1¼ cups (9 oz/280 g)
Arborio rice

½ cup (4 fl oz/125 ml) dry
white wine

1 green or red bell pepper
(capsicum), seeded, deribbed,
and cut into long strips about
¼ inch (6 mm) wide

1 yellow zucchini (courgette) or
crookneck squash, quartered
lengthwise, then cut crosswise
into pieces ¼ inch (6 mm)
thick

½ lb (250 g) asparagus, top
2 inches (5 cm) of each spear
cut on the diagonal into
½-inch (12-mm) pieces,
bottoms discarded or reserved
for another use

½ cup (2 oz/60 g) grated
Parmesan cheese

Salt and freshly ground pepper

Pour the stock into a saucepan and bring to a boil. Reduce the heat to achieve a gentle simmer, and maintain over low heat.

In a large, heavy saucepan over medium-low heat, warm the olive oil. Add the onion and mushrooms and sauté, stirring occasionally, until softened, about 3 minutes. Add the rice and stir to coat with the oil. Add the wine and cook, stirring often, until most of the liquid has been absorbed, about 3 minutes.

Reduce the heat to low and add the bell pepper and 1 cup (8 fl oz/250 ml) of the hot stock. Cook, stirring often, until most of the stock is absorbed, about 5 minutes. Add the squash and asparagus and another 1 cup (8 fl oz/250 ml) of the hot stock and simmer, stirring often, until most of it has been absorbed. Add another 1 cup (8 fl oz/250 ml) of the hot stock and simmer, stirring occasionally, until it is has been absorbed and the risotto has a creamy consistency, about 20 minutes. Taste the rice; if it is hard in the center, add the remaining ½ cup (4 fl oz/125 ml) stock and simmer, stirring, until absorbed and the grains are tender but slightly al dente.

Stir in the Parmesan and season to taste with salt and pepper. Serve at once.

*Serves 4*

# Fresh Fava Beans
# with Garlic-Lemon Dressing

Young fava beans, which are at their peak in the springtime, make this a refreshing, light, and flavorful side dish. For added color and flavor, throw in a few strips of prosciutto or poached shrimp (prawns).

Bring a large saucepan three-fourths full of water to a boil. Add the fava beans and boil for 20 seconds. Drain and let cool. Skin the beans and discard the skins. Transfer the beans to a serving bowl.

In a small bowl, whisk together the lemon juice, olive oil, garlic, parsley, and salt and pepper to taste. Add to the beans and toss well.

Transfer to a platter and garnish with lemon wedges.

*Serves 4–6*

3½ lb (1.75 kg) young fava (broad) beans, shelled

2 tablespoons fresh lemon juice

⅓ cup (3 fl oz/80 ml) extra-virgin olive oil

1 clove garlic, minced

2 tablespoons chopped fresh flat-leaf (Italian) parsley

Salt and freshly ground pepper

2 lemons, cut into small wedges

# Grilled Eggplant and Fontina Sandwiches

These vegetable "sandwiches" have a good savory flavor and are delicious warm or at room temperature. They can even be reheated on the grill or in the oven and served the next day.

1 large eggplant (aubergine)

Salt and freshly ground pepper

1/2 cup (3 fl oz/80 ml) olive oil

2 tablespoons fresh lemon juice

1 clove garlic, minced

1 tablespoon chopped fresh sage or 1 teaspoon dried sage

5 oz (155 g) fontina cheese, thinly sliced

Handful of fresh sage leaves (optional)

Line a baking sheet with paper towels. Cut the eggplant crosswise into 12 slices about 1/2 inch (12 mm) thick. Sprinkle both sides of each slice lightly with salt. Spread the slices out on the prepared baking sheet and cover with more paper towels. Let stand for at least 1 hour, then rinse the slices and pat them dry.

In a jar with a tight-fitting lid, combine the olive oil, lemon juice, garlic, dried sage, 1/2 teaspoon salt, and 1/4 teaspoon pepper. Shake vigorously.

Prepare a fire in a charcoal grill. Oil the grill rack. Arrange the eggplant slices on the rack. Grill, turning them once or twice and brushing with the oil mixture, until lightly browned, about 8 minutes. Top half of the slices with a piece of cheese and 2 or 3 sage leaves, if using, then cover with the remaining eggplant slices. Grill, turning once, until the cheese begins to melt, about 2 minutes longer.

*Serves 6*

# Italian Broccoli with Olives

Here is a simple, attractive dish that is ideal as a side dish or first course. Because it is cooked quickly over high heat, the broccoli will retain its bright color. Serve it at room temperature, as the Italians do, with pasta and a loaf of good bread.

3 or 4 stalks broccoli, about 1 lb (500 g) total weight

3 tablespoons extra-virgin olive oil

1 tablespoon red wine vinegar

Juice of 1/2 lemon

Salt and freshly ground pepper

1 tablespoon capers, rinsed and well-drained

1/2 cup (2 1/2 oz/75 g) pitted black olives, chopped

Split each broccoli stalk lengthwise into thin pieces (the number will depend on the thickness of the stalks). Cut off and discard the coarse leaves and tough lower stems.

Fill a saucepan with just enough water to cover the broccoli when it is added. Bring to a boil. Add the broccoli and cook, uncovered, over high heat until tender but firm, about 4–5 minutes.

Drain and transfer to a serving bowl. Immediately pour the olive oil over the broccoli, add the vinegar, and carefully toss. Add the lemon juice and season to taste with salt and pepper. Toss again.

Add the capers and olives, turning the broccoli gently until thoroughly combined. Serve at room temperature.

*Serves 4*

# Sautéed Pearl Onions

Based on a classic recipe from northern Italy, these delicious little onions are a complementary side dish to poultry or meat. Not to be mistaken for the slightly larger white boiling onions, pearl onions are about ¾ inch (2 cm) in diameter.

Bring a saucepan three-fourths full of water and to a boil. Have a bowl of ice water ready. Add the onions to the boiling water and boil for 2 minutes. Drain, immediately immerse in the ice water, and drain again. Using a sharp knife, cut off the root end from each onion and then cut a small, shallow X in the end. Slip off the skins and cut off the long stem tails, if necessary.

In a heavy frying pan over medium-low heat, melt the butter with the oil. Add the onions, bay leaf, oregano sprigs, stock, and salt and white pepper to taste. Cook gently, stirring occasionally, until the stock evaporates and the onions start to brown, about 10 minutes. Add the wine and continue to cook, shaking the pan often to turn the onions, until the sauce reduces to a syrupy glaze, about 2 minutes.

Discard the bay leaf and oregano sprigs and serve at once.

*Serves 4*

1¼ lb (625 g) pearl onions

1 tablespoon unsalted butter

1 tablespoon extra-virgin olive oil

1 small bay leaf

2 fresh oregano sprigs

⅔ cup (5 fl oz/160 ml) Chicken Stock (page 320)

Salt and freshly ground white pepper

⅔ cup (5 fl oz/160 ml) dry white wine

# Broccoli and Anchovy Salad

Here is an exquisite salad with the flavor of the sea. To make onion-flavored vinegar, soak onion slices in white wine vinegar for 30 minutes. Remove the onions before using. Homemade mayonnaise (page 323) would also make a good dressing for this salad.

Cut the broccoli florets off the stalks. Cut any large florets in half. Discard the stalks or reserve for another use. Bring a saucepan three-fourths full of salted water to a boil. Add the florets and boil until barely tender, about 3 minutes. Drain, cool under cold running water, and drain again. Place in a salad bowl.

Add the capers, anchovies, black and green olives, and pepper strips and toss well.

In a small bowl, stir together the vinegar and salt and pepper to taste until well mixed. Add the oil and stir vigorously until blended. Pour the dressing over the salad, toss well, and serve immediately.

*Serves 4*

2 lb (1 kg) broccoli

2 tablespoons capers, rinsed and well-drained

4 anchovy fillets in oil, cut into small pieces

1/3 cup (2 oz/60 g) black olives, pitted

1/3 cup (2 oz/60 g) green olives, pitted

1 bell pepper (capsicum), seeded, deribbed, and cut into thin strips

2 tablespoons onion-flavored vinegar (see note)

Salt and freshly ground pepper

5 tablespoons (3 fl oz/80 ml) extra-virgin olive oil

# Red Bell Peppers with Polenta

This marvelous combination of flavors and colors can be prepared in advance. Offer as an accompaniment to sautéed veal or chicken or a fish soup, or serve the peppers as part of an antipasto course.

Salt and freshly ground pepper

1/2 cup (2 1/2 oz/75 g) polenta or coarse-ground yellow cornmeal

2 large red bell peppers (capsicums)

2 tablespoons olive oil

2 large ripe tomatoes, thinly sliced

1 teaspoon dried oregano

1 cup (8 fl oz/250 ml) Vegetable Stock (page 321)

1 cup (4 oz/125 g) shredded Gruyère cheese

Preheat the oven to 375°F (190°C).

In a large saucepan, bring 4 cups (32 fl oz/1 l) water to a boil over medium heat. Add 1/2 teaspoon salt. Slowly pour in the cornmeal while stirring constantly. Reduce the heat to medium-low and simmer, stirring occasionally, until the polenta is thick and the grains are tender, about 20 minutes. (If the cornmeal becomes too stiff while simmering, add up to 1/2 cup (4 fl oz/125 ml) more water.) Set aside.

Cut the bell peppers in half lengthwise. Remove the seeds and ribs. Cut a thin slice from the rounded side of each half so it will sit upright with the hollow side up. Place hollow sides up in a baking dish.

Fill each bell pepper half with one-fourth of the polenta. Drizzle the olive oil evenly into the dish. Tuck the tomatoes around the peppers and sprinkle with the oregano and salt and pepper to taste. Pour in 1/2 cup (4 fl oz/125 ml) of the stock.

Bake until the bell peppers are tender, about 40 minutes. During baking, stir and mash the tomatoes with the back of a spoon and baste the peppers with the tomato-stock mixture several times. After the first 20 minutes of baking, pour in the remaining 1/2 cup (4 fl oz/125 ml) stock.

When the bell peppers are tender, sprinkle the cheese evenly over the tops and bake until the cheese melts, about 5 minutes. Spoon the sauce from the baking dish on top and serve hot.

*Serves 4*

# Mediterranean Potato Gratin

This zesty potato dish makes a wonderful accompaniment to grilled lamb chops or roast leg of lamb. Or serve it as a vegetarian main course with a mixed green salad. If the bell pepper is long, cut it in half crosswise before slicing.

3 tablespoons olive oil, plus extra for greasing

1 yellow onion, thinly sliced

1 red bell pepper (capsicum), seeded, deribbed, and cut into long, thin strips

2 tomatoes, peeled (page 329), seeded, and chopped

2 cloves garlic, minced

1/4 teaspoon red pepper flakes (optional)

Salt and freshly ground black pepper

4 tablespoons (1/3 oz/10 g) chopped fresh basil

4 large russet potatoes, about 2 lb (1 kg) total weight, peeled and cut into slices 1/4 inch (6 mm) thick

1 cup (4 oz/125 g) shredded Gruyère cheese

Preheat the oven to 400°F (200°C). Grease a 9-by-13-inch (23-by-33-cm) gratin dish with 2-inch (5-cm) sides.

In a large frying pan over medium heat, warm 2 tablespoons of the olive oil. Add the onion and sauté until translucent, 3–5 minutes. Add the bell pepper and sauté for 3 minutes. Add the tomatoes and cook, stirring often, for 3 minutes. Raise the heat to high and cook, stirring occasionally, until the excess moisture from the tomatoes evaporates, about 1–2 minutes longer. Add the garlic and cook for 1 minute longer. Add the red pepper flakes (if using), salt and black pepper to taste, and 2 tablespoons of the basil. Taste and adjust the seasoning.

Spread half of the potatoes on the bottom of the prepared dish. Arrange half of the vegetable mixture on top and sprinkle with half of the cheese. Repeat the layers. Drizzle the remaining 1 tablespoon olive oil evenly over the top. Cover tightly with aluminum foil.

Place the covered dish on a baking sheet. Bake for 30 minutes, then remove the foil and continue to bake until the potatoes are tender and the top is browned, 15 minutes longer. Sprinkle with the remaining 2 tablespoons basil and serve.

*Serves 4–6*

# Green Beans with Tomatoes and Prosciutto

In the Mediterranean, green beans are generally cooked until they are quite tender. In this recipe, they are combined with sautéed onion, garlic, and tomatoes and flavored with prosciutto. A Spanish version of this dish uses *presunto*, the country's famous cured ham.

1 lb (500 g) young, tender green beans, trimmed and cut into 2-inch (5-cm) pieces

3 tablespoons extra-virgin olive oil

2/3 cup (2 1/2 oz/75 g) chopped yellow onion

2 cloves garlic, minced

4–5 oz (125–155 g) prosciutto, chopped

3 cups (18 oz/560 g) peeled (page 329), seeded, and chopped tomatoes

Salt and freshly ground pepper

1/4 cup (1/3 oz/10 g) chopped fresh flat-leaf (Italian) parsley

Bring a saucepan three-fourths full of salted water to a boil. Have a large bowl of ice water ready. Add the green beans to the boiling water and boil until tender-crisp, 4 minutes. Drain, immediately immerse in the ice water and drain again. Set aside.

In a large frying pan over medium heat, warm the olive oil. Add the onion and sauté, stirring occasionally, until tender, 8–10 minutes. Add the garlic and prosciutto and cook for 1–2 minutes to release their flavors.

Add the green beans and the tomatoes to the pan and bring to a simmer over medium heat. Cover, reduce the heat to low, and cook until the tomatoes have thickened and the beans are tender, 20 minutes. Season to taste with salt and pepper. Transfer to a serving bowl and sprinkle with the parsley. Serve hot or at room temperature.

*Serves 4–6*

# Polenta with Tomato Sauce

In a heavy saucepan over medium heat, warm the oil. Add the onion and garlic and sauté, stirring often, until softened, 5–6 minutes. Stir in the tomatoes, tomato paste, sugar, chopped basil, and salt and pepper to taste. Bring to a boil, then reduce the heat to low and simmer, uncovered, until thickened, 30–40 minutes.

Meanwhile, in a deep, heavy saucepan over high heat, bring 6 1/2 cups (52 fl oz/1.6 l) water to a boil. Add 1 tablespoon salt. Reduce the heat to low to achieve a simmer and stir in the polenta. Cook, stirring often, until the polenta is thick and the grains are tender, about 20 minutes.

If soft polenta is preferred, simply spoon a bed of the polenta into warmed bowls.

If polenta squares are preferred, spread the hot polenta in an oiled, rimmed baking sheet, forming a layer 1/2 inch (12 mm) thick. Let cool until set, then cut into squares. In a large frying pan over high heat, pour in olive oil to a depth of 1/2 inch (12 mm). Working in batches, fry the squares, turning once, until crisp but not browned, about 4–6 minutes.

Top the soft polenta or polenta squares with the tomato sauce and the prosciutto. Garnish with basil sprigs, if desired, and sprinkle with Parmesan. Serve immediately.

*Serves 4–6*

2 tablespoons olive oil, plus extra if frying the polenta

1 yellow onion, chopped

3 cloves garlic, minced

3 cups (18 oz/560 g) peeled (page 329), seeded, and chopped tomatoes with their juices

3–4 tablespoons tomato paste

2 teaspoons sugar

1 tablespoon chopped fresh basil

Salt and freshly ground pepper

2 cups (10 oz/315 g) polenta or coarse-ground yellow cornmeal

2 oz (60 g) thinly sliced prosciutto, coarsely chopped

Fresh basil sprigs (optional)

Grated Parmesan cheese

# Mediterranean Stuffed Eggplant

Preheat the oven to 350°F (180°C). Oil a 9-by-13-in (23-by-33-cm) baking dish.

Using a sharp knife, cut the eggplants in half lengthwise. Sprinkle the cut sides with salt and place cut sides down in a colander to drain for 30 minutes.

Warm 2 tablespoons of the olive oil in a large frying pan over medium heat. Add the ham or veal and sauté for 3–4 minutes. Add the onion and garlic and sauté until softened, 2–3 minutes. Stir in half of the sliced tomatoes and 1/2 cup (4 fl oz/125 ml) of the stock. Cover and simmer over low heat for about 5 minutes.

Meanwhile, rinse the eggplant halves under cold water. Scoop out most of the flesh, leaving shells about 1 inch (2.5 cm) thick. Coarsely chop the flesh and stir into the tomato mixture. Set the shells aside.

Add the rice, marjoram, thyme, and 1 cup (8 fl oz/250 ml) of the stock to the frying pan, stirring to mix well. Cover and simmer over medium heat for 15 minutes, stirring a few times to prevent sticking. Discard the garlic halves. Season to taste with salt and pepper.

Fill each eggplant shell with one-fourth of the stuffing. Place in the prepared dish. Pour the remaining 2 tablespoons oil around the eggplants. Tuck the remaining sliced tomatoes around the eggplants and pour in the remaining 1/2 cup (4 fl oz/ 125 ml) stock.

Bake until the eggplants are tender, about 40–45 minutes. During baking, stir and mash the tomatoes with a spoon and baste the eggplants with the tomato-stock mixture several times.

Transfer the eggplants to a platter and sprinkle with the parsley. Serve hot with the sauce from the dish spooned over the top.

*Serves 4*

2 eggplants (aubergines),
about 1 lb (500 g) each

Salt and freshly ground pepper

4 tablespoons (2 fl oz/60 ml)
olive oil, plus extra for oiling

1 cup (6 oz/185 g) ground
(minced) ham or veal

1 cup (4 oz/125 g) chopped
red onion

2 cloves garlic, cut in half

4 ripe tomatoes, thinly sliced

2 cups (16 fl oz/500 ml)
Vegetable Stock (page 321)

1 cup (6 oz/185 g) Arborio
or other short-grain rice

1 teaspoon dried marjoram

1 teaspoon dried thyme

2 tablespoons chopped
fresh flat-leaf (Italian) parsley

# Bell Pepper and Summer Squash Skewers

Use a combination of yellow and green squashes, if you can, and keep in mind that tiny pattypan squashes, about 1 inch (2.5 cm) or so in diameter, can be skewered and grilled whole. Serve these colorful skewers with grilled meat or seafood on a large platter of rice.

1½ lb (750 g) zucchini (courgettes), crookneck squashes, or small pattypan squashes, or a mixture

1 green bell pepper (capsicum)

1 red bell pepper (capsicum)

⅓ cup (3 fl oz/80 ml) olive oil

2 tablespoons wine vinegar

1 clove garlic, minced

2 teaspoons chopped fresh thyme or ½ teaspoon dried thyme

½ teaspoon salt

¼ teaspoon freshly ground pepper

10–12 large fresh button mushrooms, stems removed and caps brushed clean

8–12 wooden skewers, soaked in water for 30 minutes, or metal skewers

If the squashes are large, cut them crosswise into pieces 1 inch (2.5 cm) long. Halve the bell peppers and remove the stems, ribs, and seeds. Cut the peppers into 1-inch (2.5-cm) squares. Bring a large pot three-fourths full of salted water to a boil. Add the squashes and bell peppers and boil for 2 minutes. Drain well and cover with cold water. Let stand for 2 minutes, then drain again and pat dry with paper towels.

In a large bowl, whisk together the olive oil, vinegar, garlic, thyme, salt, and pepper. Add the blanched vegetables and the mushrooms and toss to combine. Let stand for about 30 minutes, tossing occasionally.

Prepare a fire in a charcoal grill. Oil the grill rack. Remove the vegetables from the marinade, reserving the marinade. Thread the bell pepper and squash pieces and mushrooms alternately onto the skewers. Arrange the skewers on the rack. Grill, turning occasionally and brushing with the reserved marinade, until lightly browned, 8–10 minutes. Serve immediately.

*Serves 4*

# Risotto with Artichokes and Parmesan Cheese

There are several types of rice that Italians use to make risotto. Arborio, the most commonly available, results in a particularly creamy finish. Carnaroli is another good choice, though it can be hard to find.

Have ready a large bowl of water to which you have added half of the lemon juice. Remove the stems and tough outer leaves from the artichokes until you reach the pale green hearts. If using large artichokes, cut in half lengthwise, then scoop out the prickly chokes and discard. Cut the artichokes lengthwise into thin slices. As each is cut, place it in the bowl of water.

In a deep frying pan over medium heat, warm the olive oil. Add the onion and sauté until softened, about 10 minutes. Add the garlic and half of the parsley and sauté for 2 minutes. Drain the artichokes and add to the pan along with 1/2 cup (4 fl oz/125 ml) water and a large pinch of salt. Cover and cook over medium heat until the liquid evaporates, about 25 minutes.

Meanwhile, combine the stock and 2 cups (16 fl oz/500 ml) water in a saucepan and bring to a boil. Reduce the heat to achieve a gentle simmer and maintain over low heat.

Uncover the artichokes, add the rice, and stir for 2 minutes to coat. Add a ladleful of the simmering stock-water mixture and stir constantly over medium heat. When the liquid is almost absorbed, add another ladleful. Stir constantly to keep the rice from sticking and add more liquid, a ladleful at a time, when the previous ladleful is almost absorbed. The risotto is done when it is tender but slightly al dente and the center of each grain is no longer chalky, 20–25 minutes.

Remove from the heat and stir in the Parmesan and the remaining parsley and lemon juice. Season to taste with salt and pepper. Transfer to a warmed serving dish. Serve with lemon wedges, if you like.

*Serves 6*

Juice of 1 lemon

4 large artichokes or 20 small artichokes

2 tablespoons extra-virgin olive oil

1 very small yellow onion, minced

2 cloves garlic, minced

1/2 cup (3/4 oz/20 g) chopped fresh flat-leaf (Italian) parsley

2 1/2 cups (20 fl oz/625 ml) water

Salt and freshly ground pepper

3 cups (24 fl oz/750 ml) Chicken Stock (page 320)

1 1/2 cups (10 1/2 oz/330 g) Arborio rice

1/2 cup (2 oz/60 g) grated Parmesan cheese

1 lemon, cut into wedges (optional)

# Desserts

# Citrus Gelato

Fresh citrus gives this gelato its distinctive flavor. Garnish each serving simply with fresh mint sprigs and citrus zest curls, or serve small scoops of the gelato in frozen hollowed-out orange halves.

2 oranges

2 lemons

3 cups (24 fl oz/750 ml) whole milk

8 egg yolks

1 cup (8 oz/250 g) sugar

3 tablespoons light corn syrup

Using a vegetable peeler, remove the zest from the oranges and lemons in strips. Place the strips in a heavy saucepan and add the milk. Bring to a simmer over medium-high heat. Remove from the heat.

In a large metal bowl, whisk together the egg yolks, sugar, and corn syrup until blended. Form a kitchen towel into a ring and place the bowl on top to prevent it from moving. Gradually pour the hot milk mixture into the yolk mixture, whisking constantly. Return the mixture to the same saucepan and place over medium-low heat. Cook, stirring slowly and constantly with a wooden spatula, until the custard thickens and leaves a path on the back of the spatula when a finger is drawn across it, about 6 minutes; do not allow to boil. Pour the custard through a medium-mesh sieve set over a clean bowl. Refrigerate until cold, about 1 hour.

Transfer the custard to an ice-cream maker and freeze according to the manufacturer's instructions. For the best texture, serve the gelato immediately. Or transfer to a container, cover, and freeze until firm, at least 4 hours or for up to 3 days (the longer freezing results in a texture more like that of ice cream).

*Makes about 3 3/4 cups (30 fl oz/940 ml); serves 4–6*

# Frozen Tiramisù Cake

Mascarpone, an Italian triple-cream cheese, is available at Italian markets and some specialty food stores. If Kahlúa is unavailable, choose another coffee-flavored liqueur.

In a small, heavy saucepan over low heat, combine ½ cup (4 oz/125 g) of the sugar, ½ cup (4 fl oz/120 ml) water, and the espresso powder. Stir until the sugar dissolves, about 3 minutes. Stir in the liqueur. Remove from the heat and set aside to cool.

Bring a saucepan half full of water to a simmer. In a large metal bowl, whisk together the egg yolks, Marsala, the remaining 1 cup (8 oz/250 g) sugar, and ½ cup (2 fl oz/ 60 ml) water until blended. Place the bowl over (not touching) the simmering water. Whisk constantly until a candy thermometer registers 165°F (74°C), about 6 minutes. Remove the bowl from over the water. Using an electric mixer set on high speed, beat the yolk mixture until cool and thick, about 5 minutes. In another large bowl, whisk together the mascarpone, cream, and vanilla just until blended. Beat in the yolk mixture just until combined.

In a springform pan 9 inches (23 cm) in diameter and 3 inches (7.5 cm) deep, arrange enough of the cake slices in a single layer to cover the bottom of the pan to cover completely, trimming to fit as necessary. Brush half of the sugar syrup over the cake slices and then pour in half of the cheese mixture. Top with enough of the remaining cake slices to cover in a single layer, again trimming to fit. Brush with the remaining syrup. Pour the remaining cheese mixture over the top. Smooth with a rubber spatula, cover, and freeze overnight. Run a small, sharp knife around the pan sides to loosen the cake. Release the pan sides and carefully transfer the cake to a serving platter. Using a fine-mesh sieve, dust the top lightly with cocoa powder. Serve immediately.

*Serves 12*

1½ cups (12 oz/375 g) sugar

2 tablespoons instant espresso powder

⅓ cup (3 fl oz/80 ml) Kahlúa

8 egg yolks

6 tablespoons (3 fl oz/90 ml) sweet Marsala

2 cups (1 lb/500 g) mascarpone cheese

½ cup (4 fl oz/125 ml) heavy (double) cream

1 teaspoon vanilla extract (essence)

1 purchased pound cake, ¾ lb (375 g), cut crosswise into slices ¼ inch (6 mm) thick

Unsweetened cocoa powder

# Banana Gelato

The rich banana flavor and dense creaminess of this gelato make it a surefire favorite. Add a sprinkling of walnuts, if you like, or leave it plain to savor its perfectly smooth texture.

2 cups (16 fl oz/500 ml) whole milk

5 egg yolks

³/₄ cup (6 oz/185 g) sugar

2 tablespoons light corn syrup

½ cup (2 oz/60 g) walnuts (optional)

1½ cups (9 oz/280 g) sliced very ripe banana (about 2 large bananas)

1 tablespoon fresh lemon juice

Pour the milk into a heavy saucepan. Bring to a simmer over medium-high heat. Remove from the heat.

In a metal bowl, whisk together the egg yolks, sugar, and corn syrup until blended. Form a kitchen towel into a ring and place the bowl on top to prevent it from moving. Gradually pour the hot milk into the yolk mixture, whisking constantly. Return the mixture to the same saucepan and place over medium-low heat. Cook, stirring slowly and constantly with a wooden spatula, until the custard thickens and leaves a path on the back of the spatula when a finger is drawn across it, about 6 minutes; do not allow to boil. Pour the custard through a medium-mesh sieve set over a clean bowl. Refrigerate until cold, about 1 hour.

If using the walnuts, preheat the oven to 350°F (180°C). Spread the walnuts on a baking sheet and bake until lightly toasted and fragrant, about 10 minutes. Remove from the oven, let cool, and then chop finely. Set aside.

In a food processor fitted with the metal blade or blender, combine the sliced banana and lemon juice and purée until smooth. Stir into the chilled custard. Transfer the custard to an ice-cream maker and freeze according to the manufacturer's instructions. Add the walnuts, if using, during the final minute of processing. For the best texture, serve the gelato immediately. Or transfer to a tightly covered container, cover, and freeze until firm, at least 4 hours or for up to 3 days (the longer freezing results in a texture more like that of ice cream).

*Makes about 3¹/₂ cups (28 fl oz/875 ml); serves 4–6*

# Double Espresso Gelato

A double dose of espresso from coffee beans and espresso powder gives this gelato its deep, rich flavor. The longer freezing results in a texture more like that of ice cream.

In a heavy saucepan, combine the milk and coffee beans. Bring to a simmer over medium-high heat. Remove from the heat. Cover and let stand for 30 minutes.

Pour the milk through a medium-mesh sieve set over a bowl and set aside. Discard the coffee beans.

In a metal bowl, whisk together the egg yolks, sugar, and corn syrup until blended. Form a kitchen towel into a ring and place the bowl on top to prevent it from moving. Gradually pour the milk into the yolk mixture, whisking constantly. Return the mixture to the same saucepan and place over medium-low heat. Cook, stirring slowly and constantly with a wooden spatula, until the custard thickens and leaves a path on the back of the spatula when a finger is drawn across it, about 6 minutes; do not allow to boil. Pour the custard through the medium-mesh sieve set over a clean bowl. Add the espresso powder and vanilla and stir until the espresso dissolves. Refrigerate until cold, about 1 hour.

Transfer the custard to an ice-cream maker and freeze according to the manufacturer's instructions. For the best texture, serve the gelato immediately. Or transfer to a container, cover, and freeze until firm, at least 4 hours or for up to 3 days.

*Makes about 2 1/2 cups (20 fl oz/625 ml); serves 3 or 4*

2 cups (16 fl oz/500 ml) whole milk

1/2 cup (2 oz/60 g) whole espresso-roast coffee beans

5 egg yolks

3/4 cup (6 oz/185 g) sugar

2 tablespoons light corn syrup

1 teaspoon instant espresso powder

1/2 teaspoon vanilla extract (essence)

# Caramel Gelato

3/4 cup (6 oz/185 g) sugar

2 cups (16 fl oz/500 ml) whole milk

5 egg yolks

2 tablespoons light corn syrup

1/2 teaspoon vanilla extract (essence)

In a heavy saucepan over medium-low heat, combine the sugar and 1/4 cup (2 fl oz/60 ml) water. Stir until the sugar dissolves, about 5 minutes. Using a pastry brush dipped in water, brush down any sugar crystals that form on the pan sides. Raise the heat to high and boil without stirring until the syrup is a deep caramel color, gently swirling the pan occasionally for even caramelization, about 10 minutes (the timing will depend on the size and weight of the pan and the intensity of the heat). Gradually add the milk; the mixture will bubble vigorously. Reduce the heat to medium-low and stir until all the hard bits of caramel melt, about 5 minutes.

In a metal bowl, whisk together the egg yolks and corn syrup until blended. Form a kitchen towel into a ring and place the bowl on top to prevent it from moving. Gradually pour the hot caramel into the yolk mixture, whisking constantly. Return the mixture to the same saucepan and place over medium-low heat. Cook, stirring slowly and constantly with a wooden spatula, until the custard thickens and leaves a path on the back of the spatula when a finger is drawn across it, about 6 minutes; do not allow to boil. Pour the custard through a medium-mesh sieve set over a clean bowl. Refrigerate until cold, about 1 hour.

Stir in the vanilla. Transfer the custard to an ice-cream maker and freeze according to the manufacturer's instructions. For the best texture, serve the gelato immediately. Or transfer to a container, cover, and freeze until firm, at least 4 hours or for up to 3 days (the longer freezing results in a texture more like that of ice cream).

*Makes about 2 3/4 cups (22 fl oz/680 ml); serves 3 or 4*

# Espresso-Orange Granita

In Italy, this particular granita is traditionally topped with sweetened whipped cream. The granita will melt quickly, so be sure the wineglasses have been chilled in the freezer for at least 1 hour before filling them.

1 large orange

1/2 cup (4 oz/125 g) plus
2 tablespoons sugar

4 teaspoons instant espresso powder

1/2 cup (4 fl oz/125 ml) heavy (double) cream, chilled

1/4 teaspoon grated orange zest

Using a vegetable peeler, remove the zest from the orange in wide strips. Place the strips in a heavy saucepan and add 2 cups (16 fl oz/500 ml) water, the 1/2 cup (4 oz/125 g) sugar, and the espresso powder. Place over medium heat and stir until the sugar dissolves and the mixture is hot, about 3 minutes. Remove from the heat. Cover and let stand for 10 minutes.

Pour the mixture through a coarse-mesh sieve set over a metal bowl. Freeze, whisking every 30 minutes, until semifirm, about 3 hours. Cover and freeze without stirring until frozen solid, at least 8 hours or as long as 24 hours.

At least 1 hour before serving, place 4 wineglasses in the freezer.

In a bowl, combine the cream, the 2 tablespoons sugar, and the orange zest. Using an electric mixer set on medium-high speed, beat until soft peaks form. Cover and refrigerate until ready to use, or for up to 1 hour.

To serve, using a fork, scrape the surface of the granita to form ice crystals. Scoop the crystals into the frozen wineglasses. Top with the whipped cream and serve at once.

*Serves 4*

# Frozen Marsala Zabaglione with Strawberries

Marsala, a sherrylike fortified wine from Sicily, adds distinctive flavor to this dessert. If you prefer a crunchy texture, fold ⅔ cup (2 oz/60 g) crushed amaretto cookies into the egg yolk–cream mixture before freezing.

Line an 8½-by-4½-by-2½-inch (21.5-by-11.5-by-6-cm) metal loaf pan with plastic wrap, letting plastic overhang the edges by about 3 inches (7.5 cm). Place the pan in the freezer. Bring a saucepan half full of water to a simmer. In a large metal bowl, whisk together the Marsala, the ½ cup (4 oz/125 g) sugar, and the egg yolks until blended. Place the bowl over (but not touching) the simmering water. Whisk constantly until a candy thermometer registers 170°F (77°C), about 5 minutes. Remove the bowl from over the water.

Using an electric mixer set on high speed, beat the egg yolk mixture until cool and thick, about 5 minutes. In another bowl, using the electric mixer fitted with clean, dry beaters, beat the cream on medium-high speed until stiff peaks form. Using a rubber spatula, fold the cream into the cooled yolk mixture until no white streaks remain. Pour into the prepared loaf pan. Cover and freeze overnight.

About 1 hour before serving, place a serving platter in the freezer. Just before serving, in a bowl, toss the strawberries with the remaining 3 tablespoons sugar. Let stand for about 10 minutes.

Uncover the zabaglione. Invert the pan onto the frozen platter. Lift off the pan and peel off the plastic wrap. Using a long, sharp knife, cut the zabaglione crosswise into 10 equal slices and transfer to individual plates. Spoon the strawberries over the top and serve at once.

*Serves 10*

½ cup (4 fl oz/125 ml) sweet Marsala

½ cup (4 oz/125 g) plus 3 tablespoons sugar

5 egg yolks

1 cup (8 fl oz/250 ml) heavy (double) cream, chilled

6 cups (1½ lb/750 g) fresh strawberries, hulled and sliced

# Dark Chocolate Gelato

Pour the milk into a heavy saucepan. Bring to a simmer over medium-high heat. Remove from the heat.

In a metal bowl, whisk together the egg yolks, sugar, and corn syrup until blended. Form a kitchen towel into a ring and place the bowl on top to prevent it from moving. Gradually pour the hot milk into the yolk mixture, whisking constantly. Return the mixture to the same saucepan and place over medium-low heat. Cook, stirring slowly and constantly with a wooden spatula, until the custard thickens and leaves a path on the back of the spatula when a finger is drawn across it, about 6 minutes; do not allow to boil. Pour the custard through a medium-mesh sieve set over a clean metal bowl. Add the chocolate and cocoa powder and stir until the chocolate melts. Refrigerate until cold, about 1 hour.

Transfer the custard to an ice-cream maker and freeze according to the manufacturer's instructions. For the best texture, serve the gelato immediately. Or transfer to a container, cover, and freeze until firm, at least 4 hours or for up to 3 days (the longer freezing results in a texture more like that of ice cream).

*Makes about 4 cups (32 fl oz/1 l); serves 6*

2 cups (16 fl oz/500 ml) whole milk

5 egg yolks

3/4 cup (6 oz/185 g) sugar

2 tablespoons light corn syrup

4 oz (125 g) semisweet (plain) chocolate, chopped

1/4 cup (3/4 oz/20 g) unsweetened cocoa powder

# Dried Fruit Pizza

This pizza's topping resembles an old-fashioned dried-fruit compote, making this a satisfying brunch or dessert dish. Port, madeira, or Vin Santo are appropriate dessert wines for soaking the fruit.

½ cup (3 oz/90 g) dried apricots

⅓ cup (2 oz/60 g) prunes, pitted

⅓ cup (2 oz/60 g) raisins

⅓ cup (2 oz/60 g) dried peaches

1¼ cups (10 fl oz/310 ml) dessert wine (see note)

Milk Pizza Dough (page 319)

⅓ cup (3 oz/90 g) sugar

⅓ cup (2 oz/60 g) blanched almonds

Place all the fruits together in a shallow bowl and add the wine to cover. Leave to soak for about 24 hours, occasionally stirring gently.

Make the pizza dough. Preheat the oven to 450°F (230°C). If using a baking stone or tiles, place in the oven now.

Drain the fruits, reserving the soaking liquid, and set the fruits aside. Pour the liquid into a saucepan and add the sugar. Cook over low heat, stirring, until a syrup forms that is thick enough to coat the back of a spoon, about 10 minutes.

Shape the pizza dough and cover with the drained fruits. Drizzle the wine syrup evenly over the top and decorate with the almonds. Transfer to the oven and bake for 10 minutes. Reduce the oven temperature to 400°F (200°C) and bake until the crust is golden, about 10 minutes longer. Serve immediately.

*Serves 4*

# Italian Plum Focaccia

This popular Italian bread is quite versatile and can be served as a savory or sweet version. The inclusion of sugar, butter, and eggs in this dough makes it well-suited to sweet toppings.

1 tablespoon active dry yeast

1/2 cup (4 fl oz/125 ml) warm milk (120°F/49°C)

1/2 cup (4 oz/125 g) granulated sugar

1/4 cup (2 oz/60 g) unsalted butter, very soft, plus extra for greasing

2 extra-large eggs, lightly beaten

2 teaspoons grated lime zest or 1 teaspoon lime oil

1/2 teaspoon salt

1/2 cup (2 1/2 oz/75 g) cornmeal

3 cups (15 oz/470 g) all-purpose (plain) flour, plus extra for sprinkling

Vegetable oil for oiling bowl

8 plums, cut in half and pitted

1 egg, lightly beaten with 1 tablespoon water

1–2 tablespoons coarse sugar

Place the yeast, warm milk, and 1 teaspoon of the granulated sugar in a large bowl. Stir to dissolve the yeast. When creamy on top, after about 5 minutes, add the butter, eggs, lime zest, salt, cornmeal, flour, and the remaining granulated sugar. Stir until a soft dough forms. Turn out onto a lightly floured surface and knead until smooth and no longer sticky, 5–8 minutes. Add more flour, if necessary, to keep the dough from sticking. Form the dough into a ball and place in a well-oiled bowl. Turn the ball to coat with oil, cover the bowl with plastic wrap, and set in a warm place to rise until doubled in bulk, about 1 hour. Alternatively, refrigerate the dough overnight.

Generously grease a heavy-duty baking sheet or pizza pan with butter. Punch down the dough and turn it out onto a lightly floured surface. Pat into an 11-inch (28-cm) round. Transfer to the prepared pan. Using a finger, poke 16 holes about 1 1/2 inches (4 cm) apart across the top of the dough. Insert a plum half, cut side up, into each hole. Push the plums firmly into the dough; they should rest in the small indentations. Brush the top with the egg-water mixture and sprinkle with the coarse sugar. Let rise in a warm place until almost doubled in bulk, about 30 minutes.

Meanwhile, preheat the oven to 400°F (200°C). Bake for 15 minutes. Reduce the oven temperature to 350°F (180°C) and bake until the focaccia is golden brown, about 15 minutes longer. If it begins browning too much, cover with aluminum foil. Serve hot or warm.

*Serves 10*

# Mixed Berry Pizza

While supermarkets now have some berries available virtually year-round, this recipe will still be best in the warm months when berries — strawberries, raspberries, blueberries, black currants, or some other local specialty — are at their seasonal best.

Make the pizza dough. Preheat the oven to 450°F (230°C). If using a baking stone or tiles, place in the oven now.

In a bowl, stir the liqueur into the ricotta. Shape the pizza dough and cover with the ricotta mixture. Top evenly with the berries. Sprinkle with the sugar. Transfer to the oven and bake for 10 minutes. Reduce the oven temperature to 400°F (200°C) and bake until the crust is golden, about 10 minutes longer. Serve immediately.

*Serves 4*

Milk Pizza Dough (page 319)

6 tablespoons (3 fl oz/90 ml) kirsch or Grand Marnier

3/4 cup (6 oz/185 g) plus 2 tablespoons ricotta cheese

2¼ cup (10 oz/315 g) mixed berries

6 tablespoons (3 oz/90 g) sugar

# Coconut-Ricotta Cream Pizza

Reminiscent of an elegant cheesecake, this pizza gains flavor, richness, and texture from the combination of ricotta cheese, grated coconut, and hazelnut (filbert)–flavored Frangelico liqueur.

6 tablespoons (3 fl oz/90 ml) Frangelico or other sweet liqueur

6 tablespoons (1 oz/30 g) finely grated dried coconut

Milk Pizza Dough (page 319)

1¼ cups (10 oz/315 g) ricotta cheese

6 tablespoons (3 oz/90 g) sugar

In a bowl, stir together the Frangelico and coconut and let stand at room temperature for about 24 hours to soften the coconut.

Make the pizza dough. Preheat the oven to 450°F (230°C). If using a baking stone or tiles, place in the oven now.

Add the ricotta and sugar to the coconut mixture and stir vigorously until it has the consistency of thick cream. Shape the pizza dough and cover with the coconut-ricotta mixture. Transfer the pizza to the oven and bake for 10 minutes. Reduce the oven temperature to 400°F (200°C) and bake until the crust is golden, about 10 minutes longer. Serve immediately.

*Serves 4*

# Fresh Fruit Pizza

This pizza resembles a home-style tart. In summer, use fruits that are in abundance — peaches, nectarines, apricots, plums, and cherries — in place of the apples and pears.

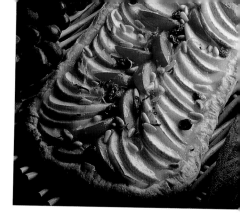

Make the pizza dough. Preheat the oven to 450°F (230°C). If using a baking stone or tiles, place in the oven now.

In a small bowl, soak the raisins in lukewarm water to cover for 30 minutes.

In a mixing bowl, vigorously stir the sugar and flour into the milk until fully dissolved. Add the eggs and whisk until well blended and a thick cream forms. Stir in the lemon zest.

Shape the pizza dough and cover with the apple and pear slices, alternating them and arranging them in attractive patterns. Pour the egg mixture evenly over the top. Drain the raisins; scatter them and the pine nuts on top. Transfer the pizza to the oven and bake for 10 minutes. Reduce the oven temperature to 400°F (200°C) and bake until the crust is golden, about 10 minutes longer. Serve immediately.

*Serves 4*

Milk Pizza Dough (page 319)

1/3 cup (2 oz/60 g) raisins

6 tablespoons (3 oz/90 g) sugar

2 tablespoons all-purpose (plain) flour

6 tablespoons (3 fl oz/90 ml) milk

2 eggs

1 tablespoon grated lemon zest

2 Golden or Red Delicious apples, peeled (optional), cored, and sliced

2 Bosc pears, peeled (optional), cored, and sliced

6 tablespoons (2 oz/60 g) pine nuts

# Gingered Pear Pizza

The red wine in which the pears are simmered gives them a lovely ruby color, while its acidity helps to keep them firm. Make sure to form the crust with a rim high enough to contain the syrup. Apples make a fine substitute for the pears.

Milk Pizza Dough (page 319)

4 Bosc pears, peeled, quartered, and cored

½ cup (4 oz/125 g) sugar

2½ cups (20 fl oz/625 ml) red wine

3 tablespoons peeled and grated fresh ginger

Make the pizza dough. Preheat the oven to 450°F (230°C). If using a baking stone or tiles, place in the oven now.

In a large saucepan over low heat, combine the pears, sugar, wine, and ginger. Cook, uncovered, until the pears are soft, about 10 minutes. Using a slotted spoon, transfer the pears to a bowl. Set aside. Cook the wine mixture over low heat, stirring occasionally, until a syrup forms that is thick enough to coat the back of a spoon, about 20 minutes.

Shape the pizza dough into one large pizza or 4 individual pizzas. Cover with the pears. Brush the pears with the wine syrup. Transfer to the oven and bake for 10 minutes. Reduce the oven temperature to 400°F (200°C) and bake until the crust is golden, about 10 minutes longer. Serve immediately.

*Serves 4*

# Orange and Grand Marnier Pizza

Pretty enough to serve for dessert, this pizza is only slightly sweet, making it an ideal dish to offer guests at breakfast, brunch, or lunch. It works just as well with apples or pears in place of the oranges.

Make the pizza dough. Preheat the oven to 450°F (230°C). If using a baking stone or tiles, place in the oven now.

Pour the sugar into a saucepan and melt it over low heat, without stirring. When the edges begin to turn gold, stir with a wooden spoon until the sugar turns gold and syrupy. Remove from the heat and add the marmalade, Grand Marnier, and orange slices. Stir gently until the slices are well coated. Using tongs, pick up the slices, one at a time, and transfer them to a wire rack to drain. Reserve the syrup and keep hot.

Shape the pizza dough and cover with the orange slices arranged in concentric circles. Transfer to the oven and bake for 10 minutes. Reduce the oven temperature to 400°F (200°C) and bake until the crust is golden, about 10 minutes longer. Arrange the strawberry slices, if using, on top and drizzle with the hot syrup. Serve immediately.

*Serves 4*

Milk Pizza Dough (page 319)

1/2 cup (4 oz/125 g) sugar

1/2 cup (5 oz/155 g) orange marmalade

1/4 cup (2 fl oz/60 ml) Grand Marnier

4 unpeeled, organic oranges, scrubbed and sliced crosswise about 1/4 inch (6 mm) thick

9 strawberries, stemmed and sliced lengthwise (optional)

# Baked Figs with Zabaglione

For this recipe, choose either green Adriatic or black Mission figs; they should be ripe and feel heavy in your hand. Zabaglione, a classic dessert traditionally flavored with Marsala, gives the dish a wonderful Italian accent.

24 small or 12 large ripe figs

¼ cup (3 oz/90 g) honey

½ cup (4 fl oz/125 ml) fresh orange juice

¼ cup (2 fl oz/60 ml) fresh lemon juice

¼ cup (2 fl oz/60 ml) anisette (optional)

4 small bay leaves

3 or 4 thin lemon or orange zest strips

FOR THE ZABAGLIONE:

1 cup (8 fl oz/250 ml) dry Marsala

7 egg yolks

½ cup (4 oz/125 g) sugar

Grated zest of 1 orange or lemon (optional)

6 orange or lemon zest strips (optional)

Preheat the oven to 350°F (180°C).

Prick the figs in a few places with a fork so they can absorb the cooking juices. Arrange them upright in a baking dish in which they fit snugly. In a small bowl, whisk together the honey and orange and lemon juices and the anisette, if using. Pour over the figs. If necessary, add a little water so that the liquid covers the bottom of the dish by a depth of about ¼ inch (6 mm). Tuck the bay leaves and 3 lemon or orange zest strips around the figs.

Cover and bake, basting occasionally with the pan juices, until the figs are soft and slightly puffy, 25–35 minutes. Remove from the oven and let cool slightly.

While the figs are cooling, make the zabaglione. Bring a saucepan half full of water to a simmer. In a large metal bowl, whisk together the Marsala, egg yolks, sugar, and the grated orange or lemon zest, if using, until foamy. Set the bowl over (not touching) the simmering water. Whisk constantly until very thick, pale, and frothy, 10–15 minutes. (If you doubt your stamina, use a handheld electric mixer set on medium speed.) Remove the bowl from over the water.

Place the warm figs on individual plates, dividing evenly. Spoon the pan juices over them. Top with the warm zabaglione, garnish with zest strips, if desired, and serve.

*Serves 6*

# Hazelnut and Date Panforte

Italy's answer to fruitcake, panforte is a specialy of Siena in Tuscany.
If you prefer a candylike texture, serve this Italian specialty chilled. To store,
wrap airtight and refrigerate for up to 1 month.

1¼ cups (6½ oz/200 g) hazelnuts (filberts), lightly toasted (page 329) and cooled

⅓ cup (2 oz/60 g) all-purpose (plain) flour

⅓ cup (1 oz/30 g) unsweetened cocoa powder, plus extra for dusting

¾ teaspoon ground cinnamon

½ teaspoon ground nutmeg

¼ teaspoon ground cloves

¾ cup (4 oz/125 g) packed coarsely chopped dried figs

¾ cup (4 oz/125 g) packed coarsely chopped pitted dates

½ cup (3 oz/90 g) diced candied orange peel or candied pineapple

1 tablespoon grated orange zest

½ cup (4 oz/125 g) plus 2 tablespoons sugar

½ cup (6 oz/185 g) honey

¼ cup (2 fl oz/60 ml) fresh orange juice

2 tablespoons unsalted butter, plus extra for greasing

8 oz (250 g) semisweet chocolate, chopped

Preheat the oven to 300°F (150°C). Grease a round cake pan 8 inches (20 cm) in diameter and 2 inches (5 cm) deep. Line the bottom with parchment (baking) paper cut to fit precisely. Generously grease the paper.

In a bowl, stir together the toasted hazelnuts, flour, the cocoa powder, cinnamon, nutmeg, cloves, figs, dates, orange peel, and orange zest. In a heavy saucepan over medium heat, stir together the sugar, honey, orange juice, and butter. Heat, stirring, until the sugar dissolves, about 3 minutes. Raise the heat to medium-high. Boil without stirring until a candy thermometer registers 250°F (120°C), 5 minutes. Remove from the heat and stir in the fruit mixture with a wooden spoon. Transfer the mixture to the cake pan, spreading it to the sides with the spoon. Bake until the top feels dry, about 50 minutes. Transfer to a wire rack and let cool in the pan for 10 minutes. Invert onto a baking sheet, peel off the paper, and let cool completely.

Place the chocolate in the top pan of a double boiler or in a heatproof bowl. Set over (not touching) simmering water. Stir until smooth and melted. Pour half of the chocolate over the top of the cake and smooth with an icing spatula. Refrigerate until set, about 1 hour.

Turn the cake over. Reheat the remaining chocolate over simmering water just until warm. Pour over the cake and, using the spatula, spread to cover the top and sides. Refrigerate for 1 hour.

Using a fine-mesh sieve, sift enough cocoa powder over both sides of the cake to cover lightly. Cut into wedges and serve.

*Makes one 8-inch (20-cm) cake; serves 12*

# Almond, Lemon, and Anise Biscotti

A new twist on a traditional recipe for mandelbrot, the Jewish version of biscotti. Anise adds an exotic flavor, but without it, the recipe turns out delicious lemon cookies. These cookies can be made in advance and stored for up to 2 weeks.

Preheat the oven to 350°F (180°C).

In a large bowl, combine the eggs, the ³/₄ cup (6 oz/185 g) granulated sugar, the oil, lemon zest, aniseeds, baking powder, vanilla, and salt. Whisk to blend. Add the flour and almonds and stir until a dough forms. Turn out onto a lightly floured work surface and knead until smooth, about 10 turns. Divide the dough in half.

Form each half into a log 2 inches (5 cm) in diameter. Carefully transfer the logs to an ungreased baking sheet, spacing them well apart, and pat to even the shapes. Sprinkle the tops with additional granulated sugar.

Bake until firm to the touch, about 30 minutes (the logs will spread during baking). Remove from the oven and let cool on the baking sheet for 10 minutes. Leave the oven set at 350°F (180°C).

Using a spatula, carefully transfer the logs to a work surface. Using a serrated knife, cut crosswise into slices ¹/₂ inch (12 mm) thick. Arrange the slices cut side down on the baking sheet. Return to the oven and bake until brown, about 20 minutes.

Transfer the cookies to wire racks to cool. Store in an airtight container at room temperature for up to 2 weeks.

*Makes about 3 dozen*

2 eggs

³/₄ cup (6 oz/185 g) granulated sugar, plus extra for sprinkling (optional)

¹/₂ cup (4 fl oz/125 ml) vegetable oil

1 tablespoon grated lemon zest

2 teaspoons aniseeds, crushed

1¹/₄ teaspoons baking powder

1 teaspoon vanilla extract (essence)

¹/₄ teaspoon salt

2 cups (10 oz/315 g) all-purpose (plain) flour

1 cup (5¹/₂ oz/170 g) whole almonds, coarsely chopped

Vanilla Sugar for sprinkling (page 323)

# Cassata alla Siciliana

This dessert is a specialty of a wonderful Italian restaurant in Provincetown, Massachusetts, called Ciro and Sal's. They make it with white pound cake, but chocolate would also work well.

FOR THE FROSTING:

4 oz (125 g) semisweet (plain) chocolate, chopped

³/₄ cup (6 oz/185 g) unsalted butter, at room temperature

¹/₂ cup (4 fl oz/125 ml) brewed espresso, or 1 tablespoon instant espresso powder or granules dissolved in ¹/₂ cup (4 fl oz/125 ml) boiling water

FOR THE CAKE:

2 cups (1 lb/500 g) whole-milk ricotta cheese

¹/₃ cup (1.5 oz/45 g) confectioners' (icing) sugar

Finely grated zest of 1 orange

2–3 oz (60–90 g) semisweet (plain), or milk chocolate, in one thick chunk

1 white or chocolate pound cake, purchased or homemade

4 tablespoons (2 fl oz/60 ml) orange-flavored liqueur

To make the frosting, place the chocolate, butter, and espresso in a small heatproof bowl or the top pan of a double boiler. Set over (not touching) a pan of gently simmering water. Stir until melted, smooth, and thoroughly combined. Remove the bowl from the heat and refrigerate, stirring every 15 minutes, until firm, about 1 hour. (To firm up the frosting more quickly, nest the bowl in a bowl of ice and stir it every 5 minutes. It will take 15–20 minutes to become firm.)

In a bowl, stir together the ricotta, confectioners' sugar, and orange zest. Using a plastic or metal grater, grate the chunk of chocolate into the bowl and fold it in using a rubber spatula.

Using a serrated knife, cut the pound cake twice horizontally to form 3 equal layers. Place 1 layer on a flat plate and sprinkle 2 tablespoons of the liqueur over it. Spread half of the ricotta mixture on top. Top with the second cake layer, sprinkle with the remaining 2 tablespoons liqueur, and spread with the remaining ricotta mixture. Top with the third cake layer. Using an icing metal spatula, frost the top and sides with the cooled frosting. Refrigerate until serving, but no longer than 8 hours.

*Serves 8*

# Espresso Tiramisù

Tiramisù (literally, "pick me up") is an Italian dessert that has become highly popular in recent years. It is traditionally made with ladyfingers, but homemade or purchased pound cake works well, too.

3 cups (1½ lb/750 g) mascarpone cheese

1½ cups (6 oz/185 g) confectioners' (icing) sugar

¼ cup (2 fl oz/60 ml) Marsala

¾ cup (6 fl oz/180 ml) cold heavy (double) cream

⅔ cup (5 fl oz/160 ml) water

5 teaspoons instant espresso powder or regular coffee powder

1 pound cake, purchased or homemade, cut crosswise into slices ¼–⅓ inch (6–9 mm) thick

Unsweetened cocoa powder for dusting

In a bowl, using an electric mixer set on medium speed, beat together the mascarpone cheese, 1 cup (4 oz/125 g) of the confectioners' sugar, and the Marsala until well blended. Add the cream and beat until fluffy, about 1 minute. Set aside.

In a small, heavy saucepan over high heat, combine ⅔ cup (5 fl oz/160 ml) water, the remaining ½ cup (2 oz/60 g) confectioners' sugar, and the espresso powder. Bring to a boil, stirring occasionally. Remove from the heat and let cool.

In a 2½-qt (2.5-l) oval or rectangular glass dish about 11 inches (28 cm) long and 2 inches (5 cm) deep, arrange enough of the cake slices in a single layer to cover the bottom completely, trimming to fit as needed. Brush half of the sugar syrup over the cake slices and then pour in half of the cheese mixture. Top with enough of the remaining cake slices to cover in a single layer, again trimming to fit. Brush with the remaining syrup. Spread the remaining cheese mixture over the top. Cover with plastic wrap and refrigerate until firm, at least 2 hours or up to 2 days.

Using a fine-mesh sieve, sift cocoa powder over the top just before serving. Using a large spoon, scoop the tiramisù onto individual plates.

*Serves 10–12*

# Poached Pears with Zabaglione

The slightly grainy texture of the cold, honeyed pears contrasts beautifully with the warm richness of Italy's famed frothy dessert. Use Comice or Bartlett (Williams') Pears, which are good for poaching.

Peel the pears and cut in half lengthwise. Using a small spoon or a melon baller, remove the core from each half to make an even cavity, then cut out the stem. In a large frying pan, combine the wine, 1 cup (8 fl oz/250 ml) water, honey, and lemon zest. Bring to a boil, stirring often. Reduce the heat to low and simmer for 5 minutes. Add the pear halves, cut sides down. Poach, turning once, until tender, 5–10 minutes. Let the pears cool in the poaching liquid, then cover and refrigerate.

To make the zabaglione, bring a saucepan half full of water to a simmer. In a large metal bowl, combine the egg yolks, whole egg, and sugar. Place the bowl over (not touching) the simmering water. Using a wire whisk or a handheld electric mixer, beat until pale yellow and fluffy, about 3 minutes. Gradually add the Marsala, beating until the mixture is just thick enough to hold its shape in a spoon, 6–7 minutes. Remove the bowl from over the water.

Divide the zabaglione among 4 individual bowls. Using a slotted spoon, transfer 2 pear halves to each bowl, cavity sides up. Mound some of the mascarpone in each cavity and garnish with mint sprigs, if desired. Serve at once.

*Serves 4*

4 firm but ripe pears

1 cup (8 fl oz/250 ml) sweet white dessert wine

1/2 cup (6 oz/185 g) honey

1 lemon zest strip, 3 inches (7.5 cm) long by 1 inch (2.5 cm) wide

FOR THE ZABAGLIONE:

5 egg yolks, plus 1 whole egg

3 tablespoons sugar

1/2 cup (4 fl oz/125 ml) Marsala wine

1/4 cup (2 oz/60 g) mascarpone or whipped cream cheese, at room temperature

Fresh mint sprigs (optional)

# Pine Nut and Honey Biscotti

The characteristic dryness of this tasty cookie makes it a wonderful companion for a cup of espresso or a glass of sweet dessert wine. For a different flavor, substitute almonds for the pine nuts.

2 cups (10 oz/315 g) all-purpose (plain) flour

1 teaspoon baking powder

1/2 teaspoon baking soda (bicarbonate of soda)

1/2 teaspoon salt

1/2 cup (4 fl oz/125 ml) vegetable oil

1/2 cup (4 oz/125 g) sugar

1/2 cup (6 oz/185 g) honey

2 eggs

2 teaspoons grated orange zest

1 teaspoon vanilla extract (essence)

1 1/2 cups (8 oz/250 g) pine nuts, lightly toasted (page 329)

In a bowl, sift together the flour, baking powder, baking soda, and salt. In a large bowl, combine the oil, sugar, honey, eggs, orange zest, and vanilla. Stir until smooth. Add the flour mixture and stir until smooth. Fold in the pine nuts. Cover and refrigerate until well chilled, about 3 hours.

Preheat the oven to 350°F (180°C). Butter and flour 2 large baking sheets. Spoon two-thirds of the batter into 2 rough log shapes on 1 sheet, spacing them well apart, and spoon the remaining batter into 1 log shape on the second sheet. Using well-floured hands, form into smooth logs 2 inches (5 cm) wide and 1 inch (2.5 cm) high.

Bake until just springy to the touch, about 25 minutes (the logs will spread during baking). Remove from the oven and let cool slightly on the baking sheets. Leave the oven set at 350°F (180°C).

Using a spatula, carefully transfer the logs to a work surface. Using a serrated knife, cut crosswise into slices 1/2 inch (12 mm) thick. Arrange the slices cut sides down on the baking sheets and bake for 5 minutes. Remove from the oven and turn the slices over. Bake until browned, about 5 minutes longer.

Transfer the cookies to wire racks to cool. Store in an airtight container at room temperature for up to 2 weeks.

*Makes about 4 dozen*

# Ginger-Almond Florentines

Here is delicious light cookie to rival any you might purchase at a premium bakery. They keep for up to 2 weeks if layered between sheets of waxed paper and refrigerated in an airtight container.

Preheat the oven to 350°F (180°C). Line 2 large, heavy baking sheets with aluminum foil. Lightly grease the foil with butter.

Combine the cream, granulated sugar, brown sugar, and 2 tablespoons butter in a heavy saucepan. Cook over medium heat, stirring constantly, just until the sugars dissolve and the butter melts. Add the almonds, flour, ginger, and orange and lemon zests. Bring the mixture to a boil, stirring constantly. Remove from the heat.

Drop 1 tablespoon batter (it will be runny) onto a prepared baking sheet. Repeat five times, spacing the cookies 3 inches (7.5 cm) apart. Repeat with the second baking sheet.

Bake until deep brown, about 10 minutes. Remove from the oven. Using a round cookie cutter or a glass 3 inches (7.5 cm) in diameter, push the hot cookie edges in toward the center to neaten them, shaping into 3-inch (7.5-cm) rounds. Slide the foil off the baking sheets. Line the same sheets with new foil, grease the foil, and repeat with the remaining batter.

Cool the cookies completely on the foil. Carefully peel the cookies off the foil and arrange them smooth side up on the baking sheets. Spoon 1 teaspoon of the hot chocolate coating in the center of each cookie and, using a small icing spatula or knife, spread to the edges. Refrigerate until the chocolate is set, about 30 minutes. Store in an airtight container in the refrigerator for up to 2 weeks.

*Makes about 2 dozen*

2 tablespoons unsalted butter, at room temperature, plus extra for greasing

1/2 cup (4 fl oz/125 ml) plus 2 tablespoons heavy (double) cream

1/2 cup (4 oz/125 g) granulated sugar

1/4 cup (2 oz/60 g) firmly packed dark brown sugar

2/3 cup (3 oz/90 g) sliced almonds, lightly toasted (page 329)

1/4 cup (1 1/2 oz/45 g) all-purpose (plain) flour

1/4 cup (1/2 oz/15 g) finely chopped crystallized ginger

2 teaspoons grated orange zest

1 1/2 teaspoons grated lemon zest

1/2 recipe chocolate coating (page 323)

# Chocolate-Hazelnut Biscotti

4 oz (125 g) semisweet (plain) chocolate, coarsely chopped

1 cup (7 oz/220 g) firmly packed light brown sugar

1³/₄ cups (9 oz/280 g) all-purpose (plain) flour

¹/₃ cup (1 oz/30 g) unsweetened cocoa powder, preferably Dutch process

1¹/₂ tablespoons instant espresso powder

1 teaspoon baking soda (bicarbonate of soda)

¹/₄ teaspoon salt

3 eggs

1¹/₄ teaspoons vanilla extract (essence)

¹/₂ teaspoon almond extract (essence)

1 cup (5 oz/155 g) hazelnuts (filberts), toasted (page 329)

Chocolate coating (page 323)

Preheat the oven to 300°F (150°C). Line a large baking sheet with parchment (baking) paper or waxed paper.

In a food processor fitted with the metal blade, combine the chocolate and brown sugar and process until the chocolate is very fine. Set aside. Alternatively, using a blender and working in 4 batches, process 1 oz (30 g) chocolate and ¹/₄ cup (2 oz/60 g) brown sugar at a time.

In a large bowl, sift together the flour, cocoa powder, espresso powder, baking soda, and salt. In another large bowl, combine the eggs, vanilla, and almond extract. Using an electric mixer set on medium speed, beat to blend. On low speed, mix in the sugar and flour mixtures until a stiff dough forms, adding the hazelnuts when about half mixed.

On a lightly floured work surface, divide the dough in half. Form each half into a log 12 inches (30 cm) long. Carefully transfer the logs to the prepared baking sheet, spacing them well apart, and pat to even the shapes. Bake until almost firm to the touch, 50 minutes (the logs will spread during baking). Remove from the oven and let cool on the baking sheet for 10 minutes. Leave the oven set at 300°F (150°C).

Using a spatula, carefully transfer the logs to a work surface. Using a serrated knife, cut on the diagonal into slices ¹/₂–³/₄ inch (12 mm–2 cm) thick. Arrange the slices cut sides down on the baking sheet. Bake 25 minutes. Turn the slices over and bake until crisp and dry, about 25 minutes longer. Turn off the oven and let cool completely in the oven with the door slightly ajar.

Dip one side of the cooled cookies in the hot chocolate coating and set, chocolate side up, on a baking sheet. Refrigerate until set. Store refrigerated in an airtight container for up to 2 weeks.

*Makes about 2¹/₂ dozen*

# Basic Recipes & Techniques

These basic recipes and techniques are used throughout *Italian Favorites*. Once you have mastered them, you'll turn to them again and again to create delicious meals.

## Basic Pizza Dough

1 tablespoon active dry yeast

3/4 cup plus 2 tablespoons
(7 fl oz/210 ml) lukewarm water
(90–105°F/32–40°C)

2 3/4 cups (14 oz/440 g)
all-purpose (plain) flour, plus
extra for dusting

1 teaspoon salt

1 tablespoon extra-virgin olive oil

In a small bowl, dissolve the yeast in the water and let stand until slightly foamy on top, about 10 minutes.

In a bowl, stir together the flour and the salt and form into a mound. Make a well in the center and add the yeast mixture to the well. Using a fork and stirring in a circular motion, gradually pull the flour into the yeast mixture. Continue stirring until a dough forms.

Transfer the dough to a lightly floured work surface. Using the heel of your hand, knead the dough until it is smooth and elastic, about 10 minutes. As you work, sprinkle additional flour on the work surface 1 tablespoon at a time only if needed to prevent sticking. Form the dough into a ball.

Brush the inside of a large bowl with the olive oil and place the dough in it. Cover with plastic wrap and let rise at room temperature until doubled, about 1–2 hours.

Turn the dough out onto a lightly floured work surface. Punch the dough down and, using your hands, begin to press it out gently into the desired shape. Then place one hand in the center of the dough and pull, lift, and stretch the dough with the other hand, gradually working your way all around the edge, until it is the desired thickness, about 1/4 inch (6 mm) for a crusty pizza base and 1/2 inch (12 mm) for a softer one. Flip the dough over from time to time as you work with it. Alternatively, roll out the dough with a rolling pin. The dough should be slightly thinner in the middle than at the edge. Lift the edge of the pizza to form a slight rim.

Transfer the dough to a baking stone or baking sheet, cover with a kitchen towel, and let rise again until almost doubled, 20 minutes. Top and bake as directed in the individual recipes.

*Makes 1 1/3 lb (650 g) dough, enough for a 12-inch (30-cm) thin-crust pizza or a 9-inch (23-cm) thick-crust pizza*

## Cornmeal Pizza Dough

To make this dough, select very fine-grind cornmeal, not the medium or coarse grind used for Italian polenta. As with the whole-wheat (wholemeal) dough, the cornmeal will weigh down the flour, producing a heavier crust well-suited to hearty toppings.

1 tablespoon active dry yeast

3/4 cup plus 2 tablespoons
(7 fl oz/210 ml) lukewarm water
(90–105°F/32–40°C)

2 1/2 cups (12 1/2 oz/390 g)
all-purpose (plain) flour, plus
extra for dusting

1/3 cup (2 oz/60 g) fine yellow
cornmeal

1 teaspoon salt

1 tablespoon extra-virgin olive oil

In a small bowl, dissolve the yeast in the water and let stand until slightly foamy on top, about 10 minutes.

In a large bowl, stir together the flour, cornmeal, and salt and form into a mound. Make a well in the center and add the yeast mixture to the well. Using a fork and stirring in a circular motion, gradually pull the flour into the yeast mixture. Continue stirring until a dough forms.

Proceed as directed for Basic Pizza Dough (left).

*Makes 1 1/4 lb (625 g) dough, enough for a 12-inch (30-cm) thin-crust pizza or a 9-inch (23-cm) thick-crust pizza*

## Herb Pizza Dough

Choose herbs such as oregano, basil, marjoram, chives, thyme, rosemary, sage, mint, and fennel seeds. It is better to choose two or three complementary herbs, or even just one herb, rather than a large mixture.

1 tablespoon active dry yeast

3/4 cup plus 2 tablespoons (7 fl oz/210 ml) lukewarm water (90–105°F/32–40°C)

2 3/4 cups (14 oz/640 g) all-purpose (plain) flour, plus extra for dusting

1 teaspoon salt

2 tablespoons minced fresh herbs or 1 tablespoon mixed dried herbs

1 tablespoon extra-virgin olive oil

Proceed as directed for Basic Pizza Dough (page 318), stirring the herbs together with the flour and salt.
*Makes 1 1/3 lb (650 g) dough, enough for a 12-inch (30-cm) thin-crust pizza or a 9-inch (23-cm) thick-crust pizza*

## Milk Pizza Dough

This soft, butter-enriched dough produces a thin, crisp crust that complements sweet toppings.

2 1/2 cups (12 1/2 oz/390 g) all-purpose (plain) flour, plus extra for dusting

3/4 cup (6 fl oz/180 ml) milk

5 tablespoons (2 1/2 oz/75 g) unsalted butter, at room temperature

1 teaspoon baking powder

1 teaspoon salt

In a large bowl, combine the flour, milk, butter, baking powder, and salt. Stir with a fork until a soft dough forms. Shape into a ball.

Turn the dough out onto a lightly floured work surface. Using a rolling pin, roll out the dough into a round 1/8 inch (3 mm) thick and 12 inches (30 cm) in diameter. Flip it over occasionally as you roll it out, sprinkling additional flour on the work surface as needed to prevent sticking. The dough should be slightly thinner in the middle than at the edge. Lift the edge of the pizza to form a slight rim. Transfer the dough to a baking stone or baking sheet. Top and bake as directed.
*Makes 1 1/4 lb (625 g) dough, enough for a 12-inch (30-cm) pizza*

## Potato Pizza Dough

The moisture content of potatoes varies, so keep an eye on how much water you add to the dough; hold a little back if your dough seems too moist, or add a little more if it is too dry.

1 boiling potato, 5 oz (150 g)

1 tablespoon active dry yeast

3/4 cup plus 2 tablespoons (7 fl oz/210 ml) lukewarm water (90–105°F/32°–40°C)

2 1/2 cups (12 1/2 oz/390 g) all-purpose (plain) flour, plus extra for dusting

1 teaspoon salt

1 tablespoon extra-virgin olive oil

Boil the potato in water to cover until tender, 20–30 minutes; drain and peel while still hot.

Meanwhile, in a small bowl, dissolve the yeast in the water and let stand until slightly foamy on top, about 10 minutes.

In a large bowl, stir together the flour and the salt. Pass the hot peeled potato through a sieve into the bowl and stir to combine. Form the mixture into a mound. Make a well in the center and add the yeast mixture to the well. Using a fork and stirring in a circular motion, gradually pull the flour and potato into the yeast mixture. Continue stirring until a dough forms.

Proceed as directed for Basic Pizza Dough (page 318).
*Makes 1 1/2 lb (750 g) dough, enough for a 12-inch (30-cm) thin-crust pizza or a 9-inch (23-cm) thick-crust pizza*

## Whole-Wheat Pizza Dough

This dough goes well with more robust pizza and calzone ingredients. Because of its increased fiber content, it will not rise as high, producing a denser, chewier crust. If you want both flavor and lightness, use half whole-wheat flour and half all-purpose (plain) flour.

1 tablespoon active dry yeast

3/4 cup plus 2 tablespoons (7 fl oz/210 ml) lukewarm water (90–105°F/32–40°C)

2 3/4 cups (14 oz/440 g) whole-wheat (wholemeal) flour, plus extra for dusting

1 teaspoon salt

1 tablespoon extra-virgin olive oil

Follow directions for Basic Pizza Dough (page 318), substituting whole-wheat (wholemeal) flour for the all-purpose (plain) flour.

*Makes 1 1/3 lb (650 g) dough, enough for a 12-inch (30-cm) thin-crust pizza or a 9-inch (23-cm) thick-crust pizza*

# Bouquet Garni

This combination of herbs and spices enhances a variety of stews. Add it to the stews as they simmer, then discard before serving.

6 whole peppercorns

1 bay leaf

1 clove garlic, sliced

3 fresh parsley sprigs

Cut a 6-inch (15-cm) square of cheese-cloth (muslin). Place the peppercorns, bay leaf, garlic, and parsley sprigs on the center of the cheesecloth, bring the corners together and tie securely with kitchen string. Alternatively, combine all the ingredients in a tea ball and secure the tip in place. Use as directed in individual recipes.

# Beef Stock

Based on beef and chicken, it can also include veal bones; avoid using lamb or pork, unless you want a broth with their distinctive flavors. Store any stock you will not be using right away in small freezer containers.

2 leeks, trimmed and carefully washed

4 lb (2 kg) meaty beef bones such as shank (shin) or short ribs

2 lb (1 kg) stewing chicken parts or wings, backs, or necks

6 cloves garlic, unpeeled

4 large carrots, unpeeled, cut into 1-inch (2.5 cm) chunks

2 celery stalks with leaves, cut into 1-inch (2.5 cm) chunks

2 large yellow onions

3 whole cloves

6 fresh parsley sprigs

3 fresh thyme sprigs

1 bay leaf

1 teaspoon peppercorns

Salt

Cut the white portion of the leeks into 1-inch (2.5 cm) chunks and place in a large stockpot; reserve the green tops. Add the beef, chicken, garlic, carrots, and celery. Stud one of the onions with the cloves and add both onions to the pot. Nestle the parsley, thyme, and bay leaf between the reserved leek tops and tie securely with kitchen string. Add to the pot along with 5 qt (5 l) water.

Over low to medium heat, slowly bring the liquid to a simmer, skimming off the foam that rises to the surface until no more forms. Add the peppercorns, cover partially, and simmer gently for 3 1/2–4 hours, skimming occasionally.

Line a strainer with a double layer of dampened cheesecloth (muslin) and set it inside a large bowl. Pour the contents of the pot into the strainer. Discard the solids. Season the stock to taste with salt and let cool to room temperature, then cover and refrigerate. A layer of fat will solidify on the surface of the stock; lift or spoon it off and discard. The stock may be stored in a tightly covered container in the refrigerator for up to 3 days or in the freezer for up to 6 months.

*Makes about 4 qt (4 l)*

# Chicken Stock

This is one of the most versatile stocks you can make. It is excellent served on its own, ladled over steamed rice or noodles. If you're not using all of it right away, freeze the unused stock in small containers. Stewing chicken parts make a particularly flavorful stock and are less costly than fryer or broiler parts.

1 leek, trimmed and carefully washed

6 lb (3 kg) stewing chicken parts

1 large yellow onion, unpeeled, root trimmed

1 large carrot, unpeeled, cut into 1-inch (2.5-cm) chunks

1 stalk celery with leaves, cut into 1-inch (2.5-cm) chunks

6 fresh parsley sprigs

3 fresh thyme sprigs

1 bay leaf

1/2 teaspoon peppercorns

Salt

Cut the white portion of the leek into 1-inch (2.5 cm) chunks and place in a large stockpot; reserve the green tops.

Add the chicken, onion, carrot, and celery to the pot. Nestle the parsley, thyme, and bay leaf between the reserved leek tops and tie securely with kitchen string. Add to the pot along with 5 qt (5 l) water.

Over low to medium heat, slowly bring the liquid to a simmer, regularly skimming off the foam that rises to the surface until no more forms. Add the peppercorns, cover partially, and continue simmering gently for about 2 hours, skimming occasionally.

Line a strainer with a double layer of dampened cheesecloth (muslin) and set it inside a large bowl. Pour the contents of the pot into the strainer. Discard the solids. Season the stock to taste with salt and let cool to room temperature then refrigerate. A layer of fat will solidify on the surface of the stock; lift or spoon it off and discard. The stock may be stored in a tightly covered container in the refrigerator for up to 3 days or in the freezer for up to 6 months.

*Makes about 4 qt (4 l)*

## Fish Stock

For a quick substitute to homemade fish stock, use bottled, canned, or frozen fish stock; or dissolve 1 fish bouillon cube in 1 cup (8 fl oz/ 250 ml) hot water for each cup of fish stock that is required. Since commercial fish stock base can be quite salty, adjust the seasoning in each recipe as necessary.

2 tablespoons olive oil

2 yellow onions, coarsely chopped

1 large leek, white part only, carefully washed and coarsely chopped

3 celery stalks with leaves, coarsely chopped

1½ lb (750 g) white fish fillets, such as cod, flounder or sole

8 cups (64 fl oz/2 l) water

bouquet garni (page 320)

½ teaspoon salt, optional

In a large stockpot over medium heat, warm the olive oil. Add the onions, leek and celery and sauté, stirring, until slightly tender but not quite translucent, about 5 minutes. Add the fish and saute, stirring, for 5 minutes longer. Pour in the water and add the bouquet garni and the salt, if desired. Bring to a simmer, then reduce the heat to low, cover and simmer gently for 20 minutes. Do not allow the stock to boil.

Remove from the heat and strain through a fine-mesh sieve lined with cheesecloth (muslin) into a clean container. Reserve the fish fillets for another use, if desired. Use stock immediately, or cover and refrigerate overnight or freeze for up to 6 months.

*Makes 6–8 cups (48–56 fl oz/1.5–1.75 l)*

## Vegetable Stock

2 large leeks, trimmed and carefully washed

2 large carrots, sliced

2 large stalks celery, sliced

2 large yellow onions, sliced

3 cloves garlic, unpeeled

3 fresh parsley sprigs

2 fresh thyme sprigs

1 bay leaf

½ teaspoon white peppercorns

Salt

2 qt (2 l) water

Slice the white portion of the leeks and place in a large stockpot; reserve the green tops. Add the carrots, celery, onions, and garlic to the pot. Nestle the parsley, thyme, and bay leaf between the reserved leek tops and tie securely with kitchen string. Add to the pot along with the 2 qt (2 l) water.

Over low to medium heat, slowly bring the liquid to a simmer, regularly skimming off the foam that rises to the surface until no more forms. Add the white peppercorns, cover partially, and continue simmering gently for 1–1 ½ hours.

Line a strainer with a double layer of dampened cheesecloth (muslin) and set it inside a large bowl. Pour the contents of the pot into the strainer. Discard the solids. Season the stock to taste with salt and let cool to room temperature. Cover tightly and refrigerate. The stock may be refrigerated for up to 3 days or frozen for up to 6 months.

*Makes about 6 cups (48 fl oz/1.5 l)*

# Fresh Egg Pasta

Cooks today have discovered what Italian home cooks knew all along: that egg-and-flour pasta is incredibly easy to make at home. Whether you do it by hand or use a machine, you can have fresh pasta ready to cook and eat in minutes. Contrary to what some modern aficionados of fresh pasta might think, Italians do not regard it as better than dried pasta; it is simply different.

The proportions given below for fresh pasta ingredients are approximate, and may vary with the actual size of the eggs you use, how you measure the flour, the absorbency of the flour, and how dry or humid the weather is when you make the pasta. In the end, your eyes and your hands are the best judges of how the fresh pasta is proceeding, so pay careful attention to the visual and tactile cues in the recipe.

2 cups (10 oz/315 g) all-purpose (plain) flour, plus extra for dusting

3 eggs

**Hand Method:** Heap the flour on a pastry board, wooden countertop, or plastic surface. Make a well in the center and break the eggs into it. Using a fork, lightly beat the eggs. With a circular movement, gradually incorporate the flour from the walls of the well. When you have pulled in enough flour to form a ball too stiff to beat with the fork, continue with the palm of your hand, until as much flour as possible is incorporated. Using the palm and heel of your hand, knead the dough as you would bread dough, pushing it against the board and turning it constantly, until it is smooth, elastic, and not too soft, about 15 minutes.

**Food Processor Method:** Combine the flour and eggs in a food processor. Pulse briefly a few times to combine the ingredients. Then process using long pulses just until the dough forms a ball around the blade, about 1 minute. Turn the dough out onto a work surface and knead with the palm of your hand as described above.

**Rolling Out the Dough:** To roll out the pasta, dust a clean work surface with flour. Flatten the ball of dough with the palm of your hand and use a rolling pin to roll it out evenly, always rolling away from you and rotating the disk as it becomes thinner and thinner. Dust the work surface with additional flour as needed to prevent sticking. The pasta sheet should be about $1/32$ inch (1 mm) thick for tagliatelle, lasagne, and taglierini, and $1/64$ inch (.5 mm) thick for filled pasta.

Lightly sprinkle a kitchen towel with flour and leave the pasta to dry a while on it, about 10 minutes, or less if the air is very dry. It should be dried until it is neither sticky nor brittle.

**Cutting the Dough:** For filled pasta, follow the individual recipe instructions for how to cut and fill specific shapes. You will need only 12 oz (375 g) of the pasta dough to make enough filled pasta for 6 people.

For noodles, roll the pasta sheet into a cylinder, flatten the top lightly with your hand, and, using a sharp knife, cut across the roll into strips a scant $1/8$ inch (2 mm) wide for taglierini, $3/8$ inch (1 cm) for tagliatelle and fettuccine, and $1 1/4$ inches (3 cm) for pappardelle. Lifting a few strips of pasta at a time, roll them into little nests about 2 inches (5 cm) wide and arrange them on a floured kitchen towel until ready to cook. To make lasagne, cut the rolled sheet into 4-inch (10-cm) strips, then cut the strips into 4-inch squares.

**Rolling and Cutting the Dough with a Pasta Machine:** Using a hand-cranked machine, cut the kneaded dough into 6 equal portions. Then, starting with the rollers set at the widest opening, roll each portion through the machine 2 or 3 times, folding each time, keeping the portions you are not working with covered to prevent drying out. Fold the flattened dough into thirds and dust with flour before putting it through each progressively narrower setting until you have a long, thin, smooth sheet of pasta. Stopping after the next-to-last setting is fine for ribbon pasta; ideally pasta for lasagne should be run through the thinnest setting. If the sheets become too long to work with easily, cut them in half. Finally, adjust the machine to the setting for cutting into the desired width and pass the rolled-out dough through the cutters. For tagliatelle or fettucine, taglierini, and pappardelle, let the sheets dry on a floured surface for 1–2 minutes before cutting.

*Makes about 1 lb (520 g) fresh egg pasta; serves 6*

# Simple Tomato Sauce

A few basic ingredients are all it takes to highlight the sweet taste of peak-of-season tomatoes in this easy sauce. It's marvelous with all fresh egg pastas, especially fettuccine and tagliatelle; with multicolored linguine; and, traditionally, with potato gnocchi. If using fresh tomatoes, make sure the they are the ripest and best quality you can find, and use only fresh basil, which is more aromatic than the dried herb. If the tomatoes' flavor is a bit acidic, add a tiny spoonful of sugar to perk them up. The butter in this recipe is typical of northern Italian cooking; substitute olive oil, if you wish.

1/3 cup (3 oz/90 g) unsalted butter

1 small white onion, thinly sliced crosswise

1 lb (500 g) fresh plum (Roma) tomatoes, peeled (page 329), seeded, and sliced lengthwise, or canned plum tomatoes, drained and chopped

Salt

8 fresh basil leaves, torn into small pieces

In a large frying pan over medium heat, melt the butter. Add the onion and 3–4 tablespoons water, cover, and cook gently, stirring occasionally, until tender and completely translucent, about 10 minutes.

Add the tomatoes, cover partially, and cook over low heat until a thickened, creamy consistency is achieved, about 20 minutes. If the sauce begins to dry out too much before the creamy state is achieved, add a few tablespoons water to the pan.

Add salt to taste and the basil and stir well. Remove from the heat and let stand, covered, for a few minutes so the basil can release its aroma.

*Serves 4*

# Mayonnaise

The flavor of the oil is important when making mayonnaise. Some people use delicately flavored extra-virgin olive oil. Others combine equal parts extra-virgin olive oil and another oil. If you need to stretch it or to make the flavor lighter, add a bit of light (single) cream.

1 egg yolk

1 tablespoon fresh lemon juice

1 teaspoon Dijon mustard

Salt and freshly ground pepper

2/3 cup (5 fl oz/150 ml) extra-virgin olive oil, grapeseed oil, or canola oil

Place the egg yolk, lemon juice, mustard, and salt and pepper to taste in a blender or food processor fitted with the metal blade; process to combine. With the motor running, add the oil in a thin, steady stream and continue to blend until smooth and thickened.

*Makes about 2/3 cup (5 fl oz/160 ml)*

# Chocolate Coating

This scrumptious coating can be used as a dip for cookies. Be sure to refrigerate chocolate-coated cookies to prevent the chocolate from softening.

8 oz (250 g) semisweet or bittersweet chocolate, chopped

2 teaspoons vegetable shortening

Combine the chocolate and shortening in the tip pan of a double boiler. Melt over (not touching) simmering water just until smooth, stirring occasionally. Remove from the heat.

To coat cookie tops with chocolate, dip the tops in the hot chocolate or, using a small icing spatula or a table knife, spread the chocolate over the tops. Set the cookies, chocolate sides up, on a baking sheet.

*Makes about 3/4 cup (6 fl oz/180 ml)*

# Vanilla Sugar

This recipe keeps for months in an airtight container.

1 1/2 vanilla beans

2 cups (1 lb/500 g) granulated sugar

Cut the vanilla beans into 1 1/2 -inch (4-cm) lengths. Place in a food processor fitted with the metal blade or in a blender and process until blended. Add 1/2 cup (4 oz/125 g) of the sugar and process until the vanilla beans are finely chopped. Add the remaining 1 1/2 cups (12 oz/375 g) sugar and process until thoroughly incorporated.

Strain the sugar through a fine-mesh sieve to remove any large pieces of vanilla bean. Store at room temperature in an airtight container.

*Makes about 2 cups (1 lb/500 ml)*

# Glossary

**Al Dente**  The Italian term, literally "to the tooth," used to describe the ideal degree of doneness for cooked pasta—tender, but still firm to the bite. Cooking time will vary with type of pasta.

**Anchovies**  Tiny saltwater fish, related to sardines, most commonly found as canned fillets that have been salted and preserved in oil. Imported anchovy fillets packed in olive oil are the most commonly available; anchovies packed in salt, available canned in some Italian delicatessens, are considered the finest. Smooth pastes made from preserved anchovy fillets and oil are sold in squeeze tubes and jars, imported from Europe. They can be found in Italian delicatessens or the specialty-food aisle of well-stocked markets.

**Arborio**  An Italian variety of rice that is commonly used in risotto dishes. It has short, round grains and is high in starch, which creates a creamy, saucelike consistency during cooking. Look for it in Italian delicatessens and well-stocked food stores.

**Baking Stone**  Also called a baking tile, pizza stone, baking stone, baker's peel, or quarry tile. This is a flat rectangular, square, or round piece of unglazed stoneware used principally for baking breads and pizzas to produce well-browned crisp crusts. Appreciated for its efficient heat distribution, it is placed on the lowest rack or sometimes on the floor of the oven and preheated for at least 45 minutes before baking. The best ones are made of the same type of clay used to line kilns, as they are less apt to crack than ordinary clay baking stones.

**Basil**  A sweet, spicy herb popular in Italian and French cooking, particularly as a seasoning for tomatoes and tomato-based sauces.

**Belgian Endive**  This leafy vegetable, also known as chicory or witloof, has refreshing, slightly bitter spear-shaped leaves that are white to pale yellow-green—or sometimes red—in color, tightly packed in cylindrical heads about 4–6 inches (10–15 cm) long.

**Biscotti**  The Italian term, literally "twice-cooked," used for crisp cookies that are first baked in loaf form, then sliced and baked again.

**Bread Crumbs**  Bread crumbs have many uses, including forming a crunchy golden topping on gratins or adding body or texture to a dish. To make bread crumbs, choose a good-quality, rustic-style loaf made of unbleached wheat flour, with a firm, coarse-textured crumb; usually sold in bakeries as "country-style," "rustic," or "peasant" bread. For fresh bread crumbs, cut away the crusts from the bread and break the bread into coarse chunks. Put them in a food processor fitted with the metal blade or in a blender and process to the desired consistency. For dried crumbs, spread the fresh crumbs on a baking sheet and bake in an oven set at its lowest temperature until they feel very dry, 30–60 minutes; do not let them brown. Store in a tightly covered container at room temperature. Dried bread crumbs, usually fine-textured, are also sold prepackaged in well-stocked markets.

**Calzone**  Italian for "pantaloon," which describes the shape of a pizza that has been folded before baking and transformed into a turnover. Virtually any pizza recipe can be made into a calzone, but the technique is best suited to more abundant fillings that cannot be served neatly atop a flat pizza.

**Cannellini Beans**  Italian variety of small, white, thin-skinned, oval-shaped beans. If using dried beans, soak for a few hours in cold water (drain before cooking). For canned beans, drain and rinse well before use. Great Northern or navy beans are acceptable substitutes.

# Cheese

In its many forms, cheese makes an excellent ingredient for Italian dishes. For the best selection and quality, buy cheese from a well-stocked market that has a frequent turnover of product. The following cheeses are used most often in the recipes in this book.

**Bel Paese** A soft-textured, delicately flavored, pale yellow Italian whole-milk cheese.

**Fontina** A firm, creamy, delicate Italian cheese with a slightly nutty taste; made from cow's milk. The best is from the Aosta Valley of northwestern Italy.

**Goat Cheese** Most cheeses made from goat's milk are fresh and creamy, with a sharp tang; they are usually sold shaped into small rounds or logs.

**Gorgonzola** An Italian variety of creamy, blue-veined cheese with a sharp flavor.

**Gruyère** A variety of Swiss cheese with a firm, smooth texture, small holes, and a relatively strong flavor.

**Mascarpone Cheese** A thick Italian cream cheese, usually sold in tubs and similar to the French crème fraîche.

**Mozzarella** A creamy, white, mild-tasting Italian variety of cheese traditionally made from water buffalo's milk and sold fresh. Look for fresh mozzarella sold immersed in water. Mozzarella is also sometimes smoked, yielding an aromatic but still mild cheese with a firmer texture.

**Parmesan** A thick-crusted Italian cow's milk cheese with a sharp, salty, full flavor resulting from at least two years of aging. Buy in block form, to grate fresh as needed, rather than already grated. The finest Italian variety is designated Parmigiano-Reggiano.

**Pecorino** Italian sheep's milk cheese, sold either fresh or aged. Two of its most popular aged forms, used primarily for grating, are pecorino romano and pecorino sardo; the latter cheese is tangier than the former.

**Provolone** An Italian whole-milk cheese, fairly firm in texture and pale yellow in color, with a slightly sweet and smoky flavor.

**Ricotta** A very light, whey-based, bland Italian cheese made from twice-cooked milk—traditionally sheep's milk, although cow's milk ricotta is far more common. Usually sold in plastic containers, as it takes no solid form.

**Capers** Small, pickled buds of a bush common to the Mediterranean, used whole as a savory flavoring or garnish.

**Deglaze** To dissolve the thin glaze of juices and browned bits on the surface of a pan in which food has been fried, sautéed, or roasted. To do this, add liquid to the pan to the pan and stir and scrape the bottom over high heat, thereby adding flavor to the liquid for use as a sauce.

**Eggplant** A vegetable-fruit, also known as aubergine, with tender, mildly earthy, sweet flesh. The shiny skins of eggplants vary in color from purple to red and from yellow to white, and their shapes range from small and oval to long and slender to large and pear shaped. The most common variety is the large, purple globe eggplant. Slender, purple Asian eggplants, more tender and with fewer, smaller seeds, are available with increasing frequency in food stores and vegetable markets.

**Eggs, Raw** Eggs are used raw in mayonnaise and other sauces. Raw eggs run a risk of being infected with salmonella or other bacteria, which can lead to food poisoning. This risk is of most concern to small children, older people, pregnant women, and anyone with a compromised immune system. If you have health and safety concerns, do not consume raw egg.

**Fennel**  A crisp, refreshing, mildly anise-flavored bulb vegetable, sometimes called by its Italian name, finocchio. Another related variety of the bulb is valued for its fine, feathery leaves and stems, which are used as a fresh or dried herb, and for its small, crescent-shaped seeds, dried and used as a spice.

**Figs**  Late summer and early-autumn fruits characterized by their many tiny edible seeds, ripe fresh figs have a sweet, slightly astringent flavor and a soft, succulent texture. It is best to use fresh figs immediately. The most common varieties are the purple-skinned Mission and the green-skinned Calimyrna.

**Gelato**  Gelato is Italian ice cream, made with less cream than other ice creams but from an egg-rich custard base. It has a lower percentage of fat, which means the finished product is denser and not quite as rich as other ice creams. The flavor of authentic gelato tends to be especially intense, too, because of a lower amount of air incorporated during churning.

**Granita**  Granita is similar to sorbet in that it is a mixture of a sugar syrup and fruit purée or other flavoring. But, instead of being churned in an ice-cream machine, a granita is poured into a shallow pan and frozen in a freezer. During the freezing process, the mixture must be scraped and stirred every 20 or 30 minutes so that it does not freeze solid. The resulting confection is granular, icy, and refreshing. Be aware that granita does not keep as long as sorbets or ice creams. It is best served on the day it is made, preferably within 4 hours of freezing for the best texture.

**Hazelnuts**  Small, usually spherical nuts with a slightly sweet flavor. Grown in Italy, Spain, and the United States, also known as filberts. Once toasted (page 329), the nuts may be stripped of their thin, papery skins by rubbing them while still warm in a folded kitchen towel.

**Indirect-Heat Cooking**  In grilling, a method of cooking larger items that would burn if direct-heat cooking were employed. The glowing coals are pushed to the perimeter of the grill's fire pan, and food is placed in the center of the grill rack and usually covered to cook more slowly in the radiant heat.

**Julienne**  Refers both to cutting food into long, thin strips and to the strips themselves. To julienne root vegetables, thinly slice lengthwise, then stack several slices at a time and slice again into thin strips; alternatively, use a mandoline or the julienne-cutting disk of a food processor. To julienne meats or cheeses, thinly slice, stack, and slice again. To julienne leaves, stack several together and thinly slice crosswise; for small leaves such as herbs, roll the stack up lengthwise into a compact bundle before slicing.

**Mandoline**  A flat, rectangular tool ideal for cutting food quickly and easily. Usually comes with several different sizes of smooth and corrugated blades so food can be sliced, julienned, or waffle-cut. The advantages of using a mandoline are precision and regularity.

**Mortadella**  Large, fine-textured, mildly spiced air-cured pork sausage, a specialty of Bologna, Italy. Best purchased in Italian food stores.

**Olives**  Throughout Mediterranean Europe, ripe black olives are cured in combinations of salt, seasonings, brines, vinegars, and oils to produce pungently flavored results. Good-quality cured olives, such as French Niçoise, Greek Kalamata, and Italian Gaeta varieties, are available in ethnic delicatessens, specialty-food shops, and well-stocked food stores.

To pit an olive, use a special olive pitter, which grips the olive and pushes out the pit in one squeeze. Or carefully slit the olive lengthwise down to the pit with a small, sharp knife. Pry the flesh away from the pit; if the flesh sticks to the pit, carefully cut it away.

**Olive Oil, Extra Virgin** Extra-virgin olive oil, extracted from olives on the first pressing without the use of heat or chemicals, is prized for its pure, fruity (sometimes peppery) taste and its golden to pale green hue. Many brands, varying in color and strength of flavor, are now widely available in well-stocked markets; choose one that suits your taste. Products labeled pure olive oil, less aromatic and flavor-ful, may be used for all-purpose cooking.

**Pancetta** Italian-style unsmoked bacon cured with salt and pepper. May be sold flat or rolled into a large sausage shape. Available in Italian deli-catessens and specialty food stores.

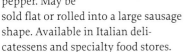

**Pesto** A traditional sauce originating from Genoa, Italy. Pesto is made of puréed basil, garlic, pine nuts, olive oil and Parmesan cheese; typically tossed with pasta and sometimes used as a seasoning. Ready-made pesto can be found in the refrigerated section of well-stocked markets.

**Pine Nuts** Small, ivory-colored seeds extracted from the cones of a species of pine tree, with a rich, slightly resinous flavor. Used whole as an ingredient or garnish, or ground into sauces, most famously pesto.

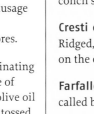

## Pastas

More than 400 distinct commercial pasta shapes exist. Some of those used in this book include:

**Angel Hair** Thin strands—capelli d'angelo in Italian.

**Armoniche** Ridged pastas shaped to resemble small harmonicas.

**Bucatini** Hollow, spaghetti-like rods, also known as perciatelli.

**Cannelloni** Pasta tubes approxi-mately 1 inch (2.5 cm) in diameter and 3 inches (7.5 cm) long.

**Conchiglie** Pasta shapes resembling conch shells.

**Cresti di gallo** "Cockscombs." Ridged, curved pasta with a wavy crest on the outer edge.

**Farfalle** Bite-sized "Butterflies." Also called bow ties.

**Fettuccine** "Ribbons," popular in both egg and spinach varieties.

**Fusilli** Short, twisted strands, also known as eliche or spirali, as well as long, twist-ed strands.

**Garganelli** Small, ridged, folded tubes.

**Gemelli** "Twins." Short intertwined strands.

**Gnocchi** Term for small dumplings, usually made of potato dough, and for small dumpling-shaped pasta.

**Linguine** "Small tongues." Long, thin, flat strands.

**Macaroni** Small to medium short, curved tubes.

**Orecchiette** Ear-shaped pasta.

**Pappardelle** Ribbons of fresh pasta, usually about $1^{1}/_{4}$ inches (3 cm) wide.

**Penne** "Quills." Tubes of egg or spinach pasta with angled ends resembling pen nibs. Avail-able smooth and ridged (rigate).

**Radiatori** "Radiators." Bite-sized, ridged shapes.

**Rigatoni** Bite-sized ridged tubes.

**Spaghetti** Classic round strands.

**Tagliatelle** Fresh pasta rolled very thin and cut into ribbons about $^{3}/_{8}$ inch (1 cm) wide.

**Taglierini** Small, narrow ribbons about $^{1}/_{8}$ inch (3 mm) wide.

**Tortelloni** Variety of large filled egg pasta; sometimes called ravioli.

**Polenta** Specially ground cornmeal cooked in either stock or water, which may be enriched with butter, cream, cheese, or eggs. When cooled, its consistency is firm enough to be sliced and grilled.

**Porcini** Widely used Italian term for Boletus edulis, a popular wild mushroom with a rich, meaty flavor. Most commonly sold in dried form, in Italian delicatessens and well-stocked markets, to be reconstituted in liquid as a flavoring for sauces, soups, stews, and stuffings. Also known by the French term cèpes.

**Prosciutto** Italian-style raw ham, a specialty of Parma, cured by dry-salting for one month, then air-drying in cool curing sheds for another 6 months. Usually cut into tissue-thin slices, the better to appreciate its intense flavor and deep pink color.

**Radicchio** A leafy vegetable related to the Belgian endive, the most common variety of radicchio has a spherical head, reddish purple leaves with creamy white ribs, and a mildly bitter flavor. Other varieties are slightly tapered and vary a bit in color. Served raw in salads, or cooked, usually by grilling. Also called red chicory.

**Risotto** A classic Northern Italian dish that is made from certain varieties of medium-grain rice that possess an outer layer of soft starch. During cooking, the rice is constantly stirred while hot liquid is gradually added, causing the starch to dissolve and form a creamy sauce that complements the chewy rice. The varieties of Italian rice most commonly used are Arborio (page 324), Carnaroli, and Vialone Nano; Arborio is by far the best known and most widely available in the United States.

**Roasting Bell Peppers** When a recipe calls for roasted and peeled bell peppers, preheat the broiler (grill). Cut the bell peppers in half lengthwise and remove the stems, seeds, and ribs. Arrange the pepper halves on a broiler pan, cut sides down, and broil until the skins blacken and blister, about 10 minutes. Transfer to a paper or plastic bag and let cool until the skins loosen, about 10 minutes. Using your fingertips or a small knife, peel off the skins, and then tear or cut the peppers as directed in the recipe.

**Saffron** An intensely aromatic spice, golden orange in color, made from the dried stigmas of a species of crocus; used to perfume and color many classic Mediterranean dishes, such as risotto. Sold either as threads—the dried stigmas—or in powdered form. Look for products that are labeled "pure saffron."

**Savoy Cabbage** Firm, round, fine-flavored variety of cabbage with dark green leaves—the outermost of which are curled—marked by a fine lacy pattern of veins.

**Shiitake** Meaty-flavored Asian mushrooms with flat, dark brown caps usually 2–3 inches (5–7.5 cm) in diameter, shiitake are available fresh with increasing frequency, particularly in Asian food shops. They are also sold dried, requiring soaking in warm water to cover for approximately 30 minutes before use.

**Sun-Dried Tomatoes** When sliced crosswise or halved, then dried in the sun, tomatoes develop an intense, sweet-tart flavor and a pleasantly chewy texture that enhance savory recipes. Available either dry or packed in oil, with or without herbs and spices. Look for them in specialty-food shops and well-stocked markets.

**Swiss Chard** Also known as chard or silverbeet, a leafy dark green vegetable with thick, crisp white or red stems and ribs. The green part, often trimmed from the stems and ribs, may be cooked like spinach, and has a somewhat milder flavor.

**Toasting Nuts**  Toasting brings out the full flavor and aroma of nuts. To toast any kind of nut, preheat an oven to 325°F (165°C). Spread the nuts in a single layer on a baking sheet and toast in the oven just until they begin to change color, 5–10 minutes for most nuts or about 3 minutes for pine nuts. Remove from the oven and let cool to room temperature.

Toasting also loosens the skins of nuts such as hazelnuts and walnuts, which may be removed by wrapping the still-warm nuts in a kitchen towel and rubbing vigorously.

**Tomatoes**  During summer, when tomatoes are in season, use the best red or yellow heirloom tomatoes you can find. At other times of year, plum tomatoes, also called Roma or egg tomatoes, are likely to have the best flavor and texture; for cooking, canned whole plum tomatoes are also a good choice. Small cherry tomatoes, barely bigger than the fruit after which they are descriptively named, also have a pronounced flavor that makes them ideal candidates for quick pasta sauces during their peak summer season.

To peel fresh tomatoes, bring a saucepan three-fourths full of water to a boil. Using a small, sharp knife, cut out the core from the stem end of the tomato. Then cut a shallow X in the skin at the tomato's base. Submerge for about 20 seconds in the boiling water, then remove and dip in a bowl of cold water. Starting at the X, peel the skin from the tomato, using your fingertips and, if necessary, the knife blade. Cut the tomatoes in half and turn each half cut-side down. Then cut as directed in individual recipes.

To seed a tomato, cut it in half crosswise. Carefully squeeze to force out the seed sacs.

**Tuna, Canned**  Most domestic brands of tuna are packed in water or vegetable oil. Imported tunas, mostly from Italy, are packed in olive oil, which gives the fish a more complex yet delicate flavor that suits it for use in Italian-style recipes.

**Vinaigrette**  Literally "little vinegar," a classic dressing or sauce for salad greens, vegetables, meats, poultry, or seafood. Made from a combination of vinegar (or some other acid such as lemon juice), seasonings, and oil. For a simple vinaigrette that will dress 3/4–1 pound (400–500 g) of salad greens, whisk together 5 tablespoons (3 fl oz/ 80 ml) extra-virgin olive oil, 1 tablespoon red wine vinegar,

and one tablespoon balsamic vinegar. Season to taste with salt and freshly ground pepper.

**Vinegar**  Literally "sour wine," vinegar results when certain strains of yeast cause wine—or some other alcoholic liquid such as apple cider or Japanese rice wine—to ferment for a second time, turning it acidic. The best-quality wine vinegars begin with good-quality wine. Red wine vinegar, like the wine from which it is made, has a more robust flavor than vinegar produced from white wine. Balsamic vinegar, a specialty of Modena, Italy, is a vinegar made from reduced grape juice and aged for many years.

**Zest**  The thin, brightly colored, outermost layer of a citrus fruit's peel, containing most of its aromatic essential oils—a lively source of flavor in baking. Zest may be easily removed by using a simple tool known as a zester, drawn across the fruit's skin to remove the zest in thin strips; with a fine hand-held grater; or in wide strips with a vegetable peeler or a paring knife held away from you and almost parallel to the fruit's skin. Zest removed with the latter two tools may then be thinly sliced or chopped on a clean cutting board. Always be careful to not remove any of the bitter white pith beneath the colored peel.

# Index

First published in the USA by Time-Life Custom Publishing.

Originally published as Williams-Sonoma Kitchen Library:
*Hors d'Oeuvres & Appetizers; Grilling; Pasta*
(© 1992 Weldon Owen Inc.)
*Beef; Chicken; Cookies & Biscotti; Fish; Pizza; Potatoes; Salads;*
*Soups; Vegetables* (© 1993 Weldon Owen Inc.)
*Beans & Rice; Fruit Desserts; Pasta Sauces; Stir-Fry*
(© 1994 Weldon Owen Inc.)
*Cakes, Cupcakes & Cheesecakes; Stews*
(© 1995 Weldon Owen Inc.)
*Cooking Basics; Ice Creams & Sorbets; Vegetarian*
(© 1996 Weldon Owen Inc.)
*Healthy Cooking; Mediterranean Cooking; Outdoor Cooking*
(© 1997 Weldon Owen Inc.)

In collaboration with Williams-Sonoma Inc.
3250 Van Ness Avenue, San Francisco, CA 94109

OXMOOR HOUSE INC.

Oxmoor
HOUSE.

Oxmoor House books are distributed by Sunset Books
80 Willow Road, Menlo Park, CA 94025
Telephone: 650-321-3600 Fax 650-324-1532
Vice President/General Manager: Rich Smeby
National Accounts Manager/Special Sales: Brad Moses

Oxmoor House and Sunset Books are divisions of
Southern Progress Corporation

WILLIAMS-SONOMA
Founder and Vice-Chairman: Chuck Williams

WELDON-OWEN INC.
Chief Executive Officer: John Owen
President and Chief Operating Officer: Terry Newell
Creative Director: Gaye Allen
Publisher: Hannah Rahill
Associate Creative Director: Leslie Harrington
Senior Designer: Charlene Charles
Assistant Editors: Donita Boles, Mitch Goldman
Editorial Assistant: Juli Vendzules
Production Director: Chris Hemesath
Production Coordinator: Libby Temple
Color Manager: Teri Bell
Glossary Illustrations: Alice Harth

*Williams-Sonoma Italian Favorites* was conceived and
produced by Weldon Owen Inc.
814 Montgomery Street, San Francisco, CA 94133
Copyright © 2004 Weldon Owen Inc.
and Williams-Sonoma Inc.

First printed in 2004.
10 9 8 7 6 5 4 3

ISBN 0-8487-2799-1

Printed in China by SNP Leefung Printers Ltd.

CREDITS
Authors: Lora Brody: Pages 209, 219, 226, 243, 292, 308, 320
(Bouquet Garni), 321 (Fish Stock); John Phillip Carroll: Pages 181,
247, 254, 274; Emalee Chapman: Pages 17, 37, 43, 216, 218, 225,
244, 260, 266, 273; Lorenza De'Medici: Pages 24, 38, 40, 49-92, 102-
107, 110, 112, 116-120, 122-132, 136, 153-157, 162, 163, 166, 173,
179, 184, 194, 200, 290, 295-301, 318, 319, 322; Joyce Goldstein:
Pages 115, 158, 188, 205-208, 211-214, 220, 224, 227-230, 233-237,
246, 248, 270, 302; Kristine Kidd: Pages 307, 312-316, 323
(Chocolate Coating, Vanilla Sugar); Norman Kolpas: Pages 26, 27,
320 (Beef Stock, Chicken Stock), 321 (Vegetable Stock); Jacqueline
Mallorca: Pages 44, 232, 263, 272, 311; Emanuela Stucchi Prinetti:
Pages 15, 16, 30-35, 45, 94-101, 108, 109, 121, 135, 138, 141-149,
161, 164, 168, 170, 175-177, 183, 185, 187, 190, 192, 195-199, 201,
265, 323 (Simple Tomato Sauce, Mayonnaise); The Scotto Sisters:
Pages 20, 21; Sarah Tenaglia: Pages 280-289, 304, 310; Joanne Weir:
Pages 18, 22, 29, 238, 250, 253, 257-258, 277; Diane Rossen
Worthington: Pages 39, 223, 268.

Photographers: Noel Barnhurst (front cover), Allan Rosenberg
(recipe photography), and Chris Shorten (recipe photography for
pages 44, 232, 262, 272, and 311).

ACKNOWLEDGEMENTS
Weldon Owen would like to thank Desne Ahlers, Carrie Bradley,
Kimberly Chun, Ken DellaPenta, Karen Kemp, Jonathan
Kauffman, Norman Kolpas, Joan Olson, and Sharon Silva for all
their expertise, assistance, and hard work.

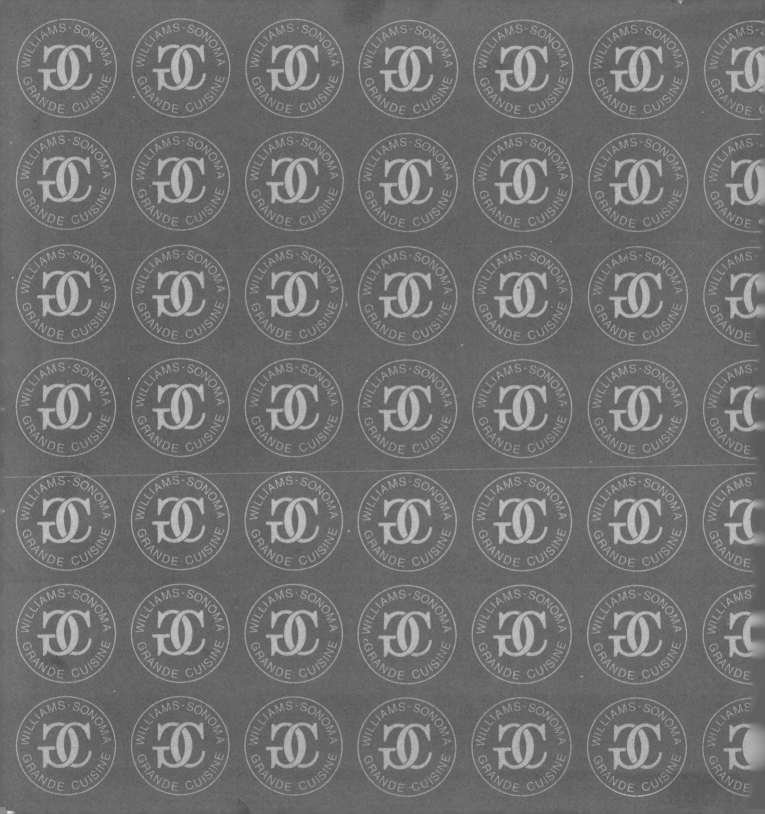